FIFTY-EIGHT LONELY MEN

FIFTY-EIGHT LONELY MEN

SOUTHERN FEDERAL JUDGES AND SCHOOL

DESEGREGATION ✳ **by J. W. PELTASON**

UNIVERSITY OF ILLINOIS PRESS ✳ *Urbana and Chicago*

To My Mother and Father

Illini Books edition, 1971

By permission from Harcourt, Brace & World, Inc.
Copyright © 1961 by J. W. Peltason
"Epilogue: 1970" and "Bibliographical Essay" copyright © 1971
by the Board of Trustees of the University of Illinois

Manufactured in the United States of America
P 9 8 7 6

Library of Congress Catalog Card Number: 61-12350
ISBN 0-252-00175-3

My good friends and colleagues, James M. Burns of Williams College and J. Austin Ranney of the University of Illinois have given generously of their time and expert skills. Except for the fact that I do not wish to involve them in any responsibility for my conclusions and presentations, I would associate their names with mine on the title page. I am also grateful to Professor Walter F. Murphy for his reading of the manuscript and his many useful comments. Professor Edward Ferguson of Southern Illinois University, East St. Louis Branch, did much of the "leg work" of gathering newspaper clippings, trial records, and other scattered materials. Because of the highly charged emotions generated by the school desegregation controversy, I refrain from thanking here those in public life who checked my manuscript and have given valuable comments. For even this minor association with my project might create political embarrassments.

My wife, Suzanne Peltason, gave encouragement and moral support at those critical moments when doubts as to whether the project would ever be finished were so destructive of morale.

Mrs. William R. Simmons, Mrs. Mary Kay Miller, and Mrs. Mary Jane Westphal have participated in the typing of my manuscript. I appreciate their hours of effort and their skill in deciphering illegible writing.

The Social Science Research Council and the Research Board of the University of Illinois provided financial assistance which permitted me to take time from my normal university chores in order to travel to the scenes of the controversy and to gather materials. Holt, Rinehart and Winston Inc. has kindly given permission to use some of the materials previously published by them in *The American Government Annual,* 1958–1959.

Needless but always necessary to say, I alone am responsible for errors of fact and interpretation.

✳ Contents

FIFTY-EIGHT LONELY MEN

1 ✳ The Men in the Middle

"It was the first day the buses were integrated. I usually don't ride the bus, but I made a point of it. A few minutes after I took my seat a young colored girl, about eighteen and very well-dressed, got on and sat down in the seat right in front of me. She was trembling. It was obvious she was scared, but determined to ride in the front. No one—it was not very crowded —said anything. I reached out, touched her on the shoulder, and said, 'Take it easy young lady, everything is fine.' "

"It seems to me, in view of the facts, that the white schools are hardly sufficient to hold the present number of white students; that it would be unthinkably and unbearably wrong to require the white students to get out so that the colored students could come in."

Both of these comments were made by United States district judges, the men who, regardless of their personal views, have the awesome assignment of forcing compliance with the Supreme Court's 1954 school segregation decisions.[1]

---

[1] Four cases challenging state segregation laws were joined under the style of *Brown v. Board of Education*, 347 U.S. 483 (1954). A fifth case,

In the District of Columbia and in the border states of Missouri, Oklahoma, West Virginia, Delaware, and Maryland, for the most part authorities have completed, or are completing, school integration. They did not wait for a judge to order them to do so. Here the courts' function is primarily to prod a few laggard districts. Those men who serve as federal judges in the eleven southern states have a much tougher assignment: school boards, responsive primarily to white voters, have been unable or unwilling to act. The full burden of forcing compliance, of presiding over this major social revolution, has fallen on forty-eight United States district judges.

This is a story of how these important but still little-known men, and their ten immediate superiors on the United States courts of appeals, have responded to the challenge. Whether they are heroes or villains depends as much upon the reader's values as upon the judges' behavior.

There was a time when southern federal judges lived serene lives. Their decisions, except for an infrequent criminal case, seldom made the front pages. As long as a judge refrained from offending local customs—and his official position seldom required him to do so—he could expect to serve out his career to the accompaniment of an occasional banquet at which he could hear himself praised as a "great judicial statesman." When he retired, he could proudly show his grandchildren editorials from the local newspapers extolling his dedicated public service.

All that has changed. Today the judge and his courtroom have become center stage for a highly charged conflict between contestants with fundamentally opposed demands. Segregationists expect the judge, himself a white southerner, to save a sacred institution; the nation as a whole, whose servant he is, and Negroes in particular, expect him to abolish segregation. Segregationists lost their case at the Supreme Court, but they demand that the district judge in the South save their cause. Negro plain-

---

Bolling v. Sharpe, 347 U.S. 497 (1955), having to do with segregation in the District of Columbia, was considered simultaneously. All five cases are commonly referred to as the school segregation cases.

tiffs insist that he turn the promise of the Supreme Court decision into a present reality. Perhaps not since pre-revolutionary years, when royal governors imposed imperial orders on colonials, have any American public officials been placed in the center of such a cross fire, a cross fire of such intensity that even the dignity of high office offers little protection.

Who are the men presiding over this revolution? All of these judges, distributed among twenty-eight district courts, are white southern males. No woman has ever served, and since Reconstruction, no Negro.[2] Only five were born outside the South; only five learned their law north of the Mason-Dixon, and of these only Judges William E. Miller of Nashville and Robert L. Taylor of Knoxville, both of whom studied at Yale, could really be charged with having gone to school with Yankees. Thirty-one are Democrats, sixteen are Republicans appointed either before 1932 or between 1952 and 1960. There is one vacancy.

The judges come from the same general social, economic, and political milieu, and reflect the same attitudes as do the men serving the South as governors, mayors, and United States senators. But there are differences: many more Republicans sit on the federal bench than hold other southern governmental posts; there is a greater sprinkling of the "Old South-aristocrats" and of the "New South-urbanites" on the bench, and less representation of the "red-suspender-populists" than is to be found in elective positions; there are proportionately fewer ardent segregationists serving as federal judges than in other southern public offices.

All these judges were appointed by the President with the consent of the Senate, but in fact those appointed by a Democratic President are really nominated by southern senators, for no man gets to be a federal district judge in the South when the Democrats control the White House unless he is acceptable to the Democratic senators of the state in which he operates. Al-

---

[2] On the Court of Appeals for the Third Circuit, however, there is a Negro, Judge William H. Hastie; and a woman, Judge Florence E. Allen, serves on the Court of Appeals for the Sixth Circuit.

though there are no Republican southern senators, even Eisenhower had to do business with the southern Democrats, who dominated the Senate Judiciary Committee to which judicial nominees are referred. Any strong opposition from the South would have delayed Senate confirmation, sometimes indefinitely.

By the time the President sends the name of a prospective federal judge to the Senate, formal approval is usually routine. Behind the scenes the candidate has been carefully screened. His name has been sent to a standing committee of the American Bar Association and to appropriate state and local bar associations. The FBI has made a full field investigation. An adverse recommendation by bar leaders is a serious handicap; an adverse report by the FBI is fatal.

To be seriously considered for a judicial appointment, a lawyer should be a member of the right political party—the one controlling the White House—a resident of the judicial district in question, of unimpeachable reputation, of good health, and preferably not too old. If he is related to the state's political leaders so much the better. The candidate's ideological position on the major issues of the day is indirectly scrutinized, approached in terms of legal competence—there seems to be a high correlation between a lawyer's economic, political, and constitutional values and the assessment of his technical proficiency. Segregationists, for example, feel that any attorney favoring integration must be an incompetent lawyer; civil rights advocates consider a segregation-minded lawyer to be ignorant of the spirit of the law.

After a candidate acceptable to party leaders, to spokesmen for the White House, and to leaders of the bar has been selected, and cleared by the FBI, a subcommittee of the Senate Judiciary Committee holds a routine public hearing, and a few days later the Senate confirms the chosen candidate, frequently without even bothering with a roll call.

Since the President, the Attorney General, and senators know that a candidate must be acceptable to a wide range of interests, they tend to select men of neutral sentiments from noncontroversial backgrounds; men whose appointments are unlikely to provoke strong opposition. In the social and political environment of the South this tends to rule out lawyers who have represented trade unions, publicly advocated civil rights, or otherwise conspicuously participated in liberal causes. Bar leaders would consider such men lacking "judicial temperament." In short, the men chosen come from bland backgrounds, men of local but not national fame, men who make *Who's Who* after rather than before appointment.

Before 1954 it was assumed as a matter of course that all southern lawyers favored segregation. Since 1954 any extreme public position, even one for segregation, lowers a man's chances of being elevated to the federal bench to near zero. To express a personal preference for segregation is permissible, but the President, Attorney General, and northern senators will veto any man whose segregationist views are expressed intemperately or publicly. And on the other hand, an attorney who had been fighting battles for civil rights is not likely to secure the endorsement of the southern senators. Lawyers aspiring to federal judgeships are thus well advised to limit their public comments to general pronouncements in favor of justice.

A sizable minority of the judges now sitting, especially among the older men and those appointed before 1954, are, however, segregationists. Among the more outspoken segregationist federal judges is Judge William H. Atwell of Dallas, an eighty-eight-year-old Harding Republican who twice refused to comply with the Supreme Court's segregation rulings and did so finally only after stern orders from the court of appeals. Atwell said: "The real law of the land is the same today as it was on May 16, 1954." [3] Nor was he unwilling to give the citizens of Dallas his advisory opinion that President Eisenhower lacked the constitutional authority to use troops to enforce court rulings in Little Rock. Judge George B. Timmerman, father of a former governor of South Carolina, and another segregationist,

[3] *Dallas Morning News,* December 15, 1957.

has accused the NAACP of spreading "poisonous propaganda." [4] And Judge Wilson Warlick of North Carolina has said: "I'm a states' rights individual and I always have been. If I had anything to do with schools in North Carolina, I wouldn't let the federal government have any part of it. . . ." [5] At the other extreme, a smaller number of judges favor integration, but they know better than to do so publicly.

Most southern federal judges are moderates who favor segregation and who feel, like most white southerners, that the Supreme Court's decision was unwise, but who do not hold segregation as a sacred and overriding principle. [6] And these pressures

---

[4] *Bryan v. Austin,* 2 Race Relations Law Reporter (hereafter cited as RRLR) 393–394 (1957).

[5] *Raleigh News and Observer,* August 28, 1955.

Rebellion in the ranks has not been limited to Deep South judges. In January 1954 District Judge John H. Druffel refused to prevent Hillsboro, Ohio—a southern Ohio community—from gerrymandering its school zones to keep Negro children from attending "white" schools. The court of appeals reversed, directing Druffel to frame a decree "which will provide for the immediate admittance to school on a non-segregated basis of school-age Negro children . . . and provide by permanent injunction for the end of all racial segregation in the Hillsboro public schools on or before the commencement of the school year in September 1956." Judge Druffel called a press conference to announce he would defy the court of appeals. He said it would take an order from the Supreme Court to make him change his mind. Eventually he backed down. See also *St. Louis Post Dispatch,* January 7, 1956.

[6] This evaluation of the personal preferences of the district judges is based on their confidential remarks and public comments, and it has been checked with observers conversant with the judges, including some of the judges themselves. It corresponds with the findings of the *U. S. News & World Report,* the leading national magazine supporting segregation, which polled 351 federal judges asking if they agreed with a critical report of the Conference of Chief Justices of the State Supreme Court. The state judges had accused the United States Supreme Court of lacking proper judicial restraint in dealing with state governments. The *U. S. News & World Report*'s question did not deal directly with the issue of segregation, but clearly there is a high correlation between a favorable attitude toward segregation and a critical view of the Supreme Court. . . . The results were surprising. Although a higher percentage of southern federal judges than those from other regions took this opportunity anonymously to criticize the Supreme Court, only thirty-three of the southern judges answered, including some judges of the court of appeals. Of these thirty-

within the judge are often more significant than those exerted upon him. A judge to whom segregation is a sacred principle is less likely to move against it than the judge to whom it is not. The district judge is very much a part of the life of the South. He must eventually leave his chambers and when he does he attends a Rotary lunch or stops off at the club to drink with men outraged by what they consider "judicial tyranny." A judge who makes rulings adverse to segregation is not so likely to be honored by testimonial dinners, or to read flattering editorials in the local press, or to partake of the fellowship at the club. He will no longer be invited to certain homes; former friends will avoid him when they meet on the street. Judge J. Skelly Wright has observed: "I never have been a gregarious type, and I've become much less so in the past few years. You never know whether people really want to talk with you and I don't see a lot of people any more." [7] The judge can never forget that any action of his against segregation will threaten his easy and prestigeous acceptance by the community. He has become a convenient target for political leaders anxious to impress the electorate with their own soundness on segregation. The judge who delays injunctions and avoids antisegregation rules, is, on the other hand, a local hero; he will hear himself referred to as one of the nation's "great constitutional scholars," a man of courage willing to risk reversal to defend the right.

Circuit Judge John R. Brown explained that "lifetime tenure insulates judges from anxiety over worldly cares for body and home and family. But it does not protect them from the unconscious urge for the approbation of their fellow-man, and

---

three, nineteen said they agreed with the state chief justices. Since the obvious purpose of the questionnaire was to embarrass the Supreme Court, it is highly probable that those who responded would include a high percentage of segregationists. *U. S. News & World Report*, October 24, 1958, pp. 36–37; see also *Washington Post & Times Herald*, October 22, 1958, and *New York Times*, October 2, 1958. (For comments critical of the poll.)

[7] William E. Giles, "Judge Wright: In the Center of the New Orleans Controversy," *Wall Street Journal*, November 10, 1960.

fellow-man most often means those of like interest and back-grounds, business and professional experiences and predilec-tions, and even prejudices." [8]

There are less gentle pressures too. Judges who have issued antisegregation orders, however mild, have been forced to dis-continue the public listing of their telephone numbers to avoid anonymous and obscene telephone calls made round-the-clock. Their mail has been loaded with threatening letters. Some have been forced to seek police protection for themselves and their families.

A judge who violates local beliefs may indeed—despite his constitutional independence—find his position so uncomfort-able that he is forced to retire. Judge J. Waties Waring, a native South Carolinian appointed to the bench by Roosevelt in 1942, had won national fame and local notoriety in 1948 when he sharply rapped South Carolina and Democratic party officials for attempting to circumvent the Fifteenth Amendment. "It is time," he told these officials, "to realize that the people of the United States expect [you] to follow the American way of elections." [9] In 1951 District Judge Waring, as one of the three judges hearing a challenge to South Carolina's segregation laws, dissented from the court's ruling that segregation was constitu-tional. He became the target of intense local abuse, his life was threatened, and his wife slandered. Shortly thereafter he retired from the bench and moved to New York.

But pressures on the judge are not all in one direction. Though he may be a white southerner living in the South, he is also a judicial officer of the national government. His position gives him some protection from local demands; at the same time it exposes him to the claims of a national constituency. The Supreme Court and courts of appeals have no formal disciplinary power over the district judge and supervise his work only sporadically, but the living traditions of the law

[8] "Hail to the Chief: Hutcheson, the Judge," *Texas Law Review,* vol. 38, December 1959, p. 145.

[9] *Brown v. Baskin,* 78 F. Supp. 933 (1948).

oblige the district judge, whatever his own views and however strong local pressures, to follow the rulings of his judicial superiors. It is a measure of his own competence to avoid reversals of his rulings by a higher court. His sense of craftsmanship and his pride in his profession force him to consider not only his local reputation but his national standing as a judge. No doubt some southern federal judges have persuaded themselves that the Supreme Court's civil rights rulings are not the "true law." No doubt some are more concerned with winning the applause of the local community than the approval of the nation. Nevertheless a judge's obligations as a federal officer, his duty to obey his superiors, and his pride in his work may be pressures upon him just as compelling as those generated within his own district.

The same man who, if serving as a state judge or a United States senator, might lead the attack on the federal courts, as a federal judge might promote civil rights. Compare, for example, two men with almost identical backgrounds and similar values —Frank M. Johnson, Jr., a federal judge, and George C. Wallace, a state judge—who found themselves on opposite sides of a civil rights issue.

Frank M. Johnson, Jr., is the United States district judge for the Middle District of Alabama, serving by appointment of President Eisenhower. A native of Alabama (1918), he graduated from the University of Alabama law school, served in World War II, became a successful practitioner of the law in Montgomery, and a federal judge in 1955. His close friend and former classmate, George C. Wallace, was a judge for the Third Judicial Circuit of Alabama, serving by election of the voters of his circuit. Except for the fact that Johnson is a Republican and Wallace a Democrat, their career patterns and backgrounds are identical.

In the fall of 1958 Wallace, making a bid for the Alabama gubernatorial nomination, defied the United States Civil Rights Commission then investigating alleged discrimination by Alabama officials against Negro voters. Wallace took charge of the voting records and announced he would go to jail rather than

turn them over to the commission. The commission appealed to
Judge Johnson, who ordered Wallace to let the commission's
staff inspect the records. Wallace refused.

On January 26, 1959, Judge Johnson looked down at Wallace from his bench in the courtroom in the Montgomery Post
Office, faced with the decision whether or not to hold his friend
in contempt of court. Wallace, for his part, had to decide
whether to persist in his defiance of the federal government.

Wallace had the easier choice. The demands of his constituents reinforced his personal inclinations, perhaps pushing him
to take a position more extreme than he might prefer, but a position certainly not distasteful to him. Still, he too was a judge.
If Stevenson had won in 1952, Wallace, as a Democrat, well
might have been sitting in Judge Johnson's chair. At the last
minute Wallace by indirection let the commission see the records, turning them over to local grand juries who in turn permitted commission inspection.

For Judge Johnson the choices were not so clear and the
pressures not so onesided. As a white southerner, he too would
endanger his stature within Alabama if he actively supported
the Civil Rights Commission. He too had "states' rights" convictions. If he served in Wallace's courtroom and were responsive to the same constituents, he might have acted as stubbornly
as Wallace. But as a federal judge he was neither so dependent
upon the white voters of Alabama, nor so independent of the
national majority. It was his job to enforce federal laws. Johnson saw to it that the Civil Rights Commission was able to inspect the records; despite Wallace's obstruction Johnson allowed
him to go unpunished. He explained that to hold Wallace in contempt would merely promote his political fortunes. "This Court,"
Johnson said, "refuses to allow its authority and dignity to be
bent or swayed by such politically-generated whirlwinds." [10]

Judge Johnson's dilemma is characteristic of the difficult position of southern district judges. These judges will do what they

[10] *In re Wallace,* 4 RRLR 97 at 121 (1959).

must; they can hardly be expected on their own initiative to move against the local power structure. If their instructions from above are ambiguous, the ambiguity will be resolved to conform to the judge's own convictions and the mores of his district. A most important question therefore is this: "What instructions did the Supreme Court give the district judges to guide their decisions in school desegregation suits?"

The directions of the United States Supreme Court are *not* clear and explicit, and this is the crucial problem. After the Supreme Court declared public school segregation unconstitutional in 1954, it refrained from issuing a decree, asking instead for another round of briefs and oral argument dealing with the precise issue of implementation. Fully aware of the explosive nature of its ruling, anxious to be reasonable, and wishing to move cautiously, the Court invited the Department of Justice, the attorneys for the Negro plaintiffs, the lawyers for the school boards in the five cases immediately before the Court, and the attorneys general of all states requiring or permitting segregation to submit briefs and join the discussion. The Court directed the lawyers to present further argument on the following questions:

Should the Supreme Court issue a decree that Negro children should forthwith be admitted to schools of their choice? or

Should the Supreme Court permit an effective gradual adjustment to be brought about from existing segregated systems not based on color distinctions?

Assuming that the Court will permit gradual desegregation, Should the Supreme Court itself formulate detailed decrees? or Should the Supreme Court remand the cases to the district judges with directions, and if so, what directions?

To the southerners this was a chance to avoid the consequence of the 1954 decision. If they could persuade the Supreme Court to leave the exact timing and precise nature of integration orders to the discretion of southern federal judges, they knew they could operate segregated schools for a long, long time. On the other side, the integrationists had little hope that the Supreme Court itself would order the immediate abolition of segregation. They recognized that the Court would probably return the suits to the district judges; it became crucial to their cause that the Supreme Court give clear commands to the district judges—otherwise segregation would merely be unconstitutional, it would not be abolished.

On April 11, 1955, the debate opened. Promptly at noon the red velvet curtains parted behind the nine chairs on the dais. The audience rose, the Court crier intoned, "The Honorable Chief Justice and Associate Justices of the Supreme Court of the United States. May God Save the United States and this Honorable Court."

Chief Justice Earl Warren took his customary seat in the center. His eight black-robed associates were arranged from right to left in order of seniority. Warren, former three-term Governor of California, appointee of Eisenhower, whispered to Justice Hugo Black on his right. Black, the New Deal liberal former senator from Alabama, nodded his head in response. On Warren's left, sat Justice Stanley Reed from Kentucky, former Solicitor General under Roosevelt, solid craftsman of the law. Two seats down on Warren's right was the brilliant and garrulous Felix Frankfurter, former Harvard law professor. Next to Frankfurter, sat Justice Harold Burton, former Ohio Senator, a Republican friend of Truman, who had appointed him. Sitting on the Court's extreme right, both ideologically and in seating arrangement, was the ailing Sherman Minton, former circuit judge and another Senate friend of Truman's.

On the left, sitting next to Justice Reed, Justice William O. Douglas, author, mountain climber, champion of liberal causes, scanned the documents before him. Justice Tom Clark, tall, informal and friendly Texan, former Attorney General under Truman, came next, and in the junior chair on the extreme left was Justice John Marshall Harlan, whose grandfather a half century earlier had been the lone dissenter in the case of *Plessy v. Ferguson,* in which the Supreme Court had sustained the constitutionality of racial segregation.

The Chief Justice rapped his gavel, and the justices settled back to hear the lawyers' arguments. Thurgood Marshall led a battery of attorneys from the National Association for the Advancement of Colored People in behalf of the Negro plaintiffs. Marshall, chief NAACP legal spokesman since 1938, was making his fifteenth appearance before the Supreme Court.

Ten states—Kansas, South Carolina, Virginia, Delaware, Florida, North Carolina, Arkansas, Oklahoma, Maryland, and Texas—had sent lawyers to advise the Court. John W. Davis, a veteran Supreme Court advocate, had represented South Carolina in the earlier hearings. He was too ill to take part in the oral arguments but he had filed a brief. Solicitor General Simon E. Sobeloff, a liberal Maryland attorney, represented the Eisenhower Administration.

From the very beginning it was apparent that the Supreme Court would not order immediate integration. Marshall and his staff concentrated on persuading the Court to issue firm instructions to the district judges. They wanted the Supreme Court to set a fixed date, either September 1955 or September 1956—in any event *some* date—by which time the district judge should order school boards to abolish segregation.

"What is needed," Marshall told the Supreme Court, "is a firm hand. . . . A district court properly instructed by this Court will supply the firm hand. . . . But the Supreme Court must arm the district judges and appellate judges with authority. If no time is set, they're [the defendants] going to argue in any event the same way they have argued here, which is nothing." Furthermore, Marshall argued, "If no time limit is included the district judges will be placed in the legislative field—their duties are merely to tell the state what it can't do." [11]

Marshall called the justices' attention to the Negro children in whose behalf the suits had been brought. Each of them had a "personal and present right" not to be discriminated against, he said, and described the case of Harry Briggs, Jr. Harry was nine years old when his father and other parents of Negro children first sued the Clarendon County South Carolina School Board. That was four years ago. If the Supreme Court allowed district

[11] *United States Law Week,* vol. 23, April 19, 1955, pp. 3256 and 3260.

judges to determine when and how schools should be integrated, Marshall predicted, young Harry would never secure his right to attend a nonsegregated school. But if the district judges were instructed to insist upon integration by a certain date, their duty would be clear, and complex litigation unnecessary. Marshall incidentally was a good prophet. In 1960 Briggs graduated from high school, a colored high school.

Then came the southerners' turn. Some argued that the Supreme Court should reverse its 1954 decision. Attorney General Thomas J. Gentry of Arkansas, confident of the southern senators' power to filibuster, wanted the Court "to leave the problem of integration . . . to Congress for appropriate legislation." [12]

Other southerners sought a "wide-open mandate" giving the district judges complete authority to determine when a community should integrate and how it should be done. Such was the view of Attorney General Richard W. Ervin of Florida, who contended that the cases should be returned to the district judges with instructions to allow a period of gradual adjustment "with broad powers of discretion vested in local school authorities and the district judge." [13]

Chief Justice Warren was disturbed. If the Supreme Court issued a "wide-open mandate" giving district judges so much latitude in formulating injunctions, what would southerners do? he asked.

S. E. Rogers, speaking for South Carolina, told the Chief Justice, "We would present our problems to the district court." [14] If this were done, Rogers admitted, there would be no integration "perhaps not until 2015 or 2045." Rogers had reason for his confidence, for in South Carolina the case would be returned to the court of Judge George Bell Timmerman, who had never made a pro-civil rights ruling.

[12] *Ibid.*
[13] *Amicus Curiae* Brief of the Attorney General of Florida, *Brown v. Board of Education*, pp. 61–65.
[14] *United States Law Week*, vol. 23, April 19, 1955, p. 3257.

Solicitor General Sobeloff, representing the federal executive, agreed with the southerners that the Supreme Court should return the cases to the district judges, but he was against giving these judges a "blank check." He argued for what he called "a middle-of-the-road concept of moderation with a degree of firmness," and urged that the Court tell the district judges to require school authorities to submit integration plans within ninety days. These plans need not call for immediate and complete integration—perhaps one grade a year—but they should satisfy the judge that local officials were making an attempt to integrate "as soon as feasible." If the board failed to come forward with a satisfactory plan, the district judge should be instructed to order immediate integration. Under such arrangements, Sobeloff argued, many districts would be able to integrate their schools immediately; in others it might take longer, but within a year at least they all would be making a start.[15]

Six weeks later the Supreme Court made its decision. It was a southern victory. The Court announced that the variety of local conditions made it unwise to formulate a single decree covering all school districts. Instead, cases would be returned to district judges for the formulation of specific orders.

The southerners secured most of what they wanted, but the Supreme Court did not quite give the district judges a "blank check." It did set some boundaries. The Supreme Court told the district judge:

1. Remember that school authorities, not the courts, have the primary duty for determining how and when schools should be integrated.

2. Require the school board, however, to make a prompt and reasonable start toward full compliance with the May 17, 1954, ruling.

3. Once such a start has been made, the board may be given additional time to complete integration.

4. The burden rests on the school board to establish the need

[15] *Ibid.*, pp. 3253 ff.

for additional time. Do not grant a postponement unless you are convinced the board is acting in good faith to bring about integration at the earliest practicable date. Among the factors which may be considered in deciding whether a school district may delay integration are necessary administrative rearrangements, adjustments of the transportation system, revisions of school district lines to accommodate the altered situation, revision of local laws and regulations.

5. Do not allow school boards to postpone integration merely because the board members or their community favor segregation.

6. Plans calling for desegregation by steps are permissible, provided authorities, acting in good faith, are proceeding with all deliberate speed.

7. Retain jurisdiction during the period of transition.

Why did the Supreme Court give the district judges so much discretion? Why did the Court fashion a remedy using such vague phrases as "with all deliberate speed," "good faith," "at the earliest practicable date," terms permitting so many divergent interpretations as to invite a "generation of litigation?" Why did the justices give the segregationists such room for maneuver?

Apparently the justices felt that the times called for a compromise. They hoped to soften the blow. And in the spring of 1955 they had good reason to believe that in the South moderate opinion would prevail; many communities were already preparing to integrate voluntarily. Furthermore, the justices might have reasoned that a decree insisting upon immediate and prompt action would so alarm southern moderates as to have an adverse impact. By issuing a flexible decree allowing for a gradual and deliberate step-by-step integration, it was hoped that southern moderates would be encouraged to take the initiative.

Southerners had the leeway they wanted. The district judges could now employ wide latitude in formulating integration mandates. Operating in uncharted regions under almost wide open mandates to consider "local conditions," the district judge could, if he wished, defeat desegregation by narrowly construing the Supreme Court's rulings, by closing his eyes to circumventions of his orders, by writing opinions encouraging segregation. On the other hand, he could do much to speed integration by interpreting broadly the Supreme Court's mandates, by keeping open access to his court, by insisting upon good faith compliance, by refusing to close his eyes to subterfuges, by insisting that his mandates be obeyed, and by writing opinions giving segregationists no loopholes. Whatever his choice, it could be supported by appropriate ritualistic citation of precedents.

Let us see how two district judges handled almost identical cases.[16]

In September 1958, just as schools were about to open, the New Orleans branch of Louisiana State University and Memphis State University denied qualified Negroes the right to enroll. In both cities Negroes sued for relief.

The Louisiana suit was assigned to the docket of Judge Herbert W. Christenberry, a native of Louisiana, a graduate of Loyola Law School in New Orleans, and a Democrat. Judge Christenberry served as United States district attorney from 1937 until his appointment to the district court by President Truman in 1947.[17]

The students told Judge Christenberry that unless he scheduled a hearing within the next ten days, the school year would be under way, and that justice delayed would be justice denied. Attorneys for the university admitted that in previous suits LSU had been ordered to cease discriminating against Negroes, but they contended these injunctions did not apply to the newly opened New Orleans branch. The issues, they contended, were

[16] The Supreme Court's 1955 Implementation Decree does not apply to institutions of higher education. At this level, as the Court subsequently made clear, the district judge is to insist upon immediate admission of otherwise qualified Negroes.

[17] Another Truman appointee, Judge J. Skelly Wright, also serves on the United States District Court for the Eastern District of Louisiana. Both Christenberry and Wright have consistently stood firm against segregationists.

too complicated to be disposed of summarily. More time was needed to prepare briefs, so the judge should stay his hand until a full-scale hearing could be held.

It took Judge Christenberry only thirty minutes to reach a decision. The constitutional situation was clear: Negroes have a constitutional right to attend public institutions of higher education on the same terms as other students. They were admittedly being denied the right to attend LSU solely because of their race. Injunction granted.

Louisiana officials rushed to the Court of Appeals for the Fifth Circuit, which also sits in New Orleans, and asked the appellate judges to stay Christenberry's decree until the court of appeals could consider it. This could have taken months. The court of appeals denied the motion for a stay, and Negroes enrolled at LSU.[18] The entire proceedings from denial by University authorities of Negroes' applications to effective order had taken ten days.

The right of Negroes to attend the Memphis State University was open to even less legal doubt. Yet here the Negroes were not successful. Their case was assigned to Judge Marion Speed Boyd who runs the United States District Court for the Western District of Tennessee. Boyd, a native Tennesseean (1900), a graduate of University of Tennessee Law School, and a Democrat, had been appointed to the bench in 1940 by President Roosevelt. He had a reputation among lawyers of his district for running his court with dispatch, in accordance with his middle name. But not so in this case.

The facts were these: in 1958, after three years of litigation, the court of appeals had told MSU it could not postpone admission of Negroes to its undergraduate division. MSU President J. M. (Jack) Smith did not like these judicial decisions, but he decided "to face it." "I am against desegregation," he said, "but I'm being forced by the courts to admit some [Negroes]. I've been backed up and have faced the jailhouse." [19]

[18] *Board of Supervisors of Louisiana University v. Wilson Fleming, Jr., et al.,* 4 RRLR 612 (1959).
[19] *Southern School News,* August 1958, p. 10.

Eight Negro students passed the entrance examinations and were all set to start school in September. As classes were about to get underway, Smith announced: "No Negroes will be admitted for at least another year." He explained: "[Desegregation] is not acceptable to a large majority of the people of Memphis." [20] The day on which Smith made his announcement, the Supreme Court in Washington handed down its Little Rock decision stating that community opposition is not a legal justification for postponing integration.

The Negro students complained to Judge Boyd, asking for early action, but he told them the issues were too important to be so quickly disposed of. Instead, he scheduled their complaint for a full hearing. The Court of Appeals for the Sixth Circuit refused to expedite proceedings, and by the time the case was heard the school year was already over! [21]

The Constitution may be what the Supreme Court says it is, but a Supreme Court opinion means, for the moment at least, what the district judge says it means. The Supreme Court said that the Constitution forbids a public institution of higher education to discriminate against Negroes. LSU was not allowed to do so; MSU was. The difference—the district judge.

District judges do not, however, have the last word. Their integration decisions are carried to one of the United States courts of appeals: if the district judge rules in favor of the Negro plaintiffs, school authorities appeal to delay; if he decides against the Negroes, the Negroes appeal, for they have learned that the court of appeals is more likely to insist upon prompt action than is the district court. Since the Supreme Court has refused to exercise its discretionary authority to review school-entry rulings, the final word in these suits has become that of the circuit judges of the court of appeals.

The United States is divided into ten numbered circuits and one for the District of Columbia, and for each circuit there is

[20] *Ibid.* For background, *Nashville Banner*, June 15, 1955, November 8, 1957; *Memphis Commercial Appeal*, October 18, 1955; *Chattanooga Times*, October 15, 1955, February 4, 1956, June 4, 1957.
[21] *Prater v. State of Tennessee Board of Education*, 4 RRLR 888 (1959).

a court of appeals, consisting of from three to nine circuit judges who usually hear cases in panels of three. Four courts of appeals have southern states within their circuits. The most prominent in segregation cases are the Fourth and Fifth, since all southern states—except Arkansas, which is part of the Eighth Circuit, and Tennessee, which is within the Sixth—fall within their jurisdiction.

The Court of Appeals for the Fourth Circuit, with headquarters in Richmond and with jurisdiction over the ten district courts in West Virginia, Maryland, Virginia, North Carolina, and South Carolina, is one of the nation's best known courts. Its judges have been more prominent than most circuit judges, and the Fourth has been a remarkably stable court. From the 1930's through the middle 1950's it consisted of three jurists: Chief Judge John J. Parker, Judge Morris A. Soper, and Judge Armistead Dobie, all three crucial policy-makers.

John J. Parker, one of the nation's most distinguished judges, was appointed to the court of appeals in 1925 and served until his death in 1958. In 1931 President Hoover nominated Parker to the Supreme Court, but the Senate refused to confirm primarily because of charges that he was antilabor and anti-Negro —as the 1920 North Carolina Republican gubernatorial candidate Parker had made disparaging racial comments, and in 1927 he had approved an injunction enforcing a "yellow dog contract." (Parker was merely applying the law as handed down by the Supreme Court.) Parker took his rebuff with dignity and proceeded to win a national reputation as a moderate and fairminded judge.

Judge Parker is the author of what has come to be the most authoritative gloss of the Supreme Court's 1954 decision. In the Briggs case he pointed out: "[The Supreme Court] has not decided that the states must mix persons of different races in the schools or must deprive them of the right of choosing the schools they attend. What it has decided, and all that it has decided, is that a state may not deny to any person on account of race the right to attend any school that it maintains. . . . The Constitution, in other words, does not require integration. It merely forbids discrimination." [22]

Parker was attempting to calm southern fears, but segregationists apparently found more comfort in Parker's words than he intended: they frequently cite and recite his comments; they make much of the fact that Parker construed the Brown decision to call for "desegregation," not "integration." Yet the Court of Appeals for the Fourth Circuit, first under Judge Parker's leadership and more recently under Judge Soboloff, with one notable exception has insisted that the district judges force school districts to begin the desegregation process. If the term "desegregation" is more palatable to southerners than "integration," the circuit judges are quite willing to use the term.

Parker's fellow jurists on the court of appeals retired just before his death. Soper left active service in 1955 at eighty-two; Judge Dobie in 1956 at seventy-five, though they continue to hear occasional cases. Soper, a Republican, was selected by Hoover. Dobie, a Democrat, was a Roosevelt selection. Prior to his appointment he was Dean of the University of Virginia School of Law, and is the only southern federal judge presently serving on the bench who came to the court from a predominantly academic background. Dobie is no integrationist. He once made a reference to "a foreign Communistic anthropologist," an obvious dig at Gunnar Myrdal. Myrdal is a distinguished Swedish social scientist—and not a Communist—whose works were cited by the Supreme Court in a footnote to its 1954 decision.[23] To replace Judge Soper, President Eisenhower nominated Solictor General Simon E. Soboloff, a liberal Republican, backed by the two Republican senators from Maryland and strongly endorsed by the three sitting judges of the Fourth Circuit. Soboloff ran into strong opposition from almost all southern senators, especially those from Virginia, North Carolina, and South Carolina, whose states are within the Fourth Circuit.

Southerners accused Soboloff of bias against the South, citing

[22] *Briggs v. Elliott,* 132 F. Supp. 776 (1955).
[23] *Southern School News,* August 1955, pp. 6–9; December 1955, p. 6.

his participation as Solicitor General in the Supreme Court oral argument over implementation of desegregation. Senator James O. Eastland went so far as to state: "The kindest thing that can be said about the nominee is that he is on the borderline of Red philosophy." [24]

Southern senators also made much of the fact that in a speech before the Judicial Conference of the Fourth Circuit Soboloff had said: "In our system the Supreme Court is not merely the adjudicator of controversies, but in the process of adjudication, it is in many instances the final formulator of national policy." This statement provoked no exceptions from the judges to whom the speech was addressed but his opponents charged that it proved he believed in "judicial legislation."

For a whole year the Senate Judiciary Committee delayed Soboloff's confirmation. Finally it was brought to the Senate floor. Senators from Virginia, North Carolina, and South Carolina attempted to invoke the rule of senatorial courtesy—the Senate practice of refusing to confirm those opposed by a Senator from the state in which a judge is to sit. In the case of *district* judges this practice is always honored if the senator belongs to the same party as the President. These southern senators called Soboloff "personally obnoxious" and insisted that President Eisenhower had violated custom by choosing a man from Maryland, since it was South Carolina's turn to have a man on the court of appeals. Despite these pleas, the Senate confirmed.

When Judge Dobie retired in 1956, President Eisenhower nominated Clement F. Haynsworth, Jr., a South Carolina Democrat, the choice of the two Democratic South Carolina senators. His confirmation was swift, giving hint to the probability that at the time of Soboloff's confirmation the Attorney General promised to permit the South Carolina senators to pick the next judge. Haynsworth, as the son of a prominent Charleston attorney and the choice of the Democratic senators, might have been expected to take the segregationists' line, but since serving on the court he has been at one with the other judges.

[24] *Congressional Record*, vol. 102, July 6, 1956, p. 12855.

When Judge Parker died in 1958, Herbert S. Boreman, a Republican who had been appointed just a few years earlier to the district bench in West Virginia, and who earlier had been a member of the West Virginia Senate and a Republican gubernatorial candidate, was elevated to take Parker's position.

In quick order, Soboleff became the senior and thus chief judge of the court of appeals. It is a somewhat amusing fact that this court, which operates in one of the strongest Democratic regions of the United States, consists today, as it has throughout its history, of two Republicans and one Democrat. Of more significance, it consists of men more moderate on civil rights issues than most of the other southern public officials.

The other court of appeals handling a large number of civil rights suits is the Fifth with seven judges. Its headquarters is in New Orleans; its panels hear appeals from the seventeen district courts covering Georgia, Florida, Alabama, Mississippi, Louisiana, and Texas.

There has been a frequent turnover of personnel on the Fifth. By 1961 only two of its seven members, both Democrats, had been appointed by a President other than Eisenhower. The senior member is Joseph C. Hutcheson, Jr., second only in age and length of service to ninety-two-year-old Justice Archibald K. Gardner of the Eighth Circuit. "The Hutch," as lawyers call him, began his judicial career in 1918 when President Wilson appointed him to the district bench. In 1931 President Hoover moved him up to the court of appeals. He served as chief judge until August 6, 1959, when the eighty-one-year-old jurist was forced to give up the center chair because of a newly enacted law requiring retirement as chief judge at age seventy.

Hutcheson continues to serve on the court. Once a Wilsonian liberal, in his older years he has become more conservative. "I am," he says, "—and proud of it—not a New Dealer but a Jeffersonian, Lincolnian American." [25] He has been a battler against bureaucrats in general and the National Labor Relations Board in particular, outspokenly critical of his superiors on the

[25] J. C. Hutcheson, Jr., "The Natural Law and the Right to Property," *Notre Dame Lawyer,* vol. 26, 1951, p. 642.

Supreme Court,[26] and personally a believer in segregation—
nonetheless he has consistently enforced the rulings against
school segregation.

Richard T. Rives, the present chief judge, a former president
of both the Montgomery and the Alabama Bar Associations,
was appointed by Truman. Judge Rives speaks the accent but
not the language of segregation. Impatient with delaying maneuvers, Chief Judge Rives has frequently reminded his fellow
southerners that they must obey the law whether they like it or
not.

Elbert P. Tuttle is next in line of seniority. He was the first
of Eisenhower's selections. He had moved to Atlanta from the
North in 1923, and had become active in Republican party
circles and community affairs, among them serving as a member
of the board of trustees of the famous Negro center of learning,
Atlanta University. He was head of the Treasury Department's
legal division at the time of his appointment to fill the vacancy
created by the death of Robert L. Russell, brother of Georgia's
Senator Richard B. Russell.

The Fifth's only ultra segregationist is Benjamin F. Cameron,
age seventy, from Meridian, Mississippi, a Republican, and a
1955 Eisenhower-Eastland selection. Insisting that what he always refers to as "the so-called civil rights statutes" should be
narrowly construed, Judge Cameron joined the two federal district judges from Mississippi in sustaining that state's "understanding test." [27] This test, adopted in 1955, requires applicants
for voter registration to demonstrate to the satisfaction of county
registrars that they "have a reasonable understanding of the
duties and obligations of citizenship." It is common knowledge
that the test was adopted to keep Negroes from voting. Yet
Judge Cameron said: "At a time when alien ideologies are mak-

[26] See speech to Fort Worth–Tarrant County Bar Association reported
in *New York Times,* November 25, 1958.

[27] Suits challenging the constitutionality of a state constitutional provision or a state law must be heard by a three-man district court. A circuit
judge joins with the district judges to hear such a case.

ing a steady and insidious assault upon constitutional government everywhere"—citing as his evidence the headlines of *U. S.
News & World Report,* October 3, 1958—"it is nothing but
reasonable that the States should be tightening their belts and
seeking to assure that those carrying the responsibility of suf-
frage understand and appreciate the form and genius of the
government of this country and of the States." [28]

President Eisenhower's next two selections are more moderate: Judge Warren L. Jones was born in Colorado, but he
moved to Florida in 1926, became a prominent attorney, bank
president, a student of Lincoln, and a circuit judge in 1955.
Judge John R. Brown was also born outside the South, in Nebraska, but he too moved to the South early in his career, becoming a leading Houston attorney, an active Republican, and
a circuit judge in 1955.

John Minor Wisdom, the junior member of the Fifth, represents the greatest departure from regional standards. Prior to
appointment he was Republican national committeeman from
Louisiana, a strong Eisenhower booster, and most significantly
a member of both the New Orleans Urban League, which promotes job opportunities for Negroes, and of the President's Committee on Government Contracts, which is responsible for federal contractors' compliance with the nondiscrimination clause.

Wisdom was strongly backed by Camille F. Gravel, Jr.,
Louisiana's Democratic national committeeman, a man whose
public endorsement of desegregation led to an unsuccessful move
by Louisiana Democrats to oust him from his party position.[29]
It could be expected that Wisdom's confirmation would have
had rough going in the Senate, though Louisiana's Democratic
Senators Allen J. Ellender and Russell B. Long refused to oppose confirmation. Wisdom was questioned by a subcommittee
of the Senate Judiciary Committee consisting of Senators James

[28] *Darby v. Daniel,* 3 RRLR 1177 at 1186 (1958).
[29] William C. Havard and Robert J. Steamer, "Louisiana Secedes: Col-
lapse of a Compromise," *Massachusetts Review,* vol. 1, October 1959, pp.
134–146.

O. Eastland, William E. Jenner, and Olin D. Johnston of South
Carolina, a trio not inclined to have much sympathy for a
southern moderate. But when Wisdom told the senators he had
served in the Urban League merely to promote harmony and
explained his service on the Government Contracts Committee
by pointing out the committee had never invoked sanctions
against noncomplying employers, Eastland announced: "I am
satisfied." [30] Washington insiders speculated that Eastland and
Attorney General Rogers must have made another of their
famous "arrangements." From then on Wisdom's confirmation
went smoothly.

The Supreme Court has refused to review most school desegregation suits, and therefore these ten circuit court judges—
three from the Fourth and seven from the Fifth—are for most of
these cases the judges of last resort. Presidents have more latitude in selecting circuit than district judges, and it is doubtful
that President Eisenhower would have been able to place a
Sobeloff or a Wisdom on the district bench in a deep southern
state. Once selected, circuit judges are less immediately a part
of the political life of a single state because of their wider jurisdiction. With a larger constituency, they are not as sensitive as
the district court judges to local pressures. In keeping with their
position in the judicial hierarchy intermediate between the Supreme Court and the district courts, are their rulings, less "national" than those of the Supreme Court but less "regional," on
the whole, than those of the district judges. Not unexpectedly,
the courts of appeals have applied the law more favorably to
the cause of civil rights than have some of the district judges.

Forty-eight district judges plus ten circuit judges: these are
the men on the spot in the eleven states of the South. What happens in their courtrooms will determine whether the Supreme

---

[30] *New Orleans Times-Picayune,* March 5, March 23, April 28, April
30, and May 1, 1957; Subcommittee of the Senate Judiciary Committee
on Nomination of John Minor Wisdom, *Hearings,* 85th Congress, 1st
Session, April 29, 1957.

Court's 1954 decision is promise or reality. Yet the litigation before these judges cannot be isolated from its political context. What happens inside the courtrooms is influenced by what happens in the halls of Congress, at the meetings of school boards, in sessions of the PTA, and in smoke-filled rooms of political conventions.

2 * The Strategy of Segregation

Every school board member in the United States takes a solemn oath to support the Constitution of the United States, anything in the constitution or laws of his own state to the contrary notwithstanding. Although the Brown decision itself applied immediately only to the five defendant school districts, the Supreme Court's ruling that segregation is unconstitutional is binding on all of the three thousand school districts operating racially separate schools. No other legal action is necessary to make it so. Since May 1955 any member of a board of education who fails to use his official position to start to integrate the schools under his control is flouting the Constitution of the United States, and violating his own sworn oath as well as the criminal laws of the United States.[1]

Have southern school board members honored their oaths? Or have they forced a lawsuit in each district?

Until 1957 there were signs that many boards of education,

---

[1] Section 242 of Title 18 of the United States Criminal Code makes it a crime for any person acting under the color of law to deprive willfully any person of any right secured to him by the Constitution. Negroes have a constitutional right not to be segregated into colored public schools. School officials who willfully continue to do so are depriving Negroes of their rights in violation of this section.

especially of the larger cities, would integrate voluntarily. The Chattanooga Board of Education announced: "The . . . board . . . will comply with the decision of the United States Supreme Court on the matter of integration in the public schools. . . . Should we have said that we would not comply, we would have been saying that each man is the sole judge of what laws he shall obey. . . . We will not be a party to what is an attack on the very foundation of our way of life." [2] In Houston, board member Mrs. A. S. Vandervoort said: "I am determined to obey the law and not to indulge in subterfuge to circumvent it." [3] Similar pronouncements were made in Little Rock, Nashville, Greensboro, Ashville, Charlotte, Arlington, and Norfolk.

Some of those who remained silent, nonetheless, were willing to desegregate. For tactical reasons they were waiting for a specific court order. Such an order would take from their shoulders the onus of an unpopular action; it would help explain to constituents why the schools must be desegregated. These officials put up only minimal opposition to the lawsuits and stood ready to carry out the judge's orders without subterfuge.

To be sure these boards of education frankly sought the least amount of integration over the longest period of time. They hoped by a judicious alteration of attendance districts and by a careful screening of applicants to retain the basic patterns of segregation. They hoped that by introducing "token" integration they could secure the judge's support and forestall more comprehensive alterations in the operation of the schools. Negro leaders denounced these programs, but as in all collective bargaining, they were willing to settle for less than they were publicly asking.

In the Upper South this good faith action by big city moderates was matched by state officials. Virginia's superintendent of public instruction stated: "There will be no defiance of the Supreme Court as far as I am concerned. We are trying to teach

[2] *The New South*, July–August 1955, pp. 6–7.
[3] *Houston Post*, February 6, 1956.

school children to obey the law of the land and we will abide by it." [4] Virginia's Governor Thomas B. Stanley promised he "would work toward a plan which will be acceptable to our citizens and in keeping with the edict of the Supreme Court." [5] The Arkansas commissioner of education announced: "Arkansas will do nothing to evade the orders of the Court. . . . State school officials will never go along with abolishing the public school system." [6] The 1955 Arkansas legislature refused to adopt a segregation program, and in 1956 Orval Faubus, who at the time was considered a moderate, was re-elected governor against the spirited challenge of segregationist Jim Johnson.

North Carolina adopted the Pearsall Plan which permitted cities to initiate limited integration, Tennessee proclaimed a four-year program to desegregate its colleges, and Texas announced that integration was a problem for each local district with which the state would not interfere. Governor Allan Shivers of that state said: "Regardless of how we feel about this unfortunate and untimely situation, we must recognize it now as part of the supreme law of the land." [7] From Texas through Virginia compliance was underway.

Everyone knew there would be pockets of resistance. Segregation was not going to be destroyed without spirited litigation in some cities. But in most metropolitan areas, the district judge's task, so it was assumed, would be limited to the issuing of an occasional order to speed the process.

Dedicated segregationists were desperate. They knew they had to bring this drift toward compliance to a stop or within a short time integration would be accomplished in the larger cities. From here it would spread into the middle-sized towns, and once it became the accepted pattern, successful opposition would be difficult to organize.

---

[4] *Atlanta Journal and Constitution*, September 12, 1954.
[5] *Ibid.*
[6] *Ibid.*
[7] *The New South*, July–August 1955, p. 13.

Who are these segregationists? Most white southerners prefer segregation, but since 1954 the extremists have appropriated the title of "segregationist" for themselves. In the political lexicon of the South, "segregationist" refers to those who oppose integration no matter how limited or how gradual, no matter whether ordered by a judge or not. To a segregationist there is no compromise: the admission of a single Negro to a "white" school is a calamity to be avoided whatever the cost. (Segregationists even objected when the Houston School Board published its teacher directory without designation of race. The board retreated and the next year resegregated the directory.) To a segregationist no school board member, federal judge, or decent American has any obligation outranking his duty to maintain racial segregation.

In the rural South almost all white southerners, regardless of their educational or economic level, are segregationists. This is not so in the cities. Moderates, if not in a majority, make up a substantial segment of the leadership. The term "moderate" came into vogue after 1954. It is used ambiguously to cover a variety of positions, but moderates, unlike segregationists, are willing to accept some degree of school integration if it becomes the price of maintaining public schools or avoiding anarchy.

Such moderation embarrasses the segregationists, and they often explain it away. One is not long in a southern city before he is told: "This is not a typical southern community"—in Miami because there are so many Yankees, in Nashville because it is not so far south, in Dallas because it is too far west, in New Orleans because of the strong French-Catholic tradition, in Atlanta because of the well-established tradition of responsible white and Negro leadership, and so on. But the fact is that most southern cities really do have more in common with their northern and western counterparts than they do with their own rural hinterlands.

Of course most white southern city dwellers prefer segregation, as undoubtedly do many white citizens of northern cities.[8]

---

[8] In one careful survey about 35 per cent of white Detroiters indicated that they opposed any kind of school integration. Again a relation be-

But if the choice is between limited integration or no public schools, between token integration or flouting the Supreme Court, in most southern cities the moderates have sufficient political backing to accept the transition from the old to the new.

And in the cities of the South the claims and aspirations of the Negro cannot be ignored. The growing Negro urban middle class has economic independence and political power; white supremacy is no longer as profitable at the ballot box as it once was. It is more than coincidence that mayors of the large cities and school board officials seldom espouse ultra segregation.

The battle between moderates and segregationists in the cities generally follows economic and educational lines. Upper- and middle-income, educated, urban southerners tend to be moderates. Not that they advocate integration, for they too prefer to send their children to schools from which Negroes are excluded. But if the Supreme Court and the local district judge say they must integrate, so be it.

The educated and more prosperous urban southerners are not terrified by the prospect of controlled school desegregation. They live in the better neighborhoods; schools where their children go will hardly be altered by the abolition of legal segregation. Better educated, exposed to the mass media, feeling a part of the national community, sensitive to outside opinion, understanding the revolution of "rising expectations" among Negroes, these southerners form the core element of the moderates.

Segregationists are strong primarily in the rural areas. There are also large numbers of them in the cities, in the neighborhoods of the least prestige among the lower-income and least educated whites. Of course, not all lower-income southern city dwellers are ardent segregationists and many of the more prosperous citizens are. But the typical hard-core resister who is willing to use force to prevent desegregation, the kind of person found in the crowds massed in front of schools, hurling invectives at Negro pupils, are blue-collar workers, with little or no education, and little or

tween attitude toward integration and formal education was discovered. *New York Times,* October 8, 1957.

no exposure to newspapers, radio, television, and national magazines.[9]

It is these people who are most directly in competition with Negroes for jobs, homes, and social prestige. Living in residential zones closest to Negro neighborhoods, they are most immediately affected by the abolition of segregation. As the former superintendent of Nashville schools, W. A. Bass, observed, "integration comes first to those least prepared for it"—the people least knowledgeable, most fearful, most susceptible to the appeals of street agitators. They are untouched by community campaigns, do not read newspaper editorials, do not belong to civic and social clubs, and even the churches they attend are presided over by ministers preaching that integration is forbidden by the Bible.

This social, economic, and educational nature of the division between segregationists and moderates has long been recognized not only by social scientists but by such acute practitioners of southern politics as Arkansas Governor Faubus. Faubus recognized the social-economic nature of the split when he described his followers as "the good, honest, hard-working people of the lower and middle classes," and charged that his opponents were "the Cadillac brigade of wealthy and prominent leaders." [10] His is a modern variant of the traditional populist appeal to the rural whites against the city slickers.

The leaders of the segregation movement, however, are often more substantial citizens, many of them well-educated and economically secure. They give moral encouragement and supporting constitutional and religious rhetoric to their cause, appealing

[9] See the findings of the following: Herbert H. Hyman and Paul B. Sheatsley, "Attitudes Toward Desegregation," *Scientific American,* December 1956; Wayne H. Holtzon, "Attitude of College Men Toward Non-Segregation in Texas Schools," *Public Opinion Quarterly,* vol. XX, Fall 1956, pp. 559–569; Melvin M. Tumin, *Desegregation: Resistance and Readiness,* Princeton: Princeton University Press, 1958; *Amicus Curiae* Brief of the Attorney General of Florida, *Brown v. Board of Education,* December 1956, pp. 107 ff., reporting study of Florida leadership made under direction of Dr. Lewis Killian. See also *Look,* "Member of the Mob," November 12, 1957, pp. 35–37.

[10] *Southern School News,* June 1959, p. 3.

to "the lower and middle classes" to provide the critical mass support.

The most vocal segregationists are the "councilmen" whose organizations are variously called states rights councils or citizens councils. Councilmen are strongest in Mississippi, Alabama, South Carolina, Georgia (except Atlanta), Eastern Arkansas, Northern Louisiana, Northern Florida, and East Texas—that is in the Black Belt, the area of large Negro concentrations.

Councilmen renounce violence, but the line between nonviolent pressures and violence is sometimes drawn rather finely. Councilmen are so positive "the people won't stand for it" that they view any attempt to integrate the schools as leading to massive upheavals. A good test to distinguish a segregationist from a moderate is to ask: "Do you think the schools in this town can be integrated without trouble?" If the answer is: "There will be blood in the streets," you are probably talking to a segregationist. Not all who predict large-scale resistance are segregationists, but almost all segregationists so predict. Councilmen are certain that, except for a few ministers or newspaper editors playing up to northerners, all southerners feel as strongly as they do, and they react angrily to any suggestion that many southerners are willing to accept a moderate degree of integration.

Running through councilmen's literature and in their public speeches is a sometimes hidden, sometimes open theme that all integrationists are Jews and Communists, and that defense of segregation is defense of Christianity. It reflects a belief that all the agitation is caused by Communists and "pinkos": Congressman E. L. (Tic) Forrester of Georgia assured the Georgia legislature: "The truth is this agitation over civil rights . . . is the work of the Communist party," and he warned his audience not to blame either Negroes or Yankees, but the "minorities." [11] And Sheriff Willis V. McCall of Lake County, Florida, commented: "We haven't had any trouble except what is being

[11] Speech before the Georgia legislature reprinted in the *Congressional Record,* vol. 104, February 18, 1958, p. A1410.

stirred up by outsiders, left-wingers, most of it communist-inspired." [12] At their meetings horror stories are told and believed; in the fall of 1957 the story was repeated that Mayor Richard J. Daley of Chicago was making every city employee force his daughter to go out with a Negro. As Robert Patterson, the executive secretary of the citizens councils of Alabama, phrased it: "We don't have to appeal to fanatics. They're on our side anyway." [13]

Councilmen are confident that their position is misunderstood, primarily because of what they consider the bias of national news media or, as R. Carter Pittman of Dalton, Georgia, wrote in an article widely circulated among segregationists: "The South is an ideal whipping boy because no magazine with national circulation is published in the South and most of her leading newspapers are owned by residents of the North—some as far north as Moscow." [14]

Most, but not all, councilmen deny that they are prejudiced against Negroes. Roy V. Harris of Georgia, a short, sixty-year-old power in Georgia politics, a former regent of the University of Georgia, president of Georgia's States' Rights Council, told one interviewer: "I have no feeling against Nigras, never called one 'nigger' in my life. I feel Nigras are different, though, in almost every respect. I feel they should have equal opportunities— for voting, too. . . . We're just not going to integrate in Georgia." [15] However, he told someone else who asked about court-ordered integration: "I can tell you what would happen in Georgia. I know of about four counties that have very few niggers where they would just run 'em out. And down in south Georgia where there's more niggers than white people, why, there'll just be some beatings at night and then they'll get the

[12] William Peters, *The Southern Temper,* Garden City: Doubleday, 1959, p. 215.

[13] *The New South,* March 1957, p. 15, quoting a United Press dispatch.

[14] R. C. Pittman, "The Supreme Court, the Broken Constitution and the Shattered Bill of Rights," reprinted in the *Congressional Record,* vol. 102, February 28, 1956, p. A1861.

[15] Peters, *op. cit.,* p. 213.

idea." [16] Furthermore, Harris's newspaper, *The Augusta Courier,* talks constantly in terms of resistance to the last southerner. It urges Georgians to be prepared to follow a policy of "withering ostracism" against Negro children. It sets forward as a proper model of behavior the antics of white students who "spit on them [Negroes], threw rocks at them, kick their shins and do everything they can to run them out." [17]

To the "gentlemen-segregationists" Negroes are children to whom one owes protection, but to some councilmen they are dangerous animals to be kept at a distance. A well-dressed woman standing in the crowded corridors outside the federal district courtroom in Little Rock said vehemently: "I don't give a damn what that stupid little judge in there says, my children are never going to school with monkeys." Directly in front of her were an elderly Negro man and woman. Others around her shrank in embarrassment, but this woman, who was a leader in the segregationist Mothers League of Central High School, made no attempt to moderate her voice as she continued to give vent to her feelings. She did not intend to insult the Negroes deliberately; she just did not see them, though she was looking directly at them. They were not part of her world.

Senator Sam Englehardt, Jr., Alabama's leading councilman and chief legislative spokesman, says that "desegregating the schools will lead to rape! Damn niggers stink; they're unwashed; they have no morals; they're just animals. . . . The nigger is depraved! Give him the opportunity to be near a white woman, and he goes berserk! . . . The nigger isn't just a dark-skinned white man. He's a separate individual altogether." [18]

To be distinguished from the councilmen are the gentlemen-segregationists who are more prevalent in the Upper than the Lower South. Among their organizations are the Patrons of North Carolina, the Tennessee Federation of Constitutional Gov-

---

[16] Interview with *Look* editor George B. Leonard, Jr., *Look,* November 12, 1957, p. 34.
[17] *The Augusta Courier,* October 28, 1957, p. 4.
[18] Peters, *op. cit.,* p. 208.

ernment, the Virginia Defenders of State Sovereignty and Individual Liberties.

Gentlemen-segregationists are less strident than councilmen. They take care to disassociate from street agitators, and, although they insist that the Supreme Court's decision does not state the law of the land, they contend that they are opposed to unlawful resistance. But perhaps one should not make too much of this difference between the gentlemen and the councilmen. One distinguished Virginian who favors segregation but opposes the tactics of segregationists insists "it is only the difference between a call girl and a prostitute."

In every state gentlemen-segregationists include some college professors and well-known journalists. They emphasize states' rights, the preservation of the noble southern traditions against northern commercialism. Their arguments are presented in the language of scholarship, often with elaborate legal citations and historical quotations. They are learned and they believe in law. But they are adamant on the issue of segregation.

A leading editorial writer of a major southern newspaper, who fervently believes that paternalism, though he does not call it this, is a natural state of race relations, is not anti-Negro himself at all. He points with pride to the many incidents of kindness between whites and Negroes in the South and contrasts the genuine affection of white southerners toward Negroes with the cold and impersonal attitude of northerners. He is proud of his relationship with his janitor. "George," he says, "is a wonderful man. When you tell him to clean the floor, you can rely on its being clean. When George had been with us for thirty years, we held a little ceremony attended by all the executives of the newspaper. It was the greatest day in George's life. It was full of warmth and companionship." [19] Such stories are told frequently. Congressman Forrester said to the Georgia legislature: "Down in Leesburg, Ga., there is an old Negro who has worked for me off and on for twenty-five or thirty years and he has as faithful a

[19] Personal interview.

heart as ever beat in a human breast. He writes to me often. In one of his letters he said this to me: 'Everything is all right down home, and the yard is all right. You take care of the Yankees, and I'll take care of the home folks.' " [20] Apparently each of the segregationists is close to a "Nigra" with whom he would trust his life. And it is this "Nigra" who always says, "Mr. Jim, I don't want to go to school with any white folks. I just wish those Yankees would leave us alone."

These are the segregationists. Their strategy is relatively simple. Mobilize political power to discourage any school board or any judge from moving against segregation. Create obstacles to make it difficult and dangerous for any Negro to carry the issue before a judge. If these moves fail, persuade the judge not to issue any injunctions, or if he does issue one, persuade him that it need not call for any actual desegregation. If all this fails, then find ways to circumvent the injunction.

But this strategy will not work unless school boards refuse to initiate desegregation and unless they resist each lawsuit with determination. The first imperative for segregationists was to persuade school officials they had no obligation to desegregate or to co-operate with the judge.

The Constitution itself could not be used as a target for segregationists; it is too secure for attack. So segregationists have aimed their shafts instead at the Supreme Court, insisting that if one wishes to obey the Constitution, he must disobey the Court. The Supreme Court, many of them charge, was misled by "communist" writers into making a decision based on sociology and contrary to law. It is the Supreme Court justices, rather than the segregationists, who are violating the Constitution.

The Supreme Court made it relatively easy for its enemies to discredit its decision. There were ample legal precedents which the justices could have cited to repudiate segregation. And such a controversial decision would have been better fortified against segregationists' attacks if it had been wrapped with the writings

[20] *Congressional Record*, vol. 104, February 18, 1958, p. A1410.

of the Founding Fathers and properly dotted with legal precedent.[21] Instead the justices handed down a brief opinion basing one of their central findings on the works of psychologists and sociologists. This gave the segregationists a tactical advantage which they have been quick to exploit. The Supreme Court's use of psychological evidence, they have charged, proves that the ruling against segregation is a departure from the traditions of the law and is based on the ideology of alien social scientists.

Yet the difference between the Supreme Court's 1896 decision (*Plessy v. Ferguson*) sustaining segregation, and its 1954 decision overruling it, is one of psychological and sociological assumptions. The Plessy decision is based on the assertion that segregation does not sanctify into law the doctrine of white supremacy or lead to discrimination. The Brown decision asserts the contrary. Of course the Supreme Court justices of 1954 were expressing value preferences; so were the justices of 1896.

On March 12, 1956, ninety-six United States congressmen from the South issued a "manifesto" and segregationists made a major breakthrough in their campaign to dignify defiance of the federal judiciary. In the manifesto some of the South's most respected leaders promised to use "all lawful means" to maintain segregation and "commended those states which have declared

[21] It is probably no accident that the segregationists' emphasis has been on the supposed sociological rather than the psychological basis of the 1954 decision despite the fact that the Court referred more to the work of the latter than the former. "Psychology, with its I.Q., aptitude, and other tests to which the public has been subjected, as well as its closeness to medicine and psychiatry, has more popular acceptance as a science. Nor is it too farfetched to note the ease in making sociologists sound like socialists." Herbert Garfinkel, "Social Science and the School Segregation Cases," paper presented before the American Political Science Association, 1957.

The introduction of evidence from social sciences is not new, dating at least from the days of the celebrated Brandeis briefs. Moreover, in thirty-two previous civil rights suits the NAACP had called over forty scientists and professional educators to the stand as expert witnesses. (*See* Appendix to Appellants Brief, 347 U.S. 483 12.) Virginia used social scientists to defend segregation in the Prince Edward case.

the intention to resist." It did much to dignify the posture of defiance, as did the interposition resolutions adopted by southern legislatures. These resolutions, varying in tone from calm protest to proclamations that the Brown decision is null and void, have no legal significance. But their use of the great names of Jefferson and Madison gave a mantle of legitimacy to the notion that it is honorable for a district judge or a school board to ignore the Supreme Court's construction of the Constitution, and that the path of honor is to disobey the Court.

The Court was also being attacked during this period from the North, but for different reasons. In its 1956 term, the Supreme Court handed down a series of decisions sustaining contentions that national-security-loyalty programs violated constitutional rights, and these decisions so antagonized many northerners, especially conservative Republicans, that in the 1957 Congressional session they opened a sustained drive "to curb the Court."

Then in August 1958, just as the Little Rock Case (*Aaron v. Cooper*) was to be heard by the Supreme Court, a resolution accusing the Court of disregarding states' rights was rushed through the Conference of State Supreme Court Chief Justices. Early in 1959 the American Bar Association threw its considerable prestige into the fray by adopting a report critical of the Supreme Court for certain of its decisions concerning internal security.

In all of these attacks on the federal judiciary segregationists "played it cool." Although active behind the scenes, segregationists let their northern allies carry the brunt of the offensive. The issue of segregation was subdued. But the cause of segregation had been immeasurably helped, for these attacks gave credence to the segregationists' charges of "judicial tyranny," and of a "communist-tainted Supreme Court," and they have powerfully supported the drive to force school boards to defy federal judges.

In order to counter these contentions that despite the Supreme Court's ruling, segregation remains constitutional, congressional liberals have proposed that Congress go on record, at least to the extent of declaring that the Brown decision states "the law of the land." The intensity of segregationists' opposition, so far successful, to such a congressional endorsement is understandable when placed in the context of this drive to persuade southerners that school boards which comply with the Court are disreputable. For if the day ever comes when southerners are convinced segregation is unconstitutional, segregationists will have lost the battle even before the lawsuits begin. No wonder Senator Richard Russell of Georgia has called these proposals for congressional endorsement of the Brown decision "the most objectionable feature" of civil rights bills.

The segregationists' ability to persuade southerners that the path of honor lies in defying desegregation decisions has had its impact on the district judges as well as the school boards. Judges are made of somewhat hardier qualities than school board members, but even judges are not accustomed to accusations of tyranny, and are hesitant to stand against the public clamor. As Oliver Wendell Holmes, Jr., wrote back in 1881, "the felt necessities of the time, the prevalent moral and political theories, institutions of public policy, avowed or unconscious, even the prejudices which judges share with their fellow-men, have had a good deal more to do than the syllogism in determining the rules by which men should be governed." Segregationists have molded the "felt necessities" of the South. Perhaps not the lasting ones, or even those most widely held, but certainly those most loudly heard.

Segregationists have nevertheless been unable to persuade all boards of education to resist. Some they cannot intimidate, and segregationists could not permit even a few cities to integrate. They turned to the state authorities for help.

If Little Rock had not been in Arkansas, Atlanta not in Georgia, Miami not in Florida, New Orleans not in Louisiana, schools could and would have been desegregated within a year or two after the Supreme Court's decision. In any city a small group of fanatics may stir up trouble, but the moderates in control of these cities would have honored their constitutional oaths. They have not done so because segregationists have been using state governments to force city moderates to resist court decrees.

Some southern governors have done their part in thwarting desegregation. Governor Faubus's interference in Little Rock is the most noted example. But Governors Marvin Griffin of Georgia and Allan Shivers of Texas were active also. On the other hand, in many states the governors have refused to interfere, leaving it up to school authorities to formulate their own programs and backing them if they run into trouble. Governors LeRoy Collins of Florida, Luther Hodges of North Carolina, and Frank Clement of Tennessee, for example, at considerable political risk have refused to fan the fires of discontent or to use their offices to aid the segregationists. The extremists have had much more consistent success with the state legislatures.

Southern legislatures are the citadels of segregation. Rural and small-town districts in which extremist sentiment is dominant are overrepresented in the legislature and give segregationists control of the leadership positions.[22] These rural-dominated legislatures, despite their avowed attachment to the virtues of local self-government, have stripped cities of their power to comply with judicial obligations. For example, in Texas, after 125 cities had integrated voluntarily, the legislature made it practically impossible for any large city to do so. Under Texas law, unless a favorable vote is first obtained in a public referendum, if a single Negro student is allowed to attend a "white" school, all the schools in the district are to lose state financial aid and the members of the

---

[22] In Alabama the sixteen Black Belt Counties—contiguous counties with a Negro-white population ratio ranging over or near 50 per cent—contain 12 per cent of the state's total population. Yet these sixteen counties elect over one-fourth of the state senators and state representatives. This same picture of overrepresentation of Black Belt counties is to be found in other southern states, most prominently in Georgia, Louisiana, and Mississippi. Black Belt legislators with their seniority have a disproportionate share of the key leadership positions. See Patrick E. McCauley, "Be It Enacted," in *With All Deliberate Speed,* edited by Don Shoemaker. New York: Harper, 1957, p. 130 ff.

board of education are subject to fine and imprisonment. In Louisiana the legislature tried to take charge of New Orleans' schools and to remove members of the school board from office in order to keep the city from complying with an integration decree. Until 1961 the Georgia legislature stipulated that all schools in a city were to be closed if a Negro was assigned to a "white" school. Virginia stripped local boards of authority over assignment of pupils, and forced them to ignore federal courts at pain of having schools closed. As Congressman William Tuck from Southside Virginia explained segregationists' policy: "We cannot allow Arlington or Norfolk to integrate. If they won't stand with us, I say make them stand." [23]

Negroes lack the political power to force school boards to integrate. Their only choice is to litigate and to persuade a judge to command the board to act. Segregationists do not fear this as long as the national government does not interfere. Segregationists do not expect the President or the Department of Justice to espouse segregation. But it suits their purpose almost as well if these officials stay out of the fight. For unless the national government throws its legal authority and political power into the battle behind southern moderates, Negro plaintiffs, and district judges, it is an unequal contest.

To immobilize federal authorities, segregationists have adroitly manipulated the states' rights symbol. Preference for states' rights, the belief that the states are "closer to the people" than the national government, is part of our conventional wisdom. Countless political speeches have dwelt on the danger of an over-reaching federal bureaucracy. By tying into these ideological commitments, segregationists have been able to win the adherence of some citizens, both in the North and in the South, who do not really care too much one way or the other about school integration. In no field is the cry of states' rights more persuasive than in education, for control over public schools is

[23] *Washington Post & Times Herald*, November 15, 1958.

traditionally a local responsibility. Segregationists have built on this tradition to question the bona fides of national intervention. The defenders of slavery were able to secure General Robert E. Lee's support, despite his distaste for slavery, by appealing to his loyalty to Virginia; similarly present-day defenders of segregation have used the doctrine of states' rights to persuade some who have no strong feelings about desegregation of the nobility of their cause.

President Eisenhower refused to provide moral leadership or to use his powers as Chief Executive in support of the Supreme Court decision. Except for his momentary intervention in Little Rock, which he did not follow up, he refused to take any part in this, the most important domestic crisis of postwar America. He criticized "extremists," and then proceeded to equate the NAACP with the citizens councils, depicting the conflict as being between two equally legitimate groups, those working for compliance with the Constitution, and those working for its defiance. He said: ". . . There are very strong emotions on the other side, people that see a picture of mongrelization of the race, they call it." [24]

Eisenhower insisted that the refusal to obey the federal courts could not be dealt with by law enforcement, but only by moral conversion,[25] yet he made little attempt to lead the people toward this conversion. In 1956, when a few southern schools were about to open for the first time on an integrated basis and segregationists were organizing student boycotts, a reporter asked the President if he would care to use his "tremendous

[24] Transcript, President's news conference, September 3, 1957.

[25] President Eisenhower's position is at variance with the findings of most social scientists who make a distinction between prejudice and discrimination. They have found that prejudice and discrimination are often independent though related variables; changes in the social and legal situation often precede rather than follow from changes in attitudes. In many areas experience confirms these findings. Take bus desegregation: southerners changed their seats before they changed their minds. On this general point of the relations between prejudice and discrimination, see Melvin M. Tumin, *Desegregation: Resistance and Readiness,* Princeton, N. J.: Princeton University Press, 1958.

reservoir of good will among the young people" and give them some advice on how they should conduct themselves. Here is what the President said: "Well, I can say what I have said so often: it is difficult through law and through force to change a man's heart. . . . We must all . . . help to bring about a change in spirit so that extremists on both sides do not defeat what we know is a reasonable, logical conclusion to this whole affair, which is recognition of equality of men." [26]

The President made no attempt to answer segregationists who on the floor of Congress, on national television, and in public forums, taught that it is honorable and profitable to defy the United States government. Since judges cannot hold press conferences or buy television time to answer their critics, the charges against them went unchallenged by any person of national stature.

President Eisenhower believed it was desirable to obey the law, but he deliberately refused to endorse the Brown decision on its merits. The only time he did state his own views, he gave aid and comfort to the segregationists. The background was this: In the summer of 1958 the Little Rock School Board asked Federal Judge Harry J. Lemley, a segregationist himself, for permission to interrupt their desegregation program. They told Judge Lemley that the illegal interference by Arkansas officials and the consequent disorder had created such chaotic educational conditions that they felt entitled to resegregate. Judge Lemley agreed.

Segregationists rushed forward with praise for Judge Lemley. Here at last was a federal judge who realized that only chaos would result if cities were forced to integrate too quickly. But their shouts of joy were silenced: the court of appeals reversed Judge Lemley, saying that to yield to the contention that disorder justifies resegregation would be to enthrone official lawlessness.

The Supreme Court was called into emergency session. Would it support Lemley or the court of appeals? Throughout the South

[26] Transcript, President's news conference, September 5, 1956.

federal judges waited, especially in Virginia, where desegregation suits were ripening into the action stage. It was in this context that the rumor spread throughout Washington that President Eisenhower wished the Supreme Court had never ruled against segregation, that he felt the Court should allow southern communities to proceed more slowly, and that he agreed with Judge Lemley.

At the August 27, 1958, Presidential press conference, a reporter asked: "Mr. President, is this rumor correct?" The President refused once again "to give an opinion about my conviction about the Supreme Court decisions." But he did say: "I might have said something about 'slower,' but I do believe that we should—because I do say, as I did yesterday or last week, we have got to have reason and sense and education, and a lot of other developments that go hand in hand as this process—if this process is going to have any real acceptance in the United States." [27]

The President's statement, hailed by Governor Faubus and Virginia segregationists as a vindication of their contentions, was hardly calculated to encourage a lonely federal judge living in the South to stand up to the importunities of segregationists. Did not the President say that the path of wisdom was to move cautiously? Perhaps "all deliberate speed" should be construed as "within the next several decades." All over the South, federal judges withheld integration decrees. Not until the Supreme Court, which despite the President's statement refused to backtrack, issued its opinion sustaining the court of appeals and rebuking Lemley, did integration litigation move forward.

What have been the consequences of President Eisenhower's unwillingness to assume political leadership? No one can say for sure. But southern moderates feel the President let them down. In the absence of Presidential leadership there was no voice of national stature to answer the Faubuses and Eastlands or the Southern manifestos, no person to challenge the segre-

[27] Transcript, President's news conference, August 27, 1958.

gationist position that each southerner could decide for himself whether or not to obey the Constitution. In the summer and fall of 1958 Attorney General Rogers insisted in several major speeches that southerners were being misled into believing they could find a constitutional way to operate segregated schools, but an Attorney General lacks the political position and personal prestige of a President. Walter Lippmann commented: "Mr. Rogers made a brave attempt to make clear much of what the President has fogged up—but on the crucial question [what the Federal Government will do about the defiance of the Southern State governments, now that the issue is not lawless mobs but the resistance of state governments] Mr. Rogers, who has no administration policy to rely upon, resorted to exhortation and to pious platitudes." [28]

Not only did Eisenhower refuse to lead the forces of civil rights, but when he did speak, whatever his intentions, his words hurt southern moderates. By defining the situation so minimally and by constantly emphasizing the need to go slow, President Eisenhower made it appear that any school board or any district judge calling for integration, no matter how limited, was taking an "extremist" stand. Eisenhower called for state and local officials to speak out, but he made it difficult for them to lead: it is politically unrealistic to expect a southern governor, or a southern school board, or even a southern district judge to take a more advanced position on school integration than the President of the United States. It is not just a question of personal courage; an elected southern official who appears to be more of a civil rights advocate than the President runs a serious political risk of jeopardizing the forces of moderation. If he gets too far out in front—and as the President defined the situation, any stand other than prosegregation was made to appear daring—he exposes himself to defeat.

Moderates have no quarrel with Eisenhower because he chose to define the issue as between law and lawlessness rather than

[28] *New York Herald Tribune,* September 2, 1958.

between integration and segregation. In fact both in terms of moral conviction and political expediency this is precisely how the southern moderates themselves phrase the issue. They know that so long as white southerners think the choice is between segregation and integration they will choose the former. It is only when they become convinced that the alternatives are token integration or no public schools, only when the community recognizes that it is a question of the preservation of ordered liberty itself, that the moderates can hope for political backing.

So it was not Eisenhower's failure to endorse integration which disturbed the moderates, but his almost total refusal to use the prestige and power of his office to support those battling for integration. In 1955 Solicitor General Simon Sobeloff in behalf of the Eisenhower Administration had assured the Supreme Court: "The responsibility for achieving compliance with the Court's decision in these cases does not rest on the judiciary alone. Every officer and agency of government, federal, state, and local, is likewise charged with the duty of enforcing the Constitution and rights guaranteed under it." [29]

Yet, until the New Orleans crisis late in 1960, President Eisenhower did practically nothing. In fact, when chided by some congressional critics for his indifference, the President told them, via special counsel: "The President would not make any assumption that the judicial branch of the Government is incapable of implementing the Supreme Court's decision." [30]

There is a fundamental public interest in school-entry suits. But President Eisenhower considered them to be only private matters between two parties in which the federal government had no concern. The President did say he intended to prevent

[29] Supplemental Memorandum for the United States on the Further Argument of the Question of Relief, *Brown v. Board of Education,* filed April 21, 1955.

[30] *New York Times,* March 20, 1956.

(Compare this with Alexander Hamilton's observation in Federalist No. 78, "The judiciary must ultimately depend upon the aid of the executive arm even for the efficacy of its judgments.")

defiance of the federal judges, but he defined defiance in its narrowest terms. All school boards which persist in operating segregated schools are defying the federal courts. But President Eisenhower considered the defiance to cover only those rare incidents where persons refused to comply with injunctions specifically directed to them, and not always even then. In the fall of 1956 Governor Allan Shivers ordered Texas Rangers to prevent Negroes from entering Mansfield High School, in the face of a federal court order that they be allowed to attend. At his press conference the President admitted he did not know what Shivers had done. Further, he said: "Until states show their inability or their refusal to grapple with this question properly, which they haven't yet, at least as any proof has been submitted, we had better be very careful about moving in and exercising police power." Since Texas authorities had restored order, Eisenhower said, "the question became unimportant." [31] It was not unimportant to the district judges who saw how a governor had been permitted to make their actions meaningless gestures.

Between 1954 and 1960 there were at least twelve incidents in which rioters, sometimes with the tacit encouragement of state and local officials, tried to thwart the execution of a federal court order. Except in Clinton, Hoxie, Nashville, Little Rock, and New Orleans, federal executive authorities refused to intervene, and they did so in these instances only after local officials begged for help. The harassed school authorities in Clinton, Tennessee, had to plead with the Department of Justice for assistance. Finally the board threatened to close the school if the Attorney General did not intervene. In desperation they wrote to Herbert Brownell, then Attorney General: "For the authorities of the federal government . . . [to] take the position that the carrying out of such an order is a 'local problem' would seem to be the height of absurdity. . . . The local F.B.I. agents and the U.S. District Attorney's officers spend considerable time in

[31] President's news conference, September 5, 1956.

this country tracking down moonshiners . . . but for some un-explained reason are oblivious to the internationally known Clinton integration problem." [32]

The same story was repeated elsewhere. When rioters challenged Nashville authorities in September 1957, Mayor Ben West asked the Department of Justice for assistance, but received none and took the matter into his own hands while the Department of Justice "dilly-dallied." [33]

The unhappy Virgil T. Blossom, then superintendent of schools in Little Rock, and his associates tried in good faith to comply with federal court orders. Hounded by Governor Faubus and harassed by local segregationists, they turned to the Department of Justice for help. But until Governor Faubus forced President Eisenhower's hand, the President refused to give any assurance to Little Rock authorities or to take a stand against potential troublemakers.

In September 1957, when riots broke out in Little Rock, federal authorities were completely unprepared. They had no alternative but to use federal troops. Federal officials failed to follow up this use of troops and stood back to permit segregationists to organize boycotts, threaten school officials, and bully Negro pupils. Attorney General Brownell, whose name was prominently associated with the more vigorous federal intervention in Little Rock, resigned and was replaced by William Rogers. Rogers announced that there would be no federal prosecution of persons who had organized and led the riots.[34] This announcement was

[32] Letter to Brownell, December 3, 1956, in 2 RRLR 27–28 (1957).

[33] *Washington Post & Times Herald,* November 15, 1958.

[34] Mr. Rogers' confirmation went smoothly past Senator. Eastland and the Senate Judiciary Committee. Many southern moderates are convinced that a "deal" had been arranged in which the confirmation was allowed to go through the Senate without question because of an understanding that Rogers would not follow Brownell's "tough policy." Whatever the arrangements, both segregationists and moderates interpreted Rogers' appointment as a repudiation of Brownell's action in intervening in Little Rock. See, for example, the comments of Senator Rainach, the segregationist leader of Louisiana, in *New York Times,* December 20, 1958.

Mrs. Lennard Thomas of Montgomery, Alabama—Democratic national

deplored by Little Rock officials, who have claimed that it was directly responsible for the terrorism which followed.

In Little Rock, the Department of Justice refused to seek an injunction to restrain the segregationists, the kind of injunction which had brought an end to the terror in Clinton and Nashville. National officials took the position that such an injunction should have been asked for by the school board. On the other hand, Little Rock authorities insisted that the school board's position was much too precarious; they did not dare act. The Department of Justice, however, was in a position to withstand local criticism and retaliation.

Little Rock made the headlines and Governor Faubus's clumsiness forced Eisenhower to intervene, but throughout his tenure Eisenhower had no program to deal with authorities flouting the judicial branch of the national government. Moderates had been telling their communities that the federal government was going to force them to integrate so that the only wise course was to accept the fact that integration must come and try to contain it. When Eisenhower let defiance go unchallenged, segregationists' pressures mounted. This is certainly what happened in North Carolina.

A highly placed official reported that Eisenhower's failure to challenge Virginia's policy of massive resistance had made it increasingly difficult for North Carolina moderates to hold the line. Under the leadership of Governor Hodges city officials in North Carolina were encouraged to admit a few Negroes to "white" schools. It was not much in the way of integration, but at least it was a start. Hodges had sold his program by contending that unless North Carolina introduced some degree of integration, the federal government would force more drastic action. But as long as Virginia was allowed to get away with complete, total, and belligerent defiance, segregationists in North Caro-

---

committeewoman—commented: "I am so delighted that we now have an attorney general who apparently believes in a return to constitutional government. . . ." Other segregationists made similar comments. See *Atlanta Journal and Constitution,* December 15, 1957, p. 13.

lina insisted that if Hodges had resisted, they too, like Virginia, could have kept total segregation. Fortunately for North Carolina's moderates, Virginia was forced to capitulate, without Eisenhower's help, before the pressures became overwhelming.

Spokesmen for the Administration excused their inaction—their failure to intervene in suits, to help the plaintiffs, or to assist the judge, except on request of school authorities or on order of the judge after a court order had been issued—on the ground that they lacked legal authority. So in 1957 a half-hearted attempt was made to secure congressional authorization to permit the Department of Justice to initiate entry suits. In the midst of the Senate debate over this provision (known as Title III of the 1957 Civil Rights Act) Eisenhower backed down. At his press conference the President was asked if he would be willing to see Title III deleted. Said Eisenhower: "Well . . . I was reading part of this bill this morning and . . . there were . . . certain phrases I didn't completely understand. . . . I would want to talk to the Attorney General and see exactly what they do mean." [35]

The President's revelation of ignorance about a bill he had recommended to Congress did not, to say the least, strengthen the hands of the senators working for Title III. Following Eisenhower's apparent withdrawal of support, the Senate deleted it. To paraphrase what President Andrew Jackson is supposed to have said about John Marshall, President Eisenhower's policy seemed to have been: "Thurgood Marshall got his decision, now let him enforce it."

Here then was the situation: school boards acting in bad faith did not have to fear federal pressure. Their segregated schools opened as scheduled, without trouble. In cities where officials did make a good faith attempt to integrate, segregationists created trouble and the moderates received no federal assistance. Thus a school board caught between the pressures of a few Negro patrons on one side and segregationists on the other, consisting itself of persons who preferred segregation, quickly learned the

[35] *Congressional Quarterly Almanac,* 1957, p. 562.

lesson: desegregate and you get into trouble; refuse to do so and you are a hero.

The President's nonintervention policy has had its impact on the judges as well. If they can find a legitimate reason for postponing an unpopular ruling they are apt to do so. Nor were those judges who did act encouraged by the fact that if they ran into opposition, the President's backing was by no means assured. In this situation the most recalcitrant judge and the most defiant school board were allowed to set the pace. When a judge allowed a school board to get away with its program of "nothingness," there was a delaying reverberation throughout the South. Other judges were afraid to get too far out in front of the pack.

So it was that by 1957 segregationists brought the movement toward integration to a stop. The day of "voluntary integration" was over. Henceforth, it was going to take a hard-fought lawsuit and a tough, resolute judge if the Supreme Court's 1954 ruling was going to mean what it said.

3 * The Rocky Road to the Federal Courthouse

The old gentleman looked like Uncle Tom—but he certainly was not. He was sitting in the front row, his hands folded on his cane. The judge had announced a fifteen-minute recess in a case brought by Negroes to win a court order directing school officials to admit their children to schools nearest their homes.

"How does it look to you?" I asked the old man.

"That judge will fix them. This is one place where they can't squirm out of it."

"Are you one of the plaintiffs?"

"No, but I know all of them. We have had lots of meetings about this."

"Is this the first time you have been here?"

"No," he said. "We vote now, but we had to come here to get it."

This was a United States district court, to southern Negroes a sanctuary—one governmental body in the South where they feel they have a chance for a fair hearing, to have their claims dealt with uninfluenced by the fact that the decision-maker depends on white votes to retain his position. Yet it was still a southern courtroom, and when the hearing resumed most of the Negroes sat on one side of the aisle, most of the whites on the other.

Federal courts have not always been hospitable to civil rights. The judiciary was the last branch of the national government to be lost by the southerners before the Civil War; it was the first regained after the War. Until 1937 the federal judiciary, whose orthodoxy on economic matters led to its famous showdown with President Roosevelt, was as conservative about civil rights as it was about economics. Then came the constitutional revolution of 1937. Federal courts, at least at the top, came to be manned by men reflecting the attitudes and values of the constituencies electing "liberal" Presidents. Judges to whom trade unions were anathema, segregation sacred, and civil rights legislation unconstitutional no longer controlled the federal courts.

Negroes were encouraged to litigate. They saw no other choice: the southern veto in the Senate deprived them of much hope of mobilizing congressional support; they were disfranchised in the South and could expect little from those in charge of southern state governments. The lawsuit became the major weapon in their struggle to secure a greater share of the nation's bounty.

By the 1950's the Negro had secured a voice in southern urban politics. But within the South at large he still remained—as he does today—"a voiceless spectator at events which [shape] his destiny but over which he [has] no control; . . . No longer a slave, he [is] no more than a disfranchised servant, sharecropper, tenant farmer, laborer." [1] The political conflict over civil rights is still being fought primarily among the white communities. The Negro's most effective weapon remains the lawsuit. Unless a federal judge orders a board to desegregate, Negroes will continue to attend separate schools.

A federal judge cannot order a board to terminate segregation until somebody with proper standing invokes the jurisdiction of his court. Since Congress has refused to authorize the Department of Justice to sue recalcitrant school boards, Negroes whose children are being discriminated against are the only persons

[1] Truman M. Pierce et al., *White and Negro Schools in the South,* Englewood Cliffs, New Jersey: Prentice Hall, 1955, p. 54.

who can initiate legal complaints. Segregationists know that if they can keep Negroes from suing in federal courts they can continue to operate segregated institutions. They have not hesitated therefore to intimidate Negro plaintiffs.

Although coercive tactics have been used in all southern states, they have been most effective in preventing legal attacks on segregation in the deepest south, especially in Mississippi. There has not been a single school-entry lawsuit in all of Mississippi, though Negroes filed desegregation petitions with the Vicksburg, Clarksdale, Natchez, Jackson, and Yazoo City school boards in 1955. Then the citizens councils circulated the names of all who had signed these petitions. Within a few days the pressures were so intense that the petitioners began "voluntarily" requesting their names be removed from the petitions. Some claimed their signatures had been forged, or that they had not understood the purpose of the petitions, and others said nothing.

In 1955 bombing of the homes of Mississippi's NAACP leaders became commonplace. During the fall a Negro a month was killed, including three of Mississippi's most outspoken Negro civil rights leaders. No one was prosecuted for these crimes, not even those who shot down Lemar Smith, a Negro leader, at midday in front of the Pike County Courthouse.[2] Since then there have been no attempts by Mississippi Negroes to bring lawsuits.

Clennon King was the only Mississippi Negro who dared to enroll at a "white" school. In June 1958, during summer school registration, he appeared on the campus of the University of Mississippi. He was immediately taken into custody by highway patrolmen. Charges of disturbing the peace and resisting arrest were filed against him, but he was not brought to trial. Instead he was committed to a state mental hospital following a lunacy hearing before a local judge. Governor James P. Coleman charged that King "went berserk" during his attempt to register. An attorney claiming to represent King was ejected from the hearing and efforts by his brother to secure his release by writ

[2] Hodding Carter, III, *The South Strikes Back,* Garden City: Doubleday, 1959, p. 119.

of habeas corpus were also unsuccessful. Twelve days later he was released after authorities decided he was sane. King left the state.

Mississippi is not the only state in which police-state tactics have been used to intimidate Negro civil rights spokesmen. There is the case of Asbury Howard. In January 1959 Howard, organizer of the Bessemer (Alabama) Voters League, which promotes Negro registration, and a vice-president of the Bessemer NAACP chapter until it was forced out of business in 1956, asked Albert McAllister, a white man operating a small printing business, to reproduce a cartoon from the *Kansas City Call,* a Negro weekly. This cartoon portrayed a shackled Negro in prayer, asking the Lord to help all Americans see that He intended human beings of all colors to have the same rights. Howard asked that the words "Vote Today for a Better Tomorrow" be added, since the poster was to hang inside the Voters League hall.

McAllister agreed to do the job for $12, but before he could finish, George Barron, Bessemer police chief, found out about the sign. Howard owned a gas station and was not dependent on any white employer, so he could not be reached by financial pressure. But Chief Barron arrested Howard without warrant, took him to city hall, and released him, ordering him to return in four days.

On January 24, before Judge James D. Hammonds, City Attorney McEniry charged Howard with violating a Bessemer ordinance by publishing matter tending "to provoke a breach of the peace" and "prejudicial to good order." Howard was fined $105 and sentenced to 180 days.

Howard posted bond pending appeal, but as he left the courtroom, he found some forty white men lined up along the walls of the lobby and stairway. As he took the last step down the stairs, the men leaped forward. His son came to the rescue, but the white men turned on him too.

There were about fifteen policemen in the courtroom. They arrested Howard's son, charged him with disorderly conduct, and placed him under $600 bond. He was sentenced to one year at hard labor. His son was released on bail pending appeal, but Howard served 180 days.[3]

Police-state tactics and terrorism have been used also in Birmingham, one of the few large southern cities to be run by segregationists. Late in the summer of 1957, after nine Negro families under the leadership of the Reverend F. L. Shuttlesworth petitioned the Birmingham School Board to admit their children to the schools nearest their homes, a group of white men beat and emasculated an unfortunate Negro who had had nothing to do with the petition. They told him: "This is what will happen if Negroes try to integrate the schools." [4] Following this attack, two families withdrew their names from the petition.[5] But not Shuttlesworth.

When schools opened, Shuttlesworth took his two daughters to the high school closest to his home, a "white" school, and asked that they be enrolled. School officials turned him down. As he left the school grounds, a gang of white men, three of whom were later arrested but not punished, attacked him.[6] The pressures on Shuttlesworth continued. His home was bombed. Police arrested him for defying an ordinance which gave the operator of a bus the right to tell passengers where to sit, an ordinance designed to circumvent court decisions against segregated seating.[7] But Shuttlesworth continued to press his suit.

In the Upper and urban South less violent, more subtle, but nonetheless coercive tactics are used against Negro plaintiffs. Some newspapers list the names and addresses of all plaintiffs, which guarantees that threatening telephone calls will be made. Even when newspapers are more cautious, segregationists get the

[3] Jeffrey E. Fuller, "The Due Processing of Asbury Howard," *The Reporter*, April 16, 1957, pp. 23–24. See also *Report of the United States Commission on Civil Rights, 1959*, Washington: U.S. Government Printing Office, 1959, pp. 96–97.

[4] *St. Louis Post-Dispatch,* September 5, 1957.

[5] *Birmingham News,* August 23, 1957.

[6] *Birmingham News,* September 9, 1957.

[7] *Washington Post & Times Herald,* October 22, 1958; *Dallas Morning News,* December 8, 1957.

list of names. In Arlington some white parents joined Negroes to ask the judge for a desegregation injunction, but the pressure against the white parents was so severe that two of them asked to have their names withdrawn. Ten other white parents unsuccessfully sought permission to become plaintiffs in order to protest these "undemocratic and nasty actions." [8]

A common tactic, used especially in Virginia, Louisiana, Florida, and South Carolina, is for a legislative committee led by segregationists and armed with subpoena power to interrogate parents and children, NAACP lawyers, and any others who have become involved one way or another in a school case. The ostensible purpose of these investigations is to determine if NAACP attorneys solicit clients or engage in subversive activities. Only a few plaintiffs have quit under these pressures, but these official investigations warn Negroes of trouble if they participate in school-entry suits.

Texas Attorney General John Ben Sheppard used a variant of these harassing tactics. In the fall of 1956, a few days before the federal judge was to hear the case, Sheppard's assistants, accompanied by armed Texas troopers, rounded up many of the plaintiffs. Here in the words of one of these plaintiffs is what happened: "About 2:30 or 3:00 o'clock P.M. on September 29, 1956, a white man came to my house and asked for me. My daughter . . . went to the door. He asked for me. My daughter called me to the door. He asked me if I was Willie Mae Goldstein; I told him yes. He told me that he has a subpoena for me to be in Judge Richburg's office right away. I asked him what I done; he stood there for a few minutes, then he told me it was pertaining to the school suit and Judge Richburg wanted me up there for questioning. He told me that if I did not come, he could arrest me. He had on a coat and there was a bulge on his side which looked like a gun. I was frightened. . . . He waited for me until I dressed. I got in the car. There was a colored man by the name of Mr. Fields already in the car. He carried me to

[8] *Washington Post & Times Herald,* Nov. 12, 1958.

Judge Richburg's office. . . . In a few minutes we were called
into Judge Richburg's office. Mr. Fields and I was asked to raise
our right hands and they swore us in. Mr. Fields were then asked
to leave the room and I was told to stay. . . . There were five of
us in the room. They were: Judge Richburg, his secretary, and
two of the men from the attorney general's office and myself.
. . . One of the men from the attorney general's office asked me
my name . . . Where was my daughter; I told him she was at
home. He asked me what does she do every day. I asked him
what did he mean; does she go to school and I told him yes.
Then he asked me if I carried my daughter up to Adamson High
School about a year ago to enroll her in school; I told him yes.
He asked me who asked me would I be interested in taking her
up there and I told him Mrs. Flannigan. He asked me had any
of the lawyers of the NAACP persuaded me to take her and I
told him no. He asked me did I know any of them personally;
I told him no. He asked me if my daughter was a graduate for
this year; I told him yes. He asked me if anyone had asked me
to sign any court papers; I told him no. I wanted my child to go
to Adamson High School because it was close to where I lived
and Lincoln High School, where she had been going, was all the
way across town. I also wanted her to go to Adamson High
School because they taught some subjects there that they did not
teach in Lincoln High School. He asked me if the lawsuit was
filed to get my child in school was filed with my consent; I told
him yes. There were some other questions asked me, but I don't
remember them right now." [9]

Only a few of the Dallas plaintiffs withdrew, but the episode,
widely reported and, like most such stories, greatly exaggerated,
furnished one more incident to warn Negroes of the risks of participation in civil rights suits.

Southern Negroes, especially the uneducated and uninformed,
tend to be terrorized by all official inquests. The "po-lice" is an

[9] Deposition, taken October 1, 1956, before Nadine Stewart, Notary
Public In and For Dallas County, Texas, on file in case of *Bell v. Rippy*.
Other similar depositions are also on file.

instrument of the white masters; their authority is unquestioned and they are to be treated with the greatest deference. The questioners are white; the hearing tribunals are white. Even with all possible safeguards, the atmosphere is coercive. But there are seldom safeguards. Oliver Hill, an NAACP attorney in Virginia, protested: "They get people with no experience in this kind of thing and ask leading questions. Nobody has an opportunity to examine witnesses to see if they understand the purpose of what they are saying. They pick certain people. The people who could give a better picture were dismissed." [10]

It is impossible to measure precisely the impact of these several pressures, but undoubtedly they discourage some Negroes from becoming parties to civil rights litigation. It is not so much that a Negro may lose his job, but that he exposes his children to danger. If he takes his child to a "white" school to enroll, often an essential prerequisite for a lawsuit, he may face taunting mobs without any assurance of police protection.

Coercive intimidation of plaintiffs is less effective in cities, especially when used against educated Negroes who are more highly motivated, less vulnerable to economic retaliation, and less dependent upon the favors of the white community. However, intimidation of plaintiffs is only one facet of the segregationists' drive to keep Negroes out of federal courts. Equally important has been their attack on the NAACP.

By far the most prominent organization working to integrate the schools is the National Association for the Advancement of Colored People. The association was established in 1909, after race riots in Springfield, Illinois, shocked into action William English Walling, a millionaire southern social reformer, and Oswald Garrison Villard, publisher of the *New York Evening Post* and grandson of William Lloyd Garrison. These two men joined forces with W. E. B. DuBois, leader of the all-Negro Niagara Movement, who had broken with Booker T. Washing-

[10] *Norfolk Pilot and Ledger,* May 15, 1957.

ton. To DuBois, Washington's views that a Negro should depend upon "powerful white friends" rather than on himself was intolerable. The NAACP goals, from the beginning, have remained essentially the same: abolition of forced segregation, equality in education, employment, and housing, and voting rights for Negroes.[11]

Without the financial help, moral encouragement, and legal know-how of the NAACP, or a similar organization, few Negroes would have the money, the knowledge, or the courage to seek legal redress for their grievances. No white southern attorney dares to serve as counsel in school-entry cases. Even in ordinary criminal prosecutions, most white lawyers are unwilling to defend Negro clients, and if they do, they are afraid to challenge exclusion of Negroes from juries or to protest other kinds of racial discrimination. Segregationists know the elimination of the NAACP would seriously cripple the ability of Negroes to litigate. In this endeavor segregationists are aided by the belief, widely shared even among moderates, that the NAACP is an extremists' organization, just as bad in its way as the white citizens councils are in their way: even southerners supporting gradual integration are apt to feel the NAACP does more harm than good.

With varying degrees of intensity, practically every instrumen-

---

[11] Nationally the NAACP is an incorporated New York nonprofit membership organization. Its membership, although biracial, is chiefly Negro. It has about 370,000 members, approximately 60 per cent of whom are in the South. These members, organized into 15,000 branches, pay dues of $2.00 and upwards. The Board of Directors includes many prominent white and Negro citizens.

The national Board of Directors charters local chapters, but each chapter is an independent association whose activities are co-ordinated on a state-wide basis through a state conference of branches. A field staff operating out of regional and national headquarters works with local chapters on organizational and political campaigns.

A separately incorporated Legal Defense and Education Fund, financed by contributions, serves as the legal arm. It has a small central staff. At the local level, lawyers who make up the National Legal Committee serve as counsel. Any branch is free to help Negroes with civil rights matters, but its charter specifically forbids the giving of general legal advice or help.

tality of government has been used to intimidate the NAACP, to round out what Arkansas Attorney General Bruce Bennett, an extreme segregationist, calls the "Southern Plan for Peace." One of the most persistent strategies is to charge the association with violating some law or other. This charge is then used as an excuse to demand, at point of banishment, that the NAACP disclose the names of all its members. Segregationists know that this is against NAACP policy because Negroes are afraid that if their NAACP membership becomes known employers will fire them, white merchants will deny them credit, and they will suffer other forms of retaliation. Although they would like to get their hands on these names, the NAACP's refusal to hand them over serves the segregationists' purpose even better. For it is used to justify imposition of heavy fines and crippling injunctions.

Many state officials are so convinced of the venality of the NAACP that they have been willing to overlook traditional constitutional rights. In this endeavor they have had the enthusiastic co-operation of many state judges.

Alabama's suppression of the NAACP illustrates how southern states have used this strategy: demand the names of members, and then banish the NAACP for refusing to give them. On June 1, 1956, then attorney general, now governor, John Patterson, a strong segregationist, appeared in the Montgomery courtroom of Alabama Circuit Judge Walter B. Jones. Judge Jones is no less of a segregationist: as one of his state's most prominent attorneys he edits the *Alabama Bar Journal* and writes a column "Off the Bench" in the *Montgomery Advertiser* which he devotes to criticism of the Supreme Court and to defense of white supremacy.

Patterson convinced Judge Jones that the NAACP was violating Alabama's corporation registration law and was fomenting racial discord. Jones immediately issued a restraining order forbidding the NAACP to conduct any business in Alabama. This restraining order was served on the NAACP, and a hearing was scheduled to determine if it should be made permanent. But prior to the hearing, and ostensibly in connection with it,

Jones, at Patterson's request, ordered the NAACP to produce its books, papers, and documents, including the names of all members. Attorneys for the NAACP contended it was not subject to the registration law, but they indicated the association would comply if given an opportunity to do so. They also agreed to produce all the documents requested except the membership lists. For this refusal Judge Jones held the NAACP in contempt and fixed the fine at $10,000, to be raised to $100,000 if the names were not produced within five days. Furthermore, he ruled that until the NAACP paid the fine and produced its membership lists, it was not even entitled to a hearing to determine if the restraining order should be lifted.

Clearly the design of the entire proceeding was to force the NAACP out of business, to keep it from sponsoring school-entry suits. Twice the association appealed to the Alabama Supreme Court; twice this court refused to set aside the contempt citation, to remove the fine, or even to order Judge Jones to give the NAACP a hearing.

Presiding over the Alabama Supreme Court is Chief Justice J. Edwin Livingston. Livingston once told two hundred Alabama students and business leaders, after criticizing federal judges for lacking restraint: "I'm for segregation in every phase of life and I don't care who knows it. . . . I would close every school from the highest to the lowest before I would go to school with colored people." [12] Apparently his fellow judges, one of whom was one of the prosecutors of the Scottsboro boys, share his sentiments.

Unable to protect their constitutional rights before Alabama jurists, the NAACP took the case to the Supreme Court. By this time two years had expired since the association had been banished by Judge Jones. It still had had no hearing.

While the case was pending before the Supreme Court, Patterson, by then the Democratic nominee for governor, asked Judge Jones to cite the NAACP for contempt once again. He contended

[12] *Birmingham News*, March 5, 1959.

the association had violated the original restraining order by continuing its operations under the name of the Alabama State Coordinating Association for Registration and Voting. The NAACP, denying Patterson's charges, asked Judge Jones to disqualify himself because in his recent election campaign he had promised his constituents: "I intend to deal the NAACP and its counterpart, the Montgomery Improvement Association, [an organization led by Dr. Martin Luther King which after the banning of the NAACP took over the civil rights fight] a mortal blow from which they shall never recover." [13]

Jones found no merit in the NAACP's contentions. This is not surprising, since he had refused to disqualify himself from hearing a similar case against the Montgomery Improvement Association, saying, "I stand legally indifferent between the parties and have neither bias for the state nor prejudice against the respondent." He did, however, postpone a hearing on this contempt motion until the NAACP could get a ruling from the Alabama Supreme Court on its request for his disqualification.[14]

Before the Alabama Supreme Court could rule on Jones's impartiality, the Supreme Court of the United States (June 30, 1958) unanimously concluded that the fine levied against the NAACP violated the Fourteenth Amendment. The Constitution, said the Supreme Court, protects the right of persons to associate for the peaceful promotion of lawful goals. The NAACP is working to protect the rights of colored people by litigation, legislation, and education—working to force Alabama to comply with the Constitution. If Alabama compelled the NAACP to identify its members, they would be exposed to economic reprisal and physical coercion, and thereby deprived of the right to association. Alabama had failed to show any legitimate or compelling reason why it needed to know the names of NAACP members. The association had been within its constitutional rights in refusing to produce membership lists.

Yet it was only a partial victory for the NAACP. The Su-

[13] *Montgomery Advertiser*, June 28, 1958.
[14] *Ibid.*, and *Southern School News*, August, 1958, p. 11.

preme Court, although setting aside the contempt citation and vacating the fine, refused to disturb the restraining order or deal with the underlying question of Alabama's right to enjoin the NAACP for allegedly violating Alabama's corporation law and fomenting racial discord. Instead, the Supreme Court told the Alabama Supreme Court to render a judgment consistent with the United States Supreme Court's opinion.

At this juncture the NAACP asked the Alabama Supreme Court to send the United States Supreme Court's mandate to Judge Jones immediately so that a hearing might be had on the merits of the restraining order. For over eight months the Alabama Supreme Court did nothing. All this time the NAACP was still under the restraint of Judge Jones's order. Then the Alabama court, instead of vacating the contempt citation, ruled the association was still in contempt. The Supreme Court, said the Alabama judges, had made its ruling "under a mistaken impression." Although Alabama might lack authority to hold the association in contempt for failure to hand over names of its members, nonetheless, the NAACP was in contempt because of failure to produce papers other than the membership lists.

The NAACP went back to the Supreme Court. In June 1959 the Supreme Court tersely pointed out to the Alabamians that in the first hearing they had relied solely on the NAACP's refusal to furnish membership lists as a reason for holding it in contempt. They were bound by their previously taken position. Nonetheless, the Supreme Court again decided to exercise restraint. Instead of issuing a mandamus to force the Alabama Supreme Court to act, the Supreme Court justices said they would rely on the good faith of the Alabama court which "thus advised, will not fail to proceed promptly with the disposition of the matters left open."

The Supreme Court's confidence was misplaced. Four years after the restraining order had first been issued, the NAACP still had had no hearing; it was still unable to operate in Alabama. In the summer of 1960 the NAACP appealed to Judge Frank M. Johnson. But he refused, telling the NAACP to seek redress in state courts. If he took jurisdiction, he said, it would amount to assuming that Alabama's judges do not take seriously their oaths to protect the constitutional rights of all citizens—an assumption he was unwilling to make.[15] Even if the NAACP does get a hearing—and it will probably have to appeal to the Supreme Court of the United States to force action—it is most likely to be before Judge Jones.

In Texas, Attorney General John Ben Sheppard, as part of his unsuccessful campaign for the United States Senate, on September 22, 1956, asked and received from State Circuit Judge Otis T. Dunagan a temporary restraining order, issued without notice to the NAACP, requiring all 122 branches of the NAACP to immediately cease their operations. (The NAACP is treated as a unit, but in Alabama and Texas, as well as in other states, the orders deal with the Legal Defense and Education Fund and the NAACP proper as separate units.) Sheppard alleged the NAACP was a profit-making corporation failing to pay franchise taxes and he accused it of inciting racial prejudice. "For over one hundred years," said Sheppard, "the white and colored races in said State have lived together peacefully and in harmony without strife or litigation, and were it not for the activities of the defendants, they would now and in the future continue to do so." [16]

In October of 1956 the case was brought to a hearing. The state took nine days to introduce 472 exhibits trying to prove the NAACP had violated 11 state laws. Sheppard, although he said little, was constantly present, bypassing Judge Dunagan's no smoking edict by chewing unlighted cigars.[17] For five days the NAACP made its rebuttal. Finally, Judge Dunagan held the NAACP was not a profit-making organization. He ordered the payment of certain taxes and required the NAACP to permit the Attorney General to search its records, but his injunction was

[15] *NAACP v. Gallion,* 5 RRLR at 813 (1960).

[16] Plaintiff's original petition, the *State of Texas v. N.A.A.C.P. et al.* In the District Court, 7th Judicial District, Smith County, Texas, filed September 21, 1956.

[17] *Dallas Morning News,* September 21, 1956; *New Orleans Times-Picayune,* September 23, 1956.

much narrower in scope than the first restraining order. It merely prohibits the NAACP from engaging in illegal lobbying or soliciting clients, practices in which the NAACP insists it never engaged anyway.

Failing to "get" the NAACP, the Texas legislature authorized a county judge to require organizations which he found "engaged in activities designed to hinder, harass and interfere with the operation of public schools" to list with him officers and members. The sponsor of this measure, Representative Joe Pool, announced that the law was not aimed at "respectable" organizations, "but it'll get the NAACP." [18]

Six months after the Supreme Court's decision in the Alabama case, the Arkansas Supreme Court, two judges dissenting, sustained a fine against NAACP officials for refusing to give city authorities the names of its members, ostensibly demanded for tax purposes. The Arkansas judges distinguished the Alabama case by saying that in Alabama "the prime purpose of the procedure . . . was to obtain information whereby Alabama could force the NAACP out of the state. . . . In the case at bar, the purpose of the ordinance is to determine the tax status of one seeking to claim immunity from occupation tax." [19]

Again the NAACP had to carry the issue to the Supreme Court. Again the Supreme Court had to point out that the Constitution protects freedom of association "not only against heavy-handed frontal attack, but also from being stifled by more subtle governmental interference." [20] Here the state was trying to get information, unnecessary to levy occupational taxes, under circumstances where compulsory disclosure of membership lists of local branches would result in a significant interference with the freedom of association of their members.

So after years of time-consuming and expensive appeals, the NAACP was able to secure some protection for its right to operate in Arkansas and some measure of relief in Alabama. But

[18] *Dallas Morning News*, November 26, 1957.
[19] *Bates v. Little Rock*, 4 RRLR 136 at 141 (1958).
[20] *Bates v. Little Rock*, 361 U.S. 516 at 523 (1960).

not in Florida. There the segregationists were permitted to go unchallenged.

In Florida, it has been the state legislature, aided and abetted by the Florida Supreme Court, well known for its distaste for United States Supreme Court decisions, that has gone after the NAACP membership lists. A legislative committee authorized to investigate "organizations advocating violence or a course of conduct which would constitute a violation of the laws of Florida" subpoenaed officers of the NAACP, including the plaintiffs in the Dade County school case, to appear and bring their records, including the names of members, especially those of the Miami branch. The committee said it was anxious to find out to what extent the Communists had infiltrated groups trying to bring about a "coercive reform of educational and social practices by litigation and pressured administrative action."

Those summoned refused to produce membership lists; some declined to answer any questions. The Florida legislators secured a court order for the production of the information. The Florida Supreme Court, after a discursive discussion of federalism and a few digs at "certain tendencies toward paternalistic nationalism, which we think we detect in the opinions of some courts . . ." held NAACP officers could be punished for contempt if they persisted in withholding membership lists. The Florida judges distinguished the Alabama case by stating: "Here, there is no showing whatsoever of the contended deterrent effect" of publication of NAACP membership and no indication that the information sought would be used to oust the NAACP from Florida.[21] By dismissing a petition for a writ of certiorari, the Supreme Court of the United States left this Florida ruling standing. Despite what the Supreme Court said in the Alabama case, Florida had found a way to get at the names of NAACP members or, if the officers refused, to put them in jail.[22]

[21] *Gibson et al. v. Florida Legislative Investigation Committee,* 4 RRLR 143 at 1954 (1958).

[22] Justice Black stayed the judgment of the Florida Supreme Court pending disposition of a petition for a writ of certiorari (petition asking

Virginia has had two legislative investigations of the NAACP. Although the Virginia Supreme Court of Appeals found the demand for membership lists to be reasonable and not infringe on freedom of association, its ruling was vacated by the Supreme Court of the United States after the Virginia Attorney General conceded that the committee concerned had expired so the issue was moot.[23]

Georgia, Mississippi, South Carolina, Tennessee, Texas, and most notably Virginia have tried to strike directly at NAACP lawyers by accusing them of barratry, champerty, and maintenance. There are technical distinctions among these several common law offenses, but they are all aimed at the unprofessional practice of the law, against attorneys who stir up litigation merely for the purpose of collecting fees or vexing persons.

The NAACP, especially its local branches, does encourage Negroes to file lawsuits. It searches for persons willing to serve as plaintiffs, instructs them on how they should proceed, defrays the cost of litigation, and otherwise takes charge. Since these practices are neither unethical nor illegal, the state legislatures have taken old common law crimes and redefined them in such a way as to make normal NAACP procedures unlawful. In Virginia, for example, barratry has been redrawn to include the payment of the expenses of litigation by persons other than the plaintiffs. Numerous exceptions are made so that the law applies only to restrain the NAACP.

Probably these so-called antibarratry laws are unconstitutional. Negroes have a constitutional right to litigate in federal courts, as do all American citizens. A state does have the power to regulate the practice of law to prevent nuisance suits and abusive use of the courts. But the NAACP's activities do not amount to solicitation of business or a stirring up of litigation of the sort condemned by either the ethical standards of the legal profes-

---

for Supreme Court review), but the Supreme Court dismissed the petition. 4 RRLR 253 (1959).

[23] *NAACP v. Committee on Offenses Against the Administration of Justice,* 3 RRLR 868 (1958).

sion or the common law. Instead, they comprise public instruction of Negroes as to the extent of their legal rights, recommendations that appeals be made to courts for the protection of these rights, offers of assistance in prosecuting cases, and the payment of legal expenses.[24]

Segregationists have been more successful in pressure against the more vulnerable Negro public school teachers, many of whom are among the NAACP's most active members. Under the guise of determining their suitability as teachers, Louisiana, Mississippi, South Carolina, and Arkansas have compelled all teachers to list their organizational affiliations, and in Arkansas and South Carolina the legislature even went so far as to make membership in the NAACP reason for dismissal. Negro teachers, and a few white ones, have chosen to challenge these anti-NAACP oath requirements in the federal, instead of the state, courts. Even so, until they took the issue to the Supreme Court, they had indifferent success.

Circuit Judge John Parker and District Judges George Bell Timmerman and Ashton H. Williams were assigned to hear a challenge to South Carolina's teacher-test-oath anti-NAACP laws—in suits seeking to enjoin enforcement of state laws on a constitutional ground a three-judge court is required. The moderate Parker and the segregationist Timmerman were joined by Williams, also a segregationist. Williams, who holds court in Charleston (in the seat vacated by the retirement of Judge J. Waties Waring in 1952), is a former member of the Democratic National Committee, and a former member of the South Carolina legislature. Judge Williams, a typical "South Carolina Democrat," not so extreme or outspoken as Timmerman, has publicly proclaimed his belief that the Supreme Court's 1954 decision is unconstitutional, and has expressed doubts whether in applying that decision he would be honoring his oath to sustain the Constitution.[25] Because of these doubts Judge Williams first dis-

[24] From *NAACP v. Patty,* 3 RRLR at 297 (1958), reversed on other grounds.
[25] *New York Times,* September 8, 1960.

qualified himself from hearing a suit challenging segregation on the Charleston Municipal Golf Course, but later he changed his mind and heard the case.

Williams and Timmerman teamed up to dismiss the complaint, Williams basing his ruling on the ground that the Negro teachers should challenge the laws before state courts prior to seeking federal relief; Timmerman basing his ruling on the grounds that since the laws were perfectly constitutional, Negroes had no right to an injunction. Timmerman staked his opinion on states' rights doctrine. He added: "The statute is designed to protect young minds from the poisonous effects of NAACP propaganda." To Judge Timmerman, South Carolina's attempt to disqualify as teachers any persons belonging to the NAACP was eminently reasonable because the organization "disturbed the peace and tranquility which has long existed between the white and negro races. . . ." [26]

Judge Parker, on the other hand, felt the laws were so clearly unconstitutional that the court should have immediately enjoined their enforcement. He pointed out that persons have a constitutionally protected right to join organizations which seek by lawful means to promote what the members regard as in the public interest. A state may inquire into the character and fitness of its teachers, but it may not pry into matters having nothing to do with their suitability to teach. For Parker the law disqualifying NAACP members from being teachers was not only unconstitutional, but the state had no right even to ask teachers if they belonged to the association.

This decision of Williams and Timmerman was destined for appeal to the Supreme Court—decisions of three-judge courts bypass the court of appeals and go directly to the Supreme Court. But the South Carolina legislature, rightly concluding that Judge Timmerman's views might not be received with much favor outside the circle of confirmed segregationists, tried to head off Supreme Court review by repealing the law making it an

---

[26] *Bryan v. Austin,* 2 RRLR 379 (1957).

offense to hire members of the NAACP. The Supreme Court dismissed the appeal as being moot. This dismissal, however, left unchallenged the provision requiring all teachers to list organizations to which they belong, and so long as South Carolina could do this, no teacher dared to join the NAACP.

Arkansas teachers were more successful. Their case was heard by Circuit Judge John B. Sanborn (Eighth Circuit), and two district judges sitting in Arkansas, John E. Miller and J. Smith Henley.

Judge Sanborn, a Republican, born in Minnesota in 1883, was appointed to the district bench in 1925 by Calvin Coolidge and promoted to the court of appeals by Hoover in January 1932, just as Hoover was about to leave the White House. Sanborn has participated in only a few school segregation cases, and has written no opinions.

Judge Miller, from Ft. Smith, in the western part of Arkansas, has taken a prominent part in desegregation suits, especially the Little Rock Case, where he has generally supported delay. A former Arkansas senator, Miller is a "McClellan Democrat."

Judge Henley has recently been selected to sit in perhaps the roughest judicial post in the United States, the Eastern District of Arkansas, which covers Little Rock. President Eisenhower had a hard time finding a man for this position. Well aware that he must appoint a man whose background would not make him a target for either segregationists or civil rights advocates, the President rejected the names of three attorneys from the Eastern District presented to him by the Republican state organization. Despite the fact that Henley lived in the Western District, Eisenhower sent his name to the Senate because Henley, having served quietly for five years in a Department of Justice office which in no way involved him in controversial questions, had no known stand on public issues. It would have been difficult for either side to find reason to oppose his confirmation. Nonetheless Senator John L. McClellan held up the appointment. He was working on a complex deal to elevate Judge Miller to the court of appeals. But McClellan was not allowed to have his way. Henley took his seat and the challenge to Arkansas teacher-oath anti-NAACP laws was the first civil rights case in which he participated.

Judges Sanborn, Miller, and Henley held that Arkansas could not fire teachers just for belonging to the NAACP. But they ruled it could require teachers to disclose whether they belong to that organization. By so doing the judges closed their eyes to the fact that Arkansas was not interested in determining if NAACP members are suitable to be teachers, but wanted to punish those teachers, white or Negro, who joined the organization.

On appeal, the Supreme Court, by a five-to-four decision—a rarity in the field of civil rights where the Supreme Court usually speaks with a single voice—reversed the trial court's ruling with respect to a state's right to inquire into NAACP membership. The minority on the Supreme Court viewed the law as if it were merely a confidential inquiry by a school board into the organizational membership of its employees. To the Supreme Court majority it was an unconstitutional attempt to deprive teachers of the right to join a lawful, even if unpopular, organization.[27] If the Supreme Court had allowed the decision to stand, southern teachers would have had three dismal alternatives: to resign from the NAACP, commit perjury, or give up teaching.

In time, the Supreme Court will declare unconstitutional most of these laws aimed at keeping Negroes from joining the NAACP and designed to force it out of existence.[28] But in the meantime, the NAACP will be forced to divert its attention from school-entry suits in order to protect its own right to exist. Prosecutions against the NAACP, even if ultimately unsuccessful, have dampened activity: after Texas's unsuccessful prosecution of the

[27] *Shelton v. E. I. McKinley, Jr.,* 4 RRLR (694) 1959; *Shelton v. Tucker, United States Law Week,* vol. 29, 1960, p. 4055.

[28] For detailed coverage: Walter F. Murphy, "The South Counter-Attacks: the Anti-NAACP Laws," *Western Political Quarterly,* vol. XII, no. 2, June 1959, pp. 371–390. *See also* American Jewish Congress, *Assault Upon Freedom of Association: A Study of the Southern Attack on the National Association for the Advancement of Colored People,* 1957.

NAACP, Roy Wilkins, executive secretary of the NAACP, reported: "Our Texas members were just as meek as lambs. In fact, they were more meek than NAACP members in Mississippi. . . ." [29]

The Supreme Court has made the NAACP's task even more difficult by adding another obstacle. The NAACP naturally prefers to challenge anti-NAACP laws in federal instead of state courts. Southern state judges elected by a white constituency have not displayed any noticeable enthusiasm for protecting the constitutional rights of Negroes. Where possible, the NAACP goes directly to federal courts, as it did to challenge a comprehensive anti-NAACP battery of laws adopted by the Virginia General Assembly in 1956.

These Virginia laws make it illegal for any organization to pay expenses of litigation; they call for the NAACP to submit detailed information about operations, including membership lists; they require the NAACP to register, but if it does register they force it in effect to admit it has violated other provisions making it a crime "to cause racial conflicts."

Circuit Judge Morris A. Soper, and Judges Walter E. Hoffman and Sterling Hutcheson, heard the Virginia case. Hoffman, a stalwart, outspoken judge, has consistently insisted upon compliance with the Brown decision; Hutcheson on the other hand has been more inclined to find reasons why school authorities should be allowed to take their time before acting. Soper and Hoffman felt that three of these laws passed "to nullify as far as possible the effect of the decision of the Supreme Court in *Brown vs. Board of Education,*" were so plainly unconstitutional that their enforcement should be enjoined. On the other three they voted to retain jurisdiction but to defer a ruling on them pending their construction by state judges. Hutcheson would have deferred ruling on all six.[30]

Since the Supreme Court has been inclined not to upset rulings of the lower courts, especially when they favor civil rights,

[29] Speech in Dallas quoted in *Texas Observer,* May 11, 1960.
[30] *NAACP v. Patty,* 3 RRLR 274 (1958).

it was something of a surprise when by a six-to-three vote it reversed Soper and Hoffman. According to the Supreme Court majority, the federal judges should have stayed their hand until state judges had been given a chance to interpret these laws. If given this opportunity, Virginia judges might construe the laws in such a fashion as to preserve constitutional rights, said the Supreme Court majority. Furthermore, Virginia promised not to enforce these laws until a final decision on their validity had been obtained.

Justice William O. Douglas wrote a strong dissenting opinion supported by Chief Justice Earl Warren and Justice William Brennan. Wrote Douglas: "Where state laws make such an assault as these do on our decisions and a State has spoken defiantly against the constitutional rights of the citizen, reasons for showing deference to local institutions vanish. The conflict is plain and apparent. . . ." But Douglas, Warren, and Brennan were in a minority. Certainly in this instance the Court bent over backward to give state judges a chance to demonstrate that they will give a higher priority to their claims as judges than to their desire for segregation. The Supreme Court of Virginia has already held that some of the anti-NAACP laws are unconstitutional, but it also ruled that the state could forbid the NAACP from providing attorneys for Negro plaintiffs. Once again the NAACP has had to ask the Supreme Court of the United States for protection.[31]

Coercive tactics have disadvantages. There is always the risk of provoking a reaction, perhaps stirring up civil rights legislation in Congress. So segregationists have turned to more subtle schemes; one of them, pupil placement. Pupil-placement laws are by far the best device segregationists have yet discovered to keep Negroes out of federal courts and to make civil rights litigation expensive, time-consuming, and frustrating. And it can all be done with the veneer of legality.

[31] *Harrison v. NAACP,* 4 RRLR 527 at 533 (1959); *NAACP v. Harrison,* 5 RRLR 1152 (1960).

Pupil-placement acts have been adopted in nine southern states. They vary in detail but their grand outline is similar. In all states except Virginia, where there is a state-wide three-man pupil-placement board, each local school board is authorized to assign pupils to particular schools on the basis of a very elaborate set of standards. All pupils are automatically assigned to the schools which they previously attended. New pupils are assigned to schools set aside for members of their race. Race is carefully avoided as the reason for making the assignments. Students who wish to transfer to a school other than the one to which they have been assigned must request a transfer on detailed forms. If their requests are denied, as they almost always are, students must appeal through an elaborate set of administrative hearings, and only then are they allowed to carry their case to the federal courts.

What do segregationists hope to gain from these programs? First, to allow school officials to segregate Negro pupils, but to do so ostensibly for a host of reasons other than race. Second, to require each Negro pupil wishing a transfer to follow such a complicated set of procedures and to attend so many hearings that many of them will become discouraged from making the attempt. Administrative procedures, even when administered in the best of fashion and with good will, are unavoidably coercive in the peculiar situation of many southern communities. The mere act of making an official appearance before a governmental agency and having children subject to questioning—"Mary Jo, don't you like the fine school where you are going? Why do you want to transfer? Who put you up to this?"—in itself intimidates many Negroes. Third, to make the procedures so involved that there will be ample opportunity to refuse transfer requests for technical reasons, such as failure to have signatures notarized, failure to meet deadlines, failure to appear at hearings, and so on. These same tactics are used by some registration officials who reject Negro applications for voting registration because of minor technical mistakes in filling out the forms.

A fourth advantage of pupil placement is that it transfers from school officials the responsibility of desegregating and puts on each Negro pupil the burden of proving he has been denied admission to a school because of his race. Finally, and perhaps most important, these schemes allow school officials to take advantage of the "doctrine of exhaustion of administrative remedies" and to prevent class suits. These last features require some explanation.

Federal rules of civil procedures and federal civil rights statutes permit class suits. A person may seek relief not only for himself but for all other persons "similarly situated." Thus, in the absence of a pupil-placement law, if a few Negro parents can by legal action force a school board to produce a desegregation plan, the court order obtained by these plaintiffs protects the right of all Negroes in the community who are being similarly discriminated against.

However, it is also a rule that before one can vindicate his legal rights in the federal courts, he must first exhaust his state administrative remedies. In states which do not have pupil-placement statutes, all Negroes must do in order to exhaust these remedies is to ask school authorities to desegregate, and perhaps have a few Negro pupils try to enroll at a "white" school. If these steps fail to bring about integration, Negroes are entitled to a hearing before a federal judge.

By using pupil placement and establishing an elaborate set of administrative remedies, segregationists hope that Negroes will exhaust themselves before they exhaust their administrative remedies. Furthermore, even if a Negro gets over these hurdles, goes to court, and obtains an injunction, it will force only his own admission. He will have to seek relief individually and not in the form of a class suit. Thus after long and expensive litigation, an individual Negro may vindicate his own right to attend a "white" school, but his victory will not affect the status of other Negro students. Nor will only one lawsuit be necessary in each school district, but each Negro pupil may have to sue.

In order to avoid a ruling against pupil placement, a state eventually must assign a few Negroes to a "white" school, but these procedures make it easy for school authorities to delay integration and to contain it when it comes. All they need to do is to announce that henceforth pupils will no longer be assigned by race, then proceed to assign Negroes to segregated schools but to do so for reasons of residence, health, educational achievement, and so on. Only a few Negro students will have the proper qualifications to make good plaintiffs, even if they do go to the bother of requesting a transfer. Those who live close to "Negro" schools will have a hard time proving that residence is not the reason for their assignment. Even in the face of *de facto* segregation, each pupil will have to prove that race has been the controlling factor in his particular assignment. If a Negro goes to court, the school officials can always find some reason why he has not properly followed the correct procedures, giving the judge a chance to dismiss the complaint without even getting to its merits. Finally, even if a Negro or two does finally secure a judicial hearing on the merits of his transfer, his victory will not disturb the assignment of other pupils. The basic pattern of segregation can be retained.

Virginia and Louisiana made the mistake of combining their first pupil-placement statutes with laws making it impossible for school boards to assign a Negro to white schools. Under such circumstances, the remedies they provided were merely futile acts offering no promise of relief. District judges quickly declared both of these assignment laws unconstitutional and did not require Negro plaintiffs to follow these procedures before invoking the jurisdiction of the federal courts.

Other southern states, following the lead of North Carolina, have been more subtle. The pioneer case involved a 1956 complaint filed by a group of Negroes against the McDowell County Board of Education, which operates no school for Negroes in the town of Old Fort but transports them to schools fourteen miles away. Here was a school district having no program of desegregation; it did not even provide *separate* schools for Negroes, let alone their being equal.

After the suit was started North Carolina adopted a pupil-assignment law; it insisted that, unless each Negro pupil individually sought a transfer and followed the procedures outlined, the federal courts should not even consider their grievances. Negroes insisted it would be futile for them to do so since obviously the board had no intention of approving the request of any Negro to transfer to schools in Old Fort. It was a notorious fact, they claimed, that the very purpose of the pupil placement was to maintain segregation. Further, the discretion given to school authorities was so broad and the standards so vague, it would be impossible to prove in individual instances that race was the reason for the denial of a transfer. Therefore, the scheme should be declared unconstitutional.

After an involved series of hearings up and down the judicial hierarchy and in and out of state and federal courts, the Court of Appeals for the Fourth Circuit, speaking through Chief Judge Parker, held the district judge had properly dismissed the complaint. North Carolina's pupil-placement law was not, said Judge Parker, inherently discriminatory or unconstitutional on its face, but he warned that if it were applied in a discriminatory fashion it could be declared unconstitutional.[32] The Supreme Court refused to review.

Taking heed of this warning, several North Carolina cities in 1957 simultaneously transferred a few Negroes to "white" schools, hoping thereby to satisfy the judge and make it difficult for Negroes to prove discrimination. However, in Old Fort the school board denied transfer requests, claiming the forms had been improperly signed. The Negroes who initiated the suit ran out of steam. They gave up the fight. Three years later and $15,000 poorer their children still take a 28-mile-a-day trip to their segregated schools.

North Carolina is the most moderate of the southern states. The state legislature, the governor, and the attorney general have refused to tolerate violence and pupil-placement programs have not been used to maintain total segregation. In such an atmosphere, where officials are making a good faith attempt to

[32] *Carson v. Warlick,* 2 RRLR 16 (1956).

move gradually toward compliance, federal judges would be more likely to consider pupil placement as not just a subterfuge, but the initial step toward compliance with the Brown decision.

Alabama is a state of "maximum resistance." The Alabama Placement Act, sponsored by the state's most ardent segregationists, was adopted, not to make token integration possible, but to prevent any integration. The act lists thirteen factors which boards are to consider in the assignment of pupils, some of which discriminate against Negroes, for example, "the effect of admission of the pupil upon the academic progress of other students . . . , the possibility or threat of friction or disorder among pupils or others."

It was Reverend F. L. Shuttlesworth who pressed the legal attack against the Alabama law. Despite the bombing of his home, despite beatings by white ruffians, despite pressures of Birmingham and Alabama officials, he insisted that the Birmingham School Board admit his children to schools "of the closest proximity to their homes on a nondiscriminatory basis." Birmingham officials, unable to persuade Shuttlesworth to withdraw, said that his children would have to take certain tests. So Shuttlesworth presented his children for the tests. Next the school board said Shuttlesworth and his wife would have to submit to an interview. This they did too.

Under the terms of the Alabama Placement Act the Birmingham board was supposed to render a decision within thirty days of a transfer request. Thirty days passed and the board said nothing. In December 1957, Shuttlesworth went to the federal court building in Birmingham and filed a complaint. He asked the judges to require the board to admit all Negro students to public schools closest to their respective homes and to enjoin the board from enforcing the Placement Act.

Sixteen months later Shuttlesworth finally was granted a hearing. The court consisted of Circuit Judge Rives, a judge whose past performance indicated that he would render a decision consistent with the constitutional rights of Negroes. The other two judges' records, however, were calculated to give the Birmingham officials confidence in the outcome.

Judge Harlan Hobart Grooms, though born in Kentucky in 1900, moved to Alabama in 1926 and was appointed to the bench by President Eisenhower. Prior to this case the most prominent integration lawsuit he had tried was that involving the University of Alabama and Autherine Lucy. That case ended with the university being formally required to admit Negroes but in reality allowed to remain segregated. Judge Grooms also heard a Birmingham bus case in which, by refusing to allow Negroes to amend their complaint to cover a law enacted after the suit had been started, he gave them no choice but to withdraw from the litigation. Similarly, Judge Grooms used Alabama's statute of limitations to defeat a civil rights complaint brought against Birmingham for its refusal to permit Negroes to take the examination for police patrolmen. In a redevelopment case, Judge Grooms ruled against Negro petitioners whose property was being taken to build housing which would be available only to whites.[33]

The third Judge, Seybourn H. Lynne, though a Truman appointee, has been at one with his Eisenhower-appointed colleague Grooms in consistently finding no merit in Negroes' civil rights complaints. Judge Lynne was the dissenting member of a three-judge court which ordered Montgomery to end bus segregation. When a Negro couple asked Judge Lynne for a declaratory judgment as to their right to use "white" railroad waiting rooms after they had been arrested for doing so, he refused. He told them: "This is but another in the growing list of cases wherein both the tutored and untutored apparently entertain the mistaken notion that the proper function of the federal courts is propaganda rather than judicature." However, on appeal, the judges of the court of appeals ruled that it was Lynne who was wrong: that it is the proper function of a federal court to protect Negroes' civil rights.[34]

---

[33] *Cherry v. Morgan,* 3 RRLR 1236 (1958); *Johnson v. Yeilding,* 3 RRLR 1166 (1958); *Barnes v. Gadsen,* 3 RRLR 1017 (1958).

[34] *Baldwin v. Morgan,* 2 RRLR 420 (1957); *Baldwin v. Morgan,* 3 RRLR 318 (1958). Judge Lynne also dismissed a complaint against a

These were the three judges whom Shuttlesworth's lawyer, Ernest D. Jackson, tried to persuade that Alabama's pupil-placement law was unconstitutional. The case was not supported by the NAACP, for the NAACP was under the ban of Judge Jones's order. Jackson argued that Alabama obviously had no intention of assigning any Negroes to "white" schools. The placement act, he contended, was a device to circumvent the Brown decision and some among the factors designated to determine assignments were relevant only in connection with race, a factor which the Supreme Court has held must not be considered.

The trial court thought otherwise. The judges conceded "No intellectually honest person would deny that these laws were passed in an effort to meet and solve problems presented by the School Segregation Cases." But even if it be assumed, Judge Rives said for the court, that the act was passed with an evil and unconstitutional intent, it would not necessarily be unconstitutional. There was no proof in the record showing that the pupils who were party to the suit had been denied admission because of their race. Nor had the Negroes proven that facilities were available in the schools which they wanted to attend. The school board had not given the Negro pupils any explanation of why their requests had not been granted, and the court did not make it clear why the burden was on Negro pupils to show seats were available in "white" schools. Thus, lacking proof of discrimination, the district court dismissed the complaint, saying: "The School Placement Law furnishes the legal machinery for an orderly administration of the public schools in a constitutional manner. . . . We must presume it will be so administered. If not, in some future proceeding it is possible that it may be declared unconstitutional in its application." [35]

---

segregated public housing project. *Watts v. Housing Authority of Birmingham,* 2 RRLR 107 (1956).

[35] *Shuttlesworth v. Birmingham,* 3 RRLR 425 at 434 (1958). Daniel J. Meador, "The Constitution and the Assignment of Pupils to Public Schools," *Virginia Law Review,* vol. 45, 1959, pp. 517–571, is the most comprehensive analysis of pupil-placement laws. Robert J. Steamer, "The

Would the Supreme Court affirm? It did, and it should be noted that the Supreme Court not only left the district court's judgment undisturbed but accepted jurisdiction and positively affirmed the ruling. The Supreme Court's *per curriam* opinion was cautiously worded: "The judgment is affirmed upon the limited grounds on which the district court rested its decisions."

The Supreme Court's decision marks a strategic retreat. That a district court or even a court of appeals sitting in the South might have hesitated to strike down pupil-placement laws could have been anticipated, but that these laws would pass muster in the Supreme Court must be chalked up as the most important prosegregation legal victory since *Plessy v. Ferguson.* The Supreme Court justices may have concluded that lacking strong support from the Executive and in the face of segregationists' political victories of 1957, it was politically impossible for the judiciary to insist upon complete desegregation. By sustaining pupil placement the Court may have hoped to strike a bargain: we will let you use pupil-assignment procedures provided you allow a few Negroes to attend "white" schools.

Federal judges have sustained pupil placement on the rather naive assumption that these laws will be applied in good faith. But if this were done these laws would lose their efficiency for maintaining segregation. This is why segregationists were so alarmed when Judge Axel J. Beck threatened to upset the plans.

In the fall of 1959 Judge Beck, a Swedish-born South Dakotan, Republican, banker, civic leader, who had been appointed to the bench in 1958, was serving in Arkansas on temporary assignment when three Negro pupils living in Dollarway, Arkansas, filed a complaint in his court. The pupils told Judge Beck that they had applied three times for admission to "white" schools and had three times been denied. They pointed out that Dollarway School Board, in the five years since the Supreme Court ruled that segregation was unconstitutional, had done nothing to desegregate their schools.

Dollarway officials asked Judge Beck to transfer the case to Judge John Miller, a native Arkansas federal judge. But Judge Beck refused, and he also declined to throw the complaint out of court. He said that the pupils, by asking three times for assignment, had done all that was necessary prior to coming to his court, and he insisted the burden was on school authorities, not on the pupils, to prove they were using the placement law in good faith. Since the board had failed so to prove, the pupils were entitled to a hearing without further ado. He ordered the pupils' immediate admission, and he refused to stay his injunction.

Here was a decision which cut through the procedural red tape. If allowed to stand, it would have forced school boards to apply pupil placement within the context of a desegregation program. Segregationists were desperate. The Dollarway School Board decided to postpone the opening of schools rather than permit the Negroes to enter. Joined by Arkansas Attorney General Bruce Bennett, they appealed Judge Beck's ruling, asking and receiving from the court of appeals an early date for a hearing. The court of appeals reversed Judge Beck's decision. Judge Beck, the appellate judges ruled, should not have heard the case because the Negro pupils had failed to follow the Arkansas assignment law.

As a consequence of the court of appeals action, Dollarway plaintiffs have little chance of ever attending nonsegregated schools. After the court of appeals decision, the Negro plaintiffs, discouraged but persistent, returned to the board to exhaust their administrative remedies. By November 1959 they had done so, and the board, as everybody knew it would, denied their applications. Again they returned to the district court, by this time presided over by Judge Henley. Dollarway attorneys tried to persuade Judge Henley that the Negroes should also be required to appeal first up through the state courts. Although Henley rejected these contentions, he refused to order the board to admit the Negro pupils because "It is too late in the school year." Instead he told the board to present a program. They could use the assignment law, he said, even considering the race of students in making transfers, provided they had a plan which would lead eventually to the elimination of segregation. Although this meant that one of the plaintiffs, a senior, would certainly, and the others might, complete their schooling in the Negro school, Henley felt that her interest in securing a nonsegregated education did not outweigh the larger interests. At least Henley's handling of this case will not allow the board to defeat the Brown ruling. He refused to treat the case as if it merely had to do with the admission of three Negro pupils; instead he held that pupil placement by itself is not sufficient. It must operate within the context of a positive desegregation program.[36]

The federal judges' willingness to permit southern states to use pupil-assignment laws is predicated on the assumption that the laws will not be administered so as to discriminate against Negroes. In practice, however, Negroes have found it most difficult even to get a federal judge to listen to their complaints that the laws are being used to discriminate against them. The story of how the Raleigh, North Carolina, Board of Education used pupil-placement regulations to keep its schools segregated well illustrates how Negroes have been prevented from securing a full hearing before federal judges.

On May 30, 1957, Joseph Hiram Holt, Jr., a Negro boy of fifteen, received a certificate from the Raleigh board telling him that he had passed the ninth grade and was assigned to Ligon Junior-Senior High School for the tenth grade, where only Negroes were enrolled. Following the procedures set up by the North Carolina Placement Act, Holt and his parents requested that he be transferred to Broughton Senior High School only eight blocks away from their home, in contrast to the more than three miles to Ligon. Only white pupils had been assigned to Broughton. The Holts filled out the forms supplied by school officials; they called upon them to give specific reasons why their child should *not* attend the school to which the board had as-

[36] *Dove v. Parham*, 5 RRLR 349 (1960). *Dove v. Parham*, 5 RRLR 43 (1959).

signed him. In addition to Broughton's closer location, the Holts stated they wanted "to remove the illegal stigma of racial segregation" from their son's "scholastic endeavor." They also made the mistake, as it turned out, of incidentally mentioning that Broughton offered a better academic and extracurricular program.

Holt's was the only request by a Negro for a transfer, but the board received sixty-five requests from white students for transfer from one "white" school to another—many of which were eventually granted. But the board, deferring action on Holt's request, announced it would consider his application at the August 6 board meeting and requested his and his parents' presence.

The Holts' attorneys notified the board that they had advised their clients not to attend the August 6 meeting since the board's initial action was not in the form of a hearing. At the meeting the board denied the transfer, stating it did so "in the public interest and interest of Holt." After notification of this action, the Holts, following the procedure specified in the law, applied for and secured a hearing. The Holts did not attend in person, but they were again represented by attorneys who were fully authorized to speak for them. Then on August 28, just a few days before schools were to open, the Raleigh board announced that Holt's request for a transfer had again been rejected. No reason was given.

That very day the Holts' attorneys went to court. They had to move quickly if there was to be any chance that Holt could get a judicial hearing before schools were underway. Don Gilliam, the resident district judge, was asked to expedite the proceedings. But Judge Gilliam became ill before he could rule on this request, and the case was turned over to Judge Edwin M. Stanley of the Eastern District of North Carolina.

Judge Stanley had just been appointed to the bench, and no sooner had he settled into his office when not only the Raleigh, but three other school suits, were dumped into his lap. A relatively young man of forty-one, Stanley had had three years of experience as district attorney. Educated at Wake Forest, a deacon of his church and a constant Bible reader, the judge also, as he said, "makes a point to read one national news magazine a week." [37] He was a Republican, but his appointment had been actively supported by Democratic Senator Samuel J. Ervin as well as Democratic Representative R. H. Cooley.[38] At the time of his appointment, Judge Stanley declined to comment on the issue of integration, saying, "I will serve with humility and to the best of my ability." [39]

Judge Stanley's handling of the Holt case certainly supports the *Raleigh News & Observer*'s characterization of him as a "methodical man." [40] But it was not completely his fault that the Holts' motion for an injunction did not even come forward for a hearing until the summer of 1958; by this time a full school year had expired. Part of the reason for the delay was Judge Gilliam's illness.

How could the Raleigh School Board answer the Holts' contention that young Joseph's request had been rejected because of his race? The board admitted it. But they contended that Judge Stanley should dismiss the Holts' motion without even raising the question of racial discrimination. The school board argued that the Holts by failing to appear personally at the hearings had not properly exhausted their state administrative remedies and thus were not entitled to federal judicial relief.[41]

Prior to the lawsuit the Raleigh School Board had not suggested that the Holts' personal absence from the hearings was the reason for refusal to transfer young Joseph to Broughton. Furthermore, under questioning, board members admitted they had granted transfer requests of white pupils without requiring personal appearances. But, they explained, they wanted the Holts personally present to be sure Holt was sincere and to discover

---

37 *Raleigh News and Observer,* October 25, 1957.

38 Hearings before Subcommittee on Judiciary, United States Senate, 85th Congress, 2nd Session, *Nomination of Edwin M. Stanley,* February 6, 1958.

39 *Raleigh News and Observer,* October 25, 1957.

40 *Ibid.*

41 *Greensboro Daily News,* July 16, 1958; *Raleigh News and Observer,* August 15, 1958.

if he were emotionally stable. The board also claimed they wanted to question his parents about their statement that Broughton was better than Ligon.

A year to the day after the Raleigh board had turned down Holt's transfer, Judge Stanley dismissed the Holts' complaint. He conceded that the questions the board wanted to put to the Holts had no relevance to the merits of Joseph's transfer, but since the Holts saw fit to include the charge that Broughton was a better school, the board had "the right" to discuss it with them personally. The North Carolina Pupil-Placement Act gives applicants a right to a hearing, but it nowhere specifies that parents and their children must appear personally. Nor do the precedents cited by Justice Stanley go to this precise point. They establish that the due process clause of the Constitution entitles persons to a hearing before administrative tribunals and that the trier of the case must personally hear the evidence. They say nothing about applicants before such tribunals appearing personally.[42]

Judge Stanley gave the Holts ten days to move that their case be retained on his docket so they could return to the board to exhaust their administrative remedies. Instead, the Holts elected to appeal Judge Stanley's decision to the court of appeals. This court had previously sustained the North Carolina Placement Act, but had done so on the assumption it would be applied in a nondiscriminatory fashion. Yet the court of appeals refused to expedite the case so it could be heard in time for a transfer for the second semester. When it did hand down its decision, the court (Soboloff, Soper, and Haynsworth) sustained Judge Stanley. The appellate judges admitted there was evidence showing the board had been influenced by racial factors, but felt Judge Stanley had been justified in refusing to consider this discrimination because of "the failure of the plaintiffs to do their part."[43]

In 1957, when Holt originally asked for a transfer, he was in the tenth grade. All Raleigh officials had to do was delay for three years. By 1960 he would graduate from high school.

---

[42] *Holt v. Raleigh Board of Education,* 3 RRLR 917 (1958).
[43] *Holt v. Raleigh Board of Education,* 4 RRLR 281 (1959).

Holt never did get a judicial hearing on the merits of his assignment.

Other North Carolina cities have had equal success in manipulating assignment procedures. In Monroe City requests were rejected because it was alleged the Negroes had failed to file them in time. In Old Fort the State Bureau of Investigation was called in and when it was discovered that some mothers had signed for fathers and vice versa, the transfer petitions were rejected because of "forgeries." Some North Carolina cities have allowed a few Negroes to attend what everybody recognizes as "white" schools. Undoubtedly the threat of a lawsuit has been an important factor. But despite considerable effort, no Negro has, as a direct result of court action, been able to force a single North Carolina school district to produce a desegregation program or to admit Negroes without regard to racial considerations. If this is how pupil-placement laws have been manipulated in North Carolina, one can imagine how they will be used in states of maximum resistance.

The Supreme Court has said that segregated schools are unconstitutional, but the judges have sustained pupil placement on the assumption that it will be used to smooth the transition from segregated to desegregated institutions. But without the right to file class suits most Negroes will remain in segregated schools. And unless the Supreme Court tightens the standards, pupil-placement procedures will forestall even limited desegregation. There are signs of such a tightening. By 1960 some of the appellate judges were taking a more critical look, suggesting that by itself a placement plan is not sufficient.

4 * With All Deliberate Delay

The law is clear: the United States district court judge has ample power to compel boards to desegregate. Yet six years of litigation produced negligible results. There were exceptions, but by and large federal judges applied the law adversely to the claims of Negroes. Some judges were so opposed to integration that they believed the safety of the nation depended upon their minimizing the scope of the Supreme Court's decisions. Others were affected by the "go slow" philosophy cultivated by President Eisenhower and segregationists. But judicial attitudes do not tell the whole story. The law is on the side of the plaintiffs, but their opponents have most of the advantages.

Southern lawmaking bodies have produced a constant stream of new laws: school boards can change the rules of the game in the midst of the litigation. Eugene Cook, Georgia's attorney general, has confessed: "We might as well be candid. Most of the laws will be stricken down by the Courts in due course." [1] Yet each law makes possible another round of motions, briefs, hearings, rulings, and appeals. As one segregationist said, "As long as we can legislate, we can segregate."

[1] Florence B. Irving, "Segregation Legislation in the South," *The New South,* February, 1957, p. 8.

In the legal battle school boards have the better talent. If one goes to a large southern city to interview the attorney for the board, one will be ushered into a posh law suite, past a battery of secretaries and young law-school graduates, and into the private office of one of the city's most successful and experienced lawyers. The carpet is thick, the furniture most chic. For representing the board, the lawyer may receive a fee as high as $25,000. The public treasury finances his court costs; he can count on the help of the state attorney general's office.[2] For example, the two attorneys defending Clarendon County, S. C., received $25,000 paid by the South Carolina legislature. In addition, John W. Davis was presented with a silver service. The attorney for the New Orleans Parish School District was on a $25,000 retainer.[3] In 1957 the Texas legislature appropriated $50,000 to be used by the attorney general to resist integration suits.[4]

When one interviews the attorney for the plaintiffs, one climbs wooden stairs to a sparsely furnished office with only linoleum on the floor. The earnest attorney answers his own phone, greets his clients, researches his own briefs. Since Negroes are seldom retained by large firms or become involved in complex litigation, their courtroom experience is limited. They are not men of wealth, and the fees they receive for handling civil rights cases are small, sometimes nothing.[5] They seldom can afford to devote much time to these cases.

[2] Samuel Krislov, "Constituency Versus Constitutionalism: The Desegregation Issue and Theories and Aspirations of Southern Attorneys General," *Midwest Journal of Political Science,* vol. III, no. 1, February 1959, pp. 75–92.

[3] *Arkansas Gazette,* May 28, 1958.

[4] *Texas Observer,* Sept. 26, 1958.

[5] "From July 1956 through September 1958, the Virginia State Conferences of NAACP branches paid $9,254 in lawyers' fees to five attorneys on the NAACP staff and $3,124 for expenses. There was a $2,413 bill for unpaid fees." Testimony of W. Lester Banks before Judge W. E. Hennings, Jr. *Washington Post & Times Herald,* Nov. 12, 1958. Thurgood Marshall, chief counsel for the NAACP, received $15,000 a year until 1960 when it was raised to $18,000. The other lawyers on his central staff get from $9,000 down to $5,800. The entire budget in 1958 for the Legal

Many of these Negro attorneys, of course, have had considerable experience in civil rights litigation; some have been at the business for twenty years. They receive help from the small but top-flight central staff of the NAACP Legal Defense and Education Fund. But as Professor Charles Alan Wright has written: "It is no disparagement of the dedicated lawyers who have worked tirelessly for the NAACP to say that, good as they are, they are not the outstanding lawyers of the South." [6]

Both the enemies and friends of the NAACP exaggerate its power. To its enemies it is a convenient "devil figure," a gigantic, well-organized, heavily financed group of clever agitators bent on forcing complete race-mixing. To friends of civil rights, the NAACP is a "father figure" with complete control over the situation. Yet stripped of the veil of mystery, on the legal side the NAACP is a small group of hard-working Negro lawyers plus a central staff who have to take on the best legal talent that the public treasuries of southern governments can find.

The NAACP has frequently been outmaneuvered. Desegregation suits are especially tricky, with rules of procedure being accommodated to unprecedented situations. If the NAACP's attorneys make the slightest procedural misstep, lawyers for the school boards will pounce on the miscue, and it can be used by the judge, if he is so minded, to dismiss the Negroes' complaints because of a technical error.

And school boards fight harder against the injunctions than Negroes fight for them. Since 1957 school boards have displayed amazing ingenuity in discovering delaying devices.

In their more optimistic moods segregationists hope that somehow and in some way they will find a formula which will win judicial approval, the political climate will change, judges will be persuaded of the error of their ways, and the Supreme Court's decision will be overthrown. But more realistically they know

---

Defense and Education Fund was $300,000. *New York Times,* Jan. 3, 1960.

[6] Charles Alan Wright, "School Integration, An Almost Lost Cause," *The Progressive,* August 1958, p. 9.

better. Their objective is of a somewhat different order: to convince the nation that the Brown decision cannot be enforced.
When the nation was convinced, they constantly point out, that
it was impossible to enforce prohibition, the Eighteenth Amendment was repealed. They believe that the nation eventually will
conclude by similar inductive reasoning that the Brown decision
is unworkable.

Why do many city school boards, controlled by moderates,
co-operate with the segregationists when many of their attorneys
privately concede that although they may gain time, a year or
two, maybe even four or five, eventually the schools must be integrated? One reason is simply that many cities have no alternative.
In Alabama (in Virginia until 1958 and in Georgia until 1961)
state law forbids local authorities to desegregate whether or not
in compliance with a federal injunction; they have had to fight
entry suits in order to keep their public schools open. But more
important, it is politically dangerous for local authorities to desegregate until they have exhausted every legal out. If this is done
then moderates can say, "We have done all we can to keep segregation; we have no choice if we wish to have public schools but
to accept integration. The judge is making us do so." Ardent
segregationists will consider anything less than absolute defiance
to be treason, but citizens who are less extreme, it is hoped, are
more likely to accept desegregation if they are convinced it must
be.

Despite contrary public statements, despite formal legal motions for postponement, many school board members privately
admit they want the judge to order them to desegregate. They
will publicly deplore such an injunction, but often they will ap-
plaud privately.

Some federal judges have failed to recognize that their primary role is to "take the heat." The judge's injunction is required
not to compel school authorities to do what they personally find
distasteful, but to take the responsibility for ordering desegregation from their shoulders. A judge who is misled into taking the
request of public officials at face value and who fails to under-

stand his duty to serve as a scapegoat, frequently undermines the political position of the moderates. In 1958, for example, the Little Rock School Board was under intense pressures from local segregationists and from Governor Faubus: it was accused of "selling out to the NAACP," and of failing to exhaust all legal weapons. To deflate these pressures, the Little Rock board petitioned Judge Lemley for permission to discontinue desegregation temporarily. They had little expectation of having their request granted. But after the anticipated rebuff, it was hoped it would be clear to all that no matter how much disorder the segregationists produced, no matter what the governor might do, integration was in Little Rock to stay.

The maneuver backfired. Even though they knew that Judge Lemley was unsympathetic to desegregation, perhaps no one was more suprised than school officials when he granted their request. Lemley was later reversed, but by granting the board's request, he had strengthened the position of the board's enemies. He had vindicated the segregationists who had been insisting that if the board had wanted to, it could have blocked desegregation.

Sometimes the school board's desire for the judge "to get them off the hook" comes to the surface. For example, after the Knoxville School Board tentatively moved to desegregate, it ran into vocal opposition. The board hastily retreated into silence. In 1959 some Negro parents sued and the case was assigned to Judge Robert Love Taylor, "Little Bob," as he is known. Judge Taylor, a member of one of East Tennessee's most distinguished families (son of a former governor), is widely known and highly respected. A close associate of Senator Kefauver, he was named to the bench in 1949. Judge Taylor personally prefers segregation, but he believes too that the law must be obeyed, and when he issues an order, he means it.[7] The board felt Judge Taylor was in a much better position to order integration than they.

At the end of the hearing, Judge Taylor announced: "I'll with-

---

[7] Note his subsequent contempt citation of Kasper.

hold action until April 8, 1960, by which time the board shall submit a plan. My setting a date, however, does not constitute an order."

S. Frank Fowler, attorney for the board, was distressed. He was distressed not because Judge Taylor asked for the submission of a plan, but because he had not *ordered* its submission. "The board," Fowler told Judge Taylor, "has stated they don't intend to present a plan unless ordered."

Judge Taylor retorted: "You tell them they're not writing this court's orders. Why does the board want to make this court make them comply with the law?"

Fowler: "The board feels its duty to desegregate is less clear than the court's duty to order desegregation."

Judge Taylor: "I've been long-suffering with you this morning. They'd better get a plan in here by April 8 or we'll see what happens." [8]

Though perhaps not a formal order, Judge Taylor gave the Knoxville board what it wanted: a firm command to act.

Sometimes judges are not so obliging. Take the Dallas situation. Texas law forbids any school board to desegregate without first holding a referendum and securing the approval of the electorate. If the Dallas board attempts to desegregate without this approval—which in any large city would be difficult to obtain—its members could be punished and the district could lose state funds. But if a federal judge should order the board to integrate, his injunction would give the board not only its political excuse, but firm legal grounds to defend the district from the withdrawal of state funds and to protect the members from state prosecution. Since a valid federal injunction takes priority over state law, Texas cannot lawfully punish school officials or withdraw funds merely because they complied with a federal integration injunction.

In Dallas, despite six years of litigation, district judges, ostensibly anxious to help the board, have refused to give the board

[8] *Southern School News,* March 1960, pp. 1 and 2.

the order it needs. Dr. Edwin L. Rippy, former school board chairman, pointed out: "I don't recall that the board has ever been asked legally to present a plan . . . it could do so with ease. . . . The board . . . has felt it inappropriate [to announce a plan] in view of litigation. . . . " [9]

The determination of school officials to oppose legal complaints is not to be explained completely as part of a deliberate strategy. Moderates in charge of the schools are personally opposed to integration. They will act if they must, but if they can delay without much cost, why not? Desegregation brings tense days. Naturally superintendents of schools and board members easily convince themselves that this year is not the best time to desegregate; it will be easier next year or the year after.

On the other side, Negroes and the NAACP, despite their reputation for extremism, have failed to press their legal claims. By 1961 there had been no suit in Mississippi and only two in South Carolina, and they had not been pressed. In Georgia, Alabama, and Louisiana, legal action was limited to the major cities. In Arkansas and Tennessee Negroes legally challenged segregation in only three cities; in Texas only Dallas, Houston, and Fort Worth faced major lawsuits. Even after complaints had been filed, Negroes did not press the issues. Only in Virginia and to a somewhat lesser extent in North Carolina did Negroes make a major attack on segregation.

Although the obstacles segregationists have imposed make it difficult, even dangerous, for Negroes to sue in some areas, in many cities there are no external barriers. Negroes can go to court if they wish. Why has there not been a flood of lawsuits?

Negroes have failed to mount a massive legal offensive partly as a matter of tactics. Especially in the first years following the Supreme Court's decision, many Negro spokesmen felt it would be premature to force the issue. They hesitated to sponsor suits for fear such action would be construed as a hostile act, as a sign of their unwillingness to co-operate. Local political consid-

[9] *Southern School News,* March 1960, p. 10.

erations have also been a factor: in Atlanta, the case was deferred until after the 1958 re-election of Mayor William B. Hartsfield, an outstanding moderate for whom litigation might have been politically embarrassing.

It was hoped that school boards would take the initiative. By 1957, however, it became clear that Negroes had an exaggerated notion of the political forces working in their favor. Their lack of aggressiveness merely allowed the segregationists to take unchallenged control of the situation. Some Negroes still are afraid that widespread litigation may force southern moderates into the extremist camp, but not as many are afraid as they used to be. Henceforth it is doubtful if Negroes will refrain from legal action because of tactical considerations.

In some communities there has been no suit for the simple reason that no person is willing to serve as a plaintiff. Even Negroes who feel intensely about segregation, who are willing to take personal abuse, who will serve as a plaintiff in a bus-desegregation or golf-course case, are hesitant to join a school case because it places their children in jeopardy. Others willing to serve as plaintiffs cannot be used, perhaps because of something in their children's school records which would give authorities a convenient excuse for rejection, perhaps because of lack of proper residential qualifications, and so on.

A more persistent deterrent to litigation is simply the lack of money. School-entry suits are expensive. It costs around $15,000 to take a case up through the judicial hierarchy. This figure excludes the services of attorneys for the central NAACP staff employed on an annual salary and the services of local attorneys who serve without fee.[10] It does not include the expenses connected with administrative hearings or fees for physicians, psychologists, and other experts frequently needed to answer school board contentions that Negroes have been rejected because they lack emotional stability, and so on.

[10] Letter from Gordon M. Tiffany, staff director of Commission on Civil Rights, to Senator Javits, dated January 29, 1960, in *Congressional Record,* vol. 106, February 27, 1960, p. 377.

The NAACP, practically the only organization supporting litigation, just does not have the resources to handle a large number of cases at any one time. It has failed to receive grass roots support. Of the seventeen million Negroes in the United States, fewer than 300,000 have joined the NAACP and they contribute to it for all purposes less than $1,000,000 a year. Does this mean that Negroes do not favor desegregation?

As far as the educated and articulate Negroes are concerned, the answer is clear: they are strongly opposed to segregation. They feel the impact of segregation intensly; they are highly sensitive to the color line. They are fighting to abolish segregation not merely because it is a symbol of servitude, but because they want their children to attend a desegregated school.

But what of the less educated Negroes—the maids, the share-croppers, the janitors, the yardmen? It is hard to discover what they want. White southerners insist these Negroes favor segregation. But many Negroes have discovered that "to get along, go along," and seldom do southern whites talk with Negroes other than those who are in a subservient status, or under circumstances in which Negroes would be encouraged to speak freely and frankly. Many southern whites get their information about Negroes only from those who are dependent upon them. Typical are the comments of a Montgomery businessman who is sure that the Montgomery bus boycott was not popular among Negroes. How does he know? His maid told him so.[11]

For decades the two races have coexisted in the South. In many areas the relations have been warm and affectionate, but there has been limited opportunity for free exchange of ideas. Even in the face of the lunch-counter protests, bus boycotts, and almost complete lack of expressed Negro sentiment for segregation, many white southerners are still convinced that all the trouble is the result of "outside agitators." On the other side, even in the face of Little Rock and the political victories of segregation leaders, many Negroes remain convinced that all the opposi-

[11] *U. S. News & World Report,* March 21, 1960, p. 74.

tion stems from a few prejudiced "politicians." The events of
the last several decades make it abundantly clear that the two
races have never really communicated with each other: Negroes
underestimate the whites' determination to maintain segregation;
whites underestimate the Negroes' desire to abolish it.

That most Negroes are opposed to segregation does not mean
that the unlearned Negro is anxious to have his own children
attend integrated schools, at least not immediately, when it means
exposing them to the dangers and tensions of being among the
first. It takes considerable sophistication and determination to
weigh the long-range advantages of destroying the pattern of
segregated schools against the short-run disadvantages for the
Negro children who have to serve as pioneers.

Throughout the South, where schools have been desegregated
there has been no mass movement of Negroes into "white"
schools. Many Negro parents are already straining their financial
resources to send their children to school. They believe, rightly
or wrongly, that if their children go to "white" schools the costs
would be prohibitive. They think of having to buy better clothes,
for their children as the center of attention will have to go to
extraordinary lengths to avoid making a "bad impression." They
are not unaffected by the feelings of inferiority generated by
decades of discrimination—many are afraid their children could
not make a go of it in a "white" school.

No doubt there are pressures within the Negro community
which make a Negro hesitant to speak out for segregation. But
Negroes who refuse to sign petitions, or who are unwilling to
serve as plaintiffs, or who refuse to send their children to "white"
schools almost never say they favor segregation. When Nashville
desegregated its first grade in 1957, for example, only nineteen
families entered children in the "white" schools, and only nine
Negro children remained when the first half of the school year
ended. An investigation into the reason why so few sent children
to these schools revealed several factors. Because of segregated
housing, only 126 out of 1400 Negro first-graders were eligible
for enrollment. Of those who were eligible, fears of physical and

economic reprisal kept many from enrolling. Others were reluctant to break the prevalent social pattern. A minister talked with parents and found among the most prominent responses the following:

"I have an older child in the Negro school and my first-grader needs his protection."

"I am not well, so I am keeping my child out of school for the first week."

"The child is not well enough to go and register."

"We are planning to move to another community within Nashville."

"I don't want to make my child a guinea pig."

"When these folks get off the school grounds and quit threatening on the telephone, I'll send my child to the integrated school." [12]

Nor does the fact that Negroes fail to join the NAACP in large numbers mean they are opposed to its goals. Negroes simply are not culturally conditioned to join political organizations or to contribute to support lawsuits. Decades of paternalism have created an attitude that these are activities for the rich and powerful. And litigation, by its complexity and technical nature and by its lack of dramatic moments, furnishes an ineffective peg around which to build a mass movement. One can hardly picket the judge or boycott the courtroom. Furthermore, the NAACP may in the eyes of the white world be the most prominent antisegregation organization, but to many Negroes their church is the more obvious and direct institution to battle against discrimination.

Negroes are opposed to segregation. Almost all feel keenly that they have to face life with handicaps imposed on no other Americans and that these handicaps flow from segregation. Dis-

[12] Anna Hoeden, *A First Step Toward School Integration,* New York Congress of Racial Equality, 1958, pp. 13–14.

crimination in education cuts deeply: an education to a Negro
is the escape from poverty, a ticket from the world of domestic
service into the life of the middle class. Nonetheless, most
Negroes are fighting against the system of segregation rather than
for the immediate opportunity to have their own children educated in integrated institutions. They do not want to go to "white"
schools so much as they want to avoid being forced to attend
"colored" schools. As one elderly Negro phrased it with respect
to bus integration: "The seats at the back are just as good as
those at the front. Most Negroes still sit in the back, even though
we got the buses integrated. But we didn't fight for seats, we
wanted to get rid of those signs."

Whatever the reason, the fact remains that whites have fought
more determinedly to keep the schools segregated than Negroes
have fought to integrate them.

In almost every instance the complaint initiating a case is the
product of group action rather than a spontaneous move of an
individual Negro. In almost every instance, the NAACP has been
the channel to recruit and instruct plaintiffs, to provide the funds
and furnish the lawyer.

The decision to litigate is not made by a small group of master
strategists sitting in New York. Thurgood Marshall and his staff
may lead, guide, suggest, but they cannot control the situation
out of which the cases spring. Nothing could have been worse,
for example, from the point of view of the NAACP's overall
strategy, than for rural-Deep-South Prince Edward and Clarendon Counties to serve as test cases. Yet when local Negroes re-
belling against deplorable schools solicited the help of the
NAACP legal staff, the lawyers felt they could not refuse it. Nor
could they allow adverse rulings to go unchallenged: events have
forced them to push a suit in areas where all the advantages are
with their opponents.

Local and national NAACP officials unapologetically encourage Negroes to petition school boards and to step forward
as plaintiffs. Forms are often prepared in state headquarters and

distributed to local chapters. In June 1955, the NAACP Conference of Virginia Branches sent out a directive urging local units to find Negroes to sign these petitions, and cautioned that persons should be selected willing "to go all the way, since it may well be only the first step to an extended court fight." [13] The national office sent a field secretary to Dallas to help prepare petitions and instruct parents and children about how to act when they appear at "white" schools.

Since it is illegal, or at least unethical, for lawyers to solicit clients, great care is taken to isolate the NAACP lawyers from these initial steps. They are not contacted until plaintiffs have come forward in search of legal assistance.

The best plaintiffs are those who are not exposed to community pressures, and who have had enough education so they cannot be led into damaging admissions. There is safety also in numbers. The larger the number of plaintiffs, the more difficult it is for school boards to find some factor other than race to explain the exclusion of Negro children from white schools. With a large number of plaintiffs, it is less likely that school authorities will be able to drag out the suit for so long that all the children will have graduated before final judgment, and thus cloud the legal picture by the issue of "mootness."

The first step to initiate legal action is to petition school authorities to integrate. In Miami and New Orleans this is all that was done prior to the suit. In Dallas, Birmingham, and other cities, in addition, some Negro pupils went to schools nearest their homes on the first day of a new term. To the surprise of no one, they were refused admission. But the effort strengthens the contentions of the plaintiffs, joins the issues more cleanly, and makes it more difficult for school officials to pretend that schools are not being operated along racial lines. Why then is this not done routinely?

Negroes are not asking that specific pupils be assigned to par-

[13] Committee on Offenses Against the Administration of Justice (Boatright Committee) of Virginia, *Report*, November 13, 1957, quoted in full in 3 RRLR 98 at 104 (1957).

ticular schools; they want the school systems integrated. But more importantly, human beings under the best of circumstances like to avoid face-to-face conflict or to postpone it for as long as possible. Many more are willing to sign petitions than to brave white hostility by taking children to white schools, an act comparable to facing enemy fire.

The plaintiffs' presentation of their case to the court is short and simple. They establish that the plaintiffs are Negroes, residents of the school district. They assert that the public schools are being operated on a segregated basis, that school authorities have not made a good faith attempt to desegregate, have moved with no speed, deliberate or otherwise. They call a few Negro parents and students to relate their attempts to secure admission to schools, and establish the fact that they live closer to "white" than to "colored" schools. Thus they contend the board of education is depriving Negroes of their rights secured by the Fourteenth Amendment and the United States civil rights laws. They ask for an early hearing on their requests for an injunction.

On the face of it, a school board is hard-pressed to find legally convincing answers. The law is on the side of the plaintiffs. So the boards first seek to avoid a head-on clash, and try to persuade the judge to dismiss the complaint without even getting to the merits. Among the arguments they have used are the following:

1) The complaint should be dismissed because the plaintiffs have failed to exhaust administrative remedies.

2) The complaint should be dismissed because the plaintiffs are not really interested in having their children admitted to "white" schools, but have been tricked into serving as plaintiffs to test the legality of the school program. In Houston, for example, the schools' lawyers charged that the fact that the plaintiffs had called in national officers of the NAACP instead of relying exclusively on local counsel proved the case was trumped up.[14]

---

[14] *Southern School News,* July 1959, p. 9. *See also* Transcript of *Borders v. Rippy* (The Dallas Case), U.S.C.A. (Fifth) 56 493 filed March 26, 1957, p. 28.

There is nothing unethical or illegal in Negroes becoming plaintiffs in order to challenge segregation, yet for political reasons, plaintiffs apparently feel compelled to insist that their only goal is to secure assignments for their own children to schools which are closer to their homes or which have better facilities. It seems obvious, however, that the first Negro students to attend "white" schools often do so at some sacrifice to their own education. The nine Negroes first assigned to Little Rock's Central High were warriors fighting for principle; it is doubtful if they personally received a better education at Central than they could have by remaining at the "colored" school, or that they went through a year of persecution just to save a few blocks' walk.

The judges have paid no attention to these charges that the plaintiffs are "insincere." But the school lawyers almost got a legal opening into which they could have driven a major wedge when a three-man district court dismissed a petition for an injunction brought by O. Z. Evers, a colored citizen of Memphis, against laws requiring segregated seating in buses. Evers admitted he was not a regular patron of the buses. The trial court ruled that since he had boarded the bus merely to institute litigation, he was in no position to represent Negro bus riders. On appeal the Supreme Court reversed, saying, "That the appellant may have boarded this particular bus for the purpose of instituting this litigation is not significant." [15] If the trial court's ruling had been allowed to stand, it would have been used by some district judges to dismiss school-entry suits on the ground that the plaintiffs were merely trying to enroll in "white" schools to institute litigation.

3) The complaint should be dismissed because the Fourteenth Amendment was ratified by southern state legislatures acting under duress, and is therefore not part of the Constitution. This contention that the Constitution itself is unconstitutional has been given national prominence by David Lawrence, publisher of the *U. S. News and World Report,* who has

[15] *Evers et al. v. Dwyer,* 358 U.S. 202 (1958).

aptly been called "the South's Own Lawyer on the National Scene." Lawyers for the Orleans Parish School Board (New Orleans) and the Tennessee Federation of Constitutional Government, among others, have submitted elaborate briefs to support this view.[16]

The short answer is that of course southern legislatures ratified the Fourteenth Amendment unwillingly. It was the price they paid for readmission to full status in the Union. The North won the Civil War; its victory terms included acceptance by southern legislatures not only of the Fourteenth, but also of the Thirteenth and Fifteenth Amendments. If southern states had had a free choice, they would not have ratified any of these amendments.

At this late date judges can scarcely be persuaded to hold the Fourteenth Amendment unconstitutional. This Amendment not only protects Negroes against governmental-imposed discrimination, but it is the primary constitutional limitation on state regulation of speech, press, and religion.

All the judges have disposed of the matter by pointing out that Congress determines the validity of the ratification of constitutional amendments; it has never been thought to be within the jurisdiction of courts.

4) The case should be dismissed because a single judge is without jurisdiction to enjoin the enforcement of state laws. Because of the seriousness of declaring a state law unconstitutional, since 1910 Congress has required the convening of a three-judge court to hear motions for injunctions against the enforcement of state statutes.[17] Furthermore, decisions of these three-judge courts are directly appellable to the Supreme Court. Sometimes it is to the advantage of the Negro plaintiffs to secure such a

---

[16] See Orleans Parish School Board v. Bush, 16, 190 U.S.C.A. (Fifth), Petition and Brief for Rehearing, March 23, 1957: Tulane Law Review, vol. 28, pp. 22–44; David Lawrence, "14th Amendment Unlawfully Adopted," New Orleans Times-Picayune, February 9, 1959.

[17] Harry L. Hudspeth, "Federal Jurisdiction and Exhaustion of Administrative Remedies," Texas Law Review, vol. 36, June 1958, pp. 812–819. Ex Parte Poresky, 290 U.S. 30 (1933); 28 U.S.C. 2281–2284.

court because it leads to faster Supreme Court review, but most of the time it has been the school boards who have challenged a single judge's jurisdiction to hear a case.

Long-established precedents make it clear that if state laws are clearly and obviously constitutional, a three-judge court need not be assembled. Otherwise, no matter how frivolous the challenge, a plaintiff would be able to demand a three-judge court and circumvent the normal channels of review. What of the converse situation, where the statute is obviously unconstitutional? Until the school-segregation controversy the question had never been raised.

It is one of the operating assumptions of our federal system that no state law is obviously unconstitutional. State legislatures are supposedly cognizant of their constitutional obligation and it is not to be thought they would pass laws clearly unconstitutional. Since 1955, however, state legislatures have sought to take advantage of this presumption by passing dozens of laws clearly in conflict with the Constitution. In most instances a single judge has felt competent to declare these laws unconstitutional.

To play it safe, three-judge courts have been used to test the validity of laws which on their face do not impose segregation but make integration impossibly difficult. Although this delays hearings and ties up judicial manpower, in the long run it may expedite desegregation. Not only are there faster appeals, but three southern judges may find enough reinforcement in collegiate activity to make an unpopular ruling collectively that they might not make separately.

School boards usually fail to persuade the judge to dismiss the Negroes' legal complaint outright. Their next line of defense is to contend that since they have acted in good faith, the judge should refrain from issuing any injunctions. If he feels he must take some kind of action, he should not call for actual desegregation, at least not for a long long time.

Under the terms of the Supreme Court's Brown decision, school boards have an obligation to make a good faith attempt to integrate. What does this obligation amount to? Not much, and they know it. Outside the courtroom many school board members have spoken otherwise. In Houston one board member said "she would go to jail rather than to have desegregation." Another said "she would not go to jail but she would never vote for any plan of integration." [18] In New Orleans a former president of the school board promised to close the public schools if necessary to prevent integration. Even moderate school board members have felt it politically necessary to promise their constituents to fight to retain segregation.

At the same time public officials are insisting on the public platform that they are doing all they can to resist integration; they come before the judge insisting they are making a good faith attempt to desegregate. In Virginia, while campaigning for governor on a pledge "to dedicate every capacity to preserve segregation in the schools," J. Lindsay Almond, as attorney general, was telling the federal judges that he and other Virginia officials were acting in good faith. In Houston the segregationists' faction, after strengthening its control over the school board in the fall of 1956, proceeded to reverse the tentative good faith steps previously taken. Then they went before Judge Ben C. Connally and cited as evidence of their good faith the very steps which they had just repudiated.

Fortunately for the school authorities, judges have refused to take judicial notice of comments of individual members or remarks made in public speeches.[19] So long as a board avoids spreading statements of outright defiance across its official minutes, its lack of good faith will probably not be made grounds for an injunction.

In short, the requirement of good faith has come to mean only that officials have thought seriously about the problem, have authorized studies to be made, and have always acted with the students' welfare in mind—a kind of character judgment rather than a legally enforceable obligation. Judge Joe E. Estes felt that

[18] *Houston Post,* May 24, 1957.
[19] *Houston Post,* May 24, 1957.

Mansfield, Texas, officials had shown good faith, for example, despite their refusing to admit Negroes to their only high school, because they had opened their meetings with prayer, studied articles in magazines, held numerous meetings, passed resolutions, and appointed committees.[20] The only boards called to task for an "attitude of intransigency" are those in Virginia, where until 1958 state laws made it obligatory for boards to show "bad faith."

But as the Court of Appeals for the Fifth Circuit has stated: "Faith by itself . . . without works, is not enough." [21] Even if a board is acting in good faith, what about its obligation to make an immediate start and move with all deliberate speed toward complete desegregation "at the earliest practicable date"? How can a board contend that it is moving with all deliberate speed when it has done nothing?

The details of the boards' contentions vary from city to city, but the argument runs something like this:

We need more time because in our city problems are more complex than those of other districts; in Houston because the district has the largest number of students of any in the South; in Prince Edward County (Virginia) because we have such a high ratio of Negroes to whites; and so on.

In New Orleans the board put up an unusually vigorous fight to persuade Judge J. Skelly Wright that their peculiar problems entitled them to retain segregation. Elaborate studies were introduced to prove that integration "would endanger the health and morals of [New Orleans'] white children." "It is only too well [known]," said the board, "that a large segment of our Negro population has little or no sense of morality and that to intermingle them with the white children in our public schools could well corrupt the minds and hearts of the white children to their lifelong and perhaps eternal injury." [22] This, it was contended,

[20] *Jackson v. Rawdon*, 1 RRLR (1955).
[21] *Jackson v. Rawdon*, 1 RRLR 655 (1956).
[22] Undated brief presented by the Orleans Parish School Board, in files of *Bush v. Orleans Parish*, Civil Action No. 3630, U.S.D.C. *See also*

made the situation in Orleans parish "substantially different from the facts in the School Segregation cases." [23]

School officials have also contended that since schools are overcrowded, no action to desegregation can be taken until more schools are built.[24]

Another argument is this: schools should remain segregated until the aptitude of Negro students has been raised. The Houston board, for illustration, insisted it was moving with deliberate speed toward desegregation because it had established a summer training program for Negro teachers.

Negro plaintiffs have countered that these several arguments are backdoor attempts to reargue the merits of segregation. The Supreme Court has already decided schools should be desegregated. Authorities may assign pupils to schools on the basis of aptitude, provided Negro and white students are treated alike. Thurgood Marshall has said: "I have no objection to academic segregation, only racial segregation. If they want to put all the dumb ones, white and black, into the same school that is fine, provided they put all the smart ones, white and black, into the same school."

Some school authorities contend that schools have already been desegregated, and that therefore no injunction is needed. The fact that all Negroes still attend "colored" schools, it is explained, comes about as a result of voluntary choice and residential location. A pupil-placement program makes such a contention plausible as long as officials avoid any formal statement that racial factors are considered in assigning pupils. Despite *de facto* segregation, the Mecklenburg County Board of Education in North Carolina told the judge in the spring of 1959 that it did not follow a policy of racial discrimination. Frank L.

Transcript of Record, pp. 108–113, and Brief on Behalf of Appellant, October 3, 1956, in Civil Action No. 16,190, before United States Court of Appeals, and Petition for Rehearing and Brief filed March 23, 1957.

[23] *Ibid.*

[24] Transcript, *Borders v. Rippy,* U.S.C.A. (Fifth), March 26, 1957, p. 6; *Orleans Parish v. Bush,* U.S.C.A., Petition for Rehearing, March 23, 1957, p. 8, and Transcript, p. 113.

Fuller, chairman of the Durham (North Carolina) board, out-side of the courtroom told a delegation of Negroes he did not believe Durham was ready for desegregation, but in court his board denied it assigned children to schools on the basis of race. Eventually the Durham board transferred a few Negroes to "white" schools.[25] A Georgia state law forbids desegregation, yet the Atlanta School Board objected when Judge Frank A. Hooper said he "assumed" Atlanta schools were segregated. The board insisted it was not pursuing a policy of racial discrimination. Judge Hooper refused to accept these assurances.

Officials of the University of Georgia also tried to argue, despite the fact that the university had been segregated for the entire 175 years of its existence, that it was not pursuing a policy of segregation when it denied admission to Hamilton E. Holmes and Charlayne Hunter, two honor students, who applied for ad-mission to the university in June 1959. For a year officials de-layed processing their applications. Then under threat of a law-suit, a preregistration interview was held.

Holmes was asked whether he had taken part in sit-in demon-strations, visited houses of prostitution, frequented beatnik joints, been to interracial parties, or been arrested. He answered "no" to all these questions. But his application was rejected by university officials because they contended he had been untruth-ful since they had information he had been arrested for speeding. After Miss Hunter's interview, the university ruled that she would not be admitted because there was no space in the dormitories, but indicated she might be allowed to attend the university in September 1961.

At a five-day hearing lawyers for the university and the state of Georgia tried to persuade Judge William A. Bootle that the fact of race had not caused them to reject Holmes's and Hunter's applications. Judge Bootle—a former dean of the Mercer law school, native Georgian, staunch Republican, and a 1954 ap-pointee of President Eisenhower—on January 6, 1961, three

[25] *Southern School News,* May 1959, p. 10.

days before winter-quarter registration, ruled, "Had plaintiffs been white applicants to the University of Georgia both would have been admitted to the university not later than the beginning of the fall quarter, 1960." [26]

When the arguments are over, and the judge returns to his chambers and takes off his robe, the decision is up to him. He has read the Supreme Court's opinions, studied the briefs, listened to the arguments of both sides. He weighs the arguments. He assesses the political factors of life, those factors which are not mentioned but are very much a part of the decision-making process. What are the judge's choices? He can:

1. Dismiss the complaint.

2. Retain jurisdiction, but refuse to deal with the complaint on its merits and send Negroes elsewhere to seek relief.

3. Order school authorities "from and after such time as may be necessary to make arrangements for admission of children to such schools on a racially nondiscriminatory basis with all deliberate speed," but specify no date or set a date in the far future.

4. Order school authorities to come forward by a specified date with a plan at which time there will be further hearings to determine if it meets the minimum requirements as outlined in the Brown decisions.

5. Order school authorities to admit on a certain date certain named Negro pupils to certain named schools.

6. Order authorities to begin desegregation by a certain date, doing so by stages.

7. Order school authorities to admit all Negroes to public schools on the same terms as other pupils.

With exceptions, in the border states federal judges have held school authorities to a strict accounting; they have called for the immediate integration of schools or have forced authorities to come forward promptly with a desegregation proposal. In Dela-

[26] *Southern School News,* February 1961, p. 8.

ware, for example, Judge Paul Leahy required state educational authorities to force reluctant districts in the southern part of the state to desegregate, thus avoiding the necessity of a suit against each and every school board.[27] Again, despite the fact that Hopkins County (Kentucky) officials were acting in good faith, Judge Henry L. Brooks rejected a proposal to stretch desegregation over a twelve-year period, disapproved a second plan to do it in four years, and ordered complete desegregation within a year.[28] The judges operating in the border states have not tolerated plans subjecting Negro students to admission tests or standards not being required of white students, not even during a transitional phase.

In the South itself the judges have ordered very little desegregation. A few have even dismissed the Negroes' complaints. In Miami, Judge Emett C. Choate ruled that Negroes, by asking for an integration injunction rather than asking for assignment to particular schools, had failed to present a valid complaint; in Dallas, Judge Atwell ruled the suit had been started prematurely. In both instances the respective courts of appeals reversed; even so the second time around the district judges dismissed the complaints again.

In other cases, for example in Birmingham, in all the North Carolina cases, and in Dollarway, Arkansas, judges retained jurisdiction but refused to deal with the complaints on their merits and sent Negroes back to the school boards in order to exhaust their administrative remedies. By this means, a judge avoids further action for a year or so.

Some judges have been a bit bolder: In Houston, in New Orleans, in Clarendon County and Prince Edward County, Virginia, and eventually in Dallas, the judges ordered school authorities to cease segregating Negroes "from and after such time as may be necessary" to make arrangements. But the judges carefully avoided specifying any date. They reiterated the Brown decision, making it apply specifically to the district in question. School

[27] *Southern School News,* January 1958, p. 14.
[28] *Mitchell v. Pollock,* 2 RRLR 305 (1957).

authorities are subject to possible punishment for violating these injunctions, but the obligation imposed is so vague, the chance of their being punished without future action so slight, as to be insignificant. The granting of these "from and after" injunctions is a major victory for the board.

It took the Dallas plaintiffs two years, three district court hearings, and three interventions by the court of appeals even to secure one of these mild and almost meaningless "from and after" injunctions. After the court of appeals told Judge Atwell he should not have peremptorily dismissed the complaint, he held another hearing. In a decision outspokenly critical of the Supreme Court and in favor of the right of white students to remain segregated from Negroes, Atwell again refused to order the Dallas board to take any action. The school board, he insisted, had the right to determine when schools should be integrated. He would not interfere. Again the court of appeals reversed.

Finally in September 1957, two years after the Negroes had first come to his court, Atwell, in what can only be described as a fit of pique, ordered Dallas to desegregate all its schools and to do so by the beginning of the second semester in January 1958. This order, issued without giving the board an opportunity to present its own plan, was so obviously uncalled for that many observers speculated that Atwell had issued it in the expectation it would be reversed.

At any rate, Andrew J. Thuss, lawyer for the Dallas board, secured an early hearing from the court of appeals, where he told the judges (R. T. Rives, J. R. Brown, and W. L. Jones): "Judge Atwell just came in and said he wanted his judgment. . . . It didn't take but a few minutes."

The circuit judges were disturbed by Atwell's failure to give the board a chance to present a plan for gradual desegregation. On the other hand, they were equally disturbed by the board's failure to take any initiative. Judge Brown told Thuss, "You've taken two years and you're not a step further." Judge Jones tried to get a commitment from Thuss: "When do you expect to present a plan?"

Said Thuss, "I think this summer."

Judge Jones persisted. "What do you think deliberate speed means in regard to this situation?"

Thuss smiled.[29]

The court of appeals vacated Atwell's injunction, and taking a somewhat unusual step itself issued a "from and after" undated injunction.

School boards have demonstrated no greater willingness to initiate desegregation action under these undated injunctions than they have under the Brown decision itself. Even after a "from and after" injunction has been issued, schools have remained segregated until Negroes again return to court.

Despite its reputation of being an extremist organization, the NAACP made no attempt to force the Dallas board to comply with the injunction until the summer of 1959, four years after filing the first complaint and two years after the "from and after" injunction was issued. They merely asked the judge to make the school board come up with a plan.

By this fourth go-round, Judge Atwell had fully retired, so the Dallas suit was assigned to Atwell's younger colleague, Judge T. Whitfield Davidson, age eighty-two, who was only in semi-retirement.[30] The Dallas suit has never been heard by a judge under eighty. Davidson, who studied law at Columbia University and the University of Chicago before the turn of the century, was admitted to the bar in 1903. He practiced in East Texas, was active in Democratic circles, served as a state senator and

[29] *Dallas Morning News,* November 23, 1957.

[30] Democrat Davidson and Republican Atwell were old antagonists. In February 1954 Atwell had publicly criticized Judge Davidson, suggesting that if Davidson did his work the problem of crowded dockets could be solved. Davidson, who was then seventy-seven, retorted: "In your ruffled . . . moments you probably feel that I should retire, but it has possibly not occurred to you that many feel that you could set me an example. . . . My dockets are of course not so clear of cases as yours. We have a different idea about this. If the end of the courtroom is primarily to have clear dockets, then you're right. . . . I think it is better to give (time) to them than to force them to take a nonsuit and go to trial." Letter from Davidson to Atwell, *Dallas Morning News,* Feb. 20, 1954.

lieutenant governor, and was appointed to the bench in 1932. Davidson had said he was ready to retire in 1954, provided "the powers that be" would "accept a judge, a man who had voted for Eisenhower, if such was required, that had the endorsement of the Abilene and Fort Worth Bars," but in 1959 he was still hearing non-jury cases.[31]

When the Dallas case was heard for the fourth time, Dr. W. T. White, superintendent of schools, testified that the authorities were acting in good faith with all deliberate speed and cited as evidence the fact that the board was studying the problems. Schools were overcrowded, he said; Negro students had lower aptitudes than white students, and many white parents and teachers objected to desegregation. In fact, said Dr. White, the problems were so overwhelming that it would take Dallas twenty to twenty-five years to desegregate.

Thurgood Marshall had come down from New York to join C. B. Bunkley, Jr., the local NAACP lawyer and one of the best, to see if they could not get the Dallas suit off the ground. Marshall and Bunkley insisted that Dallas was merely going through "tongue-in-cheek steps." The board could integrate if it wanted to, at least it could start, but obviously it had no intention of ever doing so unless Judge Davidson insisted upon it.

At the conclusion of the hearing Judge Davidson delivered a lecture to the Negroes in his courtroom. "I have had dealings with Negroes all my life," he told them. "I received my first nourishment from a Negro woman's breast. There is no animosity, no hatred of any kind in my heart. The southern white gentleman does not feel unkindly toward the Negro." He loved the Old South tradition, he told his audience, and continued: "As long as he [the Negro] begins imitating his white brother he is not at his best. If you want to rise in life, there is a way. . . . That is to excel." Following additional remarks about the virtues of patience and Christian charity, Judge Davidson said: "The Supreme Court has placed your state, your country, and your

[31] *Dallas Morning News,* February 20, 1954.

schools . . . to use a street term . . . over the barrel. . . . You are going to integrate your schools. The question is when." However, he continued, Negroes should recognize "that the white man has a right to maintain his racial integrity and it can't be done so easily in integrated schools . . . We will not name any date or issue any order. . . . The School Board should further study this question and perhaps take further action, maybe an election." [32]

Thurgood Marshall threw his pencil on the table with a look of strong disappointment. Nor was he comforted by the fact that Judge Davidson set another hearing for April 1960. Five years after the original complaint, six years after the Brown decision, the Dallas Independent School District was as segregated as ever.

For the fifth time the NAACP was forced to go to the court of appeals in New Orleans. This time, February 1960, the panel consisted of Chief Judge Rives, Judge John Minor Wisdom, and Judge Benjamin F. Cameron. The NAACP could expect no more from Cameron than they had been able to get from Atwell or Davidson, but it was obvious that Rives and Wisdom were losing patience with Dallas.

Dallas was represented by R. H. Brin, Jr. Rives and Wisdom gave him a rough time. At one point, when Brin commented, "I am not sure what the Negro plaintiffs want," Chief Judge Rives interrupted: "Everybody knows what they want. They want desegregation as soon as they can get it. . . . We've been engaging in legal literature for five years without action. . . . Actually the first step has not been taken on this matter. The school board has not yet come forward with a desegregation plan. Do you think that a mere study over a period of five years is a prompt and immediate start as ordered by the Supreme Court?"

Brin responded: "The Board fully recognizes its duties. The study cannot be indefinite."

Rives: "You have been telling us that all along."

Judge Wisdom entered the discussion, pointing out that the board kept saying it recognized its obligations under the Brown

[32] A.P. dispatch, July 30, 1959.

decision, but still it had done nothing. "Don't you think," he asked, "the school board should come up with a plan without a court order?"

Brin did not answer. Clearly what the board needed was a court command to present a plan. Clearly, it would not present such a plan unless such an order was issued.

C. B. Bunkley, Jr., speaking for the plaintiffs, told the court of appeals: "A gradual stair-step integration plan would be workable and acceptable to us. We are not asking that the whole system be desegregated, but we want a start by September." [33]

The court of appeals (March 1960), with Judge Cameron dissenting, ordered Dallas to present a desegregation plan to Judge Davidson and to do it soon.[34] The court of appeals' mandate was unequivocal: it would be hard for either the school authorities or even Judge Davidson to ignore it.

Late in May Davidson once again called his court to order. Once again the clerk called the Dallas case from the docket— still known as *Borders v. Rippy* though by this time Borders and most of the Negro plaintiffs in whose behalf the suit had been first instituted had graduated and Rippy had retired as chairman of the school board.

Harry W. Strasburger, attorney for the board, came forward to present Dallas's desegregation plan: nothing would be done until September 1961, but then the first grade would be desegregated. Thereafter, another grade would be desegregated each year. Attorneys for the NAACP, though preferring to see Dallas move at a faster pace, did not object to the stair-step program. From their point of view Dallas did not offer much. Yet, after all these years and hearings, Dallas did promise to begin.

Would Judge Davidson accept the Dallas plan? Six years after the Supreme Court's original decision, Dallas proposed to delay for another year and then to take until 1973 to complete desegregation. Everybody knew how Davidson felt; he was expected to rule that the Dallas plan was adequate.

[33] *Dallas Morning News,* February 14, 1960, March 16, 1960; *Texas Observer,* February 26, 1960; *Southern School News,* March 1960.
[34] *Borders v. Rippy,* 5 RRLR 392 (1960).

Judge Davidson rejected Dallas's proposals—not because the school board was moving too slowly, but because it was moving too rapidly. He became the first, and so far the only, judge to reject a proposed desegregation program on the ground it was too sweeping.

For over two hours Davidson held forth. "The Dallas Plan," he later reiterated, "would lead, in the opinion and the light of history and unquestionable sources to an amalgamation of the races. . . . In no clime and in no nation have the races ever amalgamated that it has not been to the disadvantage of both. . . . When the President's guard was shot, when the halls of Congress were shot up, they were not from Negroes that were raised in the South. They were from the integrated people of Puerto Rico." [35]

After further recitation, Judge Davidson instructed Dallas to set aside its own plans and substitute a program, to begin in September 1961, of "voluntary preference," or what is known in Dallas as "salt and pepper." Under the Davidson plan (which he adopted from a program long urged by the *Dallas Morning News*) all the schools in Dallas would remain segregated for the indefinite future, except for a school or two which the board was told to set aside for those students desiring to attend integrated institutions. "Let those integration advocates of both races have their children transferred there," said Davidson. "If that school succeeded, then the entire town could be integrated by consent."

Thurgood Marshall, who has made a practice of attending these Dallas hearings, was bewildered. So was Attorney Strasburger. Said Marshall, "I don't know what the ruling is . . . let me out of here." Said Strasburger, "The board prefers its graduate-a-year system, but it will as ordered submit a 'voluntary' program." [36]

During the summer of 1960 Dallas held a referendum to determine if its citizens would support desegregation, for under Texas law a city is not supposed to abandon segregation without prior favorable public vote. Such a referendum has no relation

[35] *Borders v. Rippy*, 5 RRLR 679 at 685 (1960).
[36] *Southern School News*, June 1960, p. 3.

to Dallas's constitutional obligation to desegregate its schools, but Judge Davidson was anxious for it to be held. He did his part to guarantee that the voters would reject integration. On the eve of the election he announced that if the vote were favorable to desegregation, he would order "immediate wholesale integration."

Judge Davidson's plan for Dallas went before the court of appeals. For the sixth time the court of appeals reversed the district judge. Circuit Judges Rives, Tuttle, and Jones refused to take charge of the Dallas case, although they agreed that the NAACP's request that they do so had been made "with much reason in view of the frustrating history of this litigation." [37] The circuit judges, however, directed Davidson to approve the stair-step plan presented by the Dallas board, but to eliminate a transfer provision which introduced racial factors. Yet despite the unequivocal mandate to Davidson, as long as he retains jurisdiction over the Dallas suit, it is difficult to predict what will happen.

The Houston case has been handled by Judge Ben C. Connally. The son of former Senator Tom Connally, a 1949 Truman appointee when he was 39, Judge Connally, more than any other judge, worked behind the scenes and outside the courtroom in an attempt to work out a compromise. At the outset of the Houston suit in December 1956, he persuaded the plaintiffs to withdraw their motion for a temporary injunction in exchange for an agreement that their suit would be scheduled for a comprehensive hearing on a permanent injunction in the spring of 1957, still plenty of time, it was thought, before schools opened in September.[38]

After an extended hearing, Connally called the two sides (lawyers for the plaintiffs and all members of the board) into his chambers for a secret meeting in which he tried to persuade the

---

[37] *Borders v. Rippy,* Opinion of the Court of Appeals, in *Southern School News,* March 1961, p. 12.

[38] Transcript, *Ross. v. Houston Independent School District,* Civil Docket 10,444, May 20, 1957.

board to come up with a plan, something acceptable to the board and something "plaintiff's lawyer could sell to his people." The board refused to do so.[39]

Connally took the case under advisement. Three months later schools opened. Judge Connally still had not handed down his ruling. Sometimes he woke up in the middle of the night and pondered the school integration case,[40] but it was not until October 16, a good month after school started, that he made his ruling public. It did no more than to tell the board it should desegregate with all deliberate speed.

For two years the Houston School Board—one of the few large city boards which has more defiantly resisted desegregation than even the state legislatures or the governors—did nothing. In 1956 the segregationist faction on the board had been strengthened and the board prepared to resist desegregation even more determinedly. In the summer of 1959 the plaintiffs asked for another hearing, telling Judge Connally that the board had ignored his earlier order to proceed and asking for an injunction to compel a start in September 1959. The board responded by submitting a 100,000-word report saying that problems of housing, academic achievement, and finances made it impossible for them to present a desegregation program and that they were already doing all that could reasonably be expected.

Judge Connally, holding back his ruling until after schools opened, in the fall of 1959 told the Houston board to report on progress by the following summer. Still he did not instruct the board that it must begin with desegregation, although he made it clear that he expected some action.

In the spring of 1960, after the court of appeals in the Dallas suit had indicated its displeasure with the way Davidson had handled that suit, Judge Connally sent the Houston board a letter to the effect that he expected it to file a desegregation plan by June 1. Connally warned unless it did so he had no alternative "but to grant the relief which the plaintiffs have sought" by

[39] *Houston Post,* September 29, 1957.
[40] *Ibid.*

ordering the immediate abolishment of segregation.[41] Judge Connally was losing patience. He took command and was determined that when Houston's schools opened in the fall, desegregation would begin.

During the summer the Houston board held a public referendum, ostensibly to comply with a state law requiring approval of district patrons or else withdrawal of state funds. Prior to the referendum (which went against integration by a large majority) Stone Wells, a member of the Houston board, announced: "The people should know that the areas which want desegration first are going to get it. And the ones that vote for it are going to get it first. That's what this election is for." [42]

This was too much for Connally. He publicly rebuked Wells by releasing a letter he wrote to Joe H. Reynolds, attorney for the board: "Your clients must recognize," the judge wrote, "that this is not a popularity contest, but is the performance of a duty which the law imposes. In our many conferences and hearings, I have always been led to believe that some plan adopted by other Texas cities, and which experience has shown to be workable, will be submitted here." [43]

Nonetheless when the deadline came all the Houston board did was submit to Connally a "salt-and-pepper" plan similar to the one the Dallas board a few days before had prepared at the request of Judge Davidson. But Judge Connally is no Davidson. The Houston plan "does not constitute compliance . . . nor does it constitute a good faith attempt at compliance; but is a palpable sham and subterfuge designed only to accomplish further evasion and delay." [44]

Since the Houston board refused to present an acceptable plan, Judge Connally himself ordered Houston to desegregate its first

---

[41] *Southern School News,* May 1960, p. 12. *See also* 5 RRLR 707–705 (1960) for complete text of letter.

[42] *Southern School News,* June 1960, p. 4.

[43] *Ibid.*

[44] *Ross v. Peterson,* 5 RRLR 703 at 709 (1960).

grade in September 1960, progressively including another grade each year.

Stone Wells commented: "Judge Davidson in Dallas recommended the very same plan that we as a board submitted to the judge here. Apparently federal judges differ quite a bit on their outlook on plans." [45]

The court of appeals refused to stay Judge Connally's order. September was fast approaching. The Houston board searched for an out. They tried to construe Judge Connally's order to mean that desegregation should start with kindergarten, but Judge Connally checked this move by clarifying his order.[46] Then the board adopted new standards for admission to the first grade in order to reduce the number of Negroes eligible to attend integrated institutions. However, they could not design standards which would keep all Negroes out of desegregated first grades without running afoul of Judge Connally.

Governor Price Daniel refused to interfere, and the Houston board lost their last excuse for delay when Texas Attorney General Will Wilson ruled that the Texas law depriving school districts of state funds if they desegregated without a favorable vote of their patrons did not apply when integration resulted from a court order.[47] (Wilson's ruling also stripped Dallas of any further excuse.) With the last avenue of escape cut off, the Houston School Board, the Houston mayor, and the local newspapers became last-minute moderates and urged compliance. The most defiant sounds came from the school board, which delayed the transfer. But two weeks after schools started eleven six-year-old Negro children started to study their ABC's in "white" schools. Houston is no longer the nation's largest completely segregated school district.

The New Orleans case has been handled by Judge J. Skelly Wright, a native of New Orleans. Wright, a Democrat, slight of

---

[45] *Southern School News,* September 1960, p. 16.
[46] *Ross v. Peterson,* 5 RRLR 703 at 709–710 (1960).
[47] Opinion of State Attorney General, 5 RRLR 711 (1960).

stature and decisive in action, taught for two years after gradu-
ating from Loyola University Law School in 1933. After service
as United States attorney and war duty, in 1948 he was named
United States attorney in New Orleans and a year later at thirty-
eight was appointed to the bench by President Truman.

At first Judge Wright issued a meaningless "from and after"
injunction. Since then he has been much less willing to tolerate
delay than his fellow judges sitting in Texas. The New Orleans
suit too has been a long-drawn-out affair, but less because of the
judge than because of the lack of aggressive pressing of the case
by the Negro plaintiffs and intense resistance by the school board.
Judge Wright's opinions and public comments, unlike those of
Atwell and Davidson, have given little comfort to confirmed
segregationists. For example, he concluded his opinion in which
he ordered New Orleans to desegregate with all deliberate speed
by saying, "We are, all of us, free-born Americans, with a right
to make our way, unfettered by sanctions imposed by man because of the work of God" [48]—perhaps the most cogent and brief
argument against segregation penned in the entire controversy.

Even though Wright's first injunction required New Orleans to
do nothing, at least for a while, the school board appealed all the
way up the judicial hierarchy. Except to consume time, this
maneuver accomplished little. Until the fall of 1960 the lawyers
for the board kept up a running fire of motions asking Wright to
set aside the injunction, each time for some new and ingenious
reason—once because it was claimed that the plaintiffs had not
proved they were in fact Negroes. Judge Wright denied all these
motions.

The New Orleans board persisted in its refusal to initiate desegregation, but the plaintiffs waited for almost three years before returning to court. Then in the summer of 1959 they asked
Judge Wright to put some teeth into his earlier "from and
after" injunction. After a brief hearing, he told the Orleans Parish
School Board that "all deliberate speed" in their case had already

[48] *Bush v. Orleans Parish School Board*, 1 RRLR 306 at 308 (1956).

run to six years and he ordered them to present a plan by May 1960, suggesting they start with the first grade.

Again the board appealed unsuccessfully. Again they tried to persuade Wright to vacate his order. May came and the board still had no plan. The board complained it could not produce a plan because of restrictive state laws. To take the board off the spot the judge himself put forth a token desegregation plan. He ordered the board to integrate the first grade in September 1960.

Certainly the New Orleans School Board had done all it could to delay desegregation. No other board had fought harder or longer. By the summer of 1960, however, all except one of the board members recognized that their legal battles were over. Judge Wright's order would stick. They prepared to comply. But would the state let them? To that phase of the story we shall return later.

In time these "from and after" injunctions do force authorities to desegregate. Other judges have moved the proceedings along more swiftly by setting in their original injunctions a fixed date for the submission of a plan. This is what Judge Frank A. Hooper did in Atlanta, Judge William E. Miller in Nashville, Judge Robert L. Taylor in Knoxville, and Judge John E. Miller in Little Rock. These judges gave the boards plenty of time, but their decrees had more meaning than those in which the courts failed to set a target date. The setting of a date forces the community to face its alternatives; it clarifies the choices, and offers earlier action.

Most of the judges have refused to order the admission of certain students to particular schools on the ground that the assignment of pupils is the duty of the school board and not of the courts. The judge's task is to see to it that the board desegregates, not to tell the board how it should be done. However, in Norfolk, after school authorities refused to transfer a single one of the 151 Negro students requesting a transfer, Judge Walter Hoffman, not a man to be lightly trifled with, gave the board four days to reconsider. He told them it was all right if they

wished to make Negro pupils take tests and submit to oral interviews; however, he warned them that they could not refuse a
transfer merely because they felt it would be bad for Negro students to attend "white" schools. The board then approved the
request of fourteen students, but later rescinded its action in the
face of a state court injunction and pressure from state officials.
At this juncture Judge Hoffman himself ordered the fourteen
students admitted. Similarly, Judge Wright in New Orleans and
Judge Connally in Houston themselves had instituted twelve-year
desegregation plans beginning with the first grade when school
officials in those cities refused to come forward with their own
programs. And then there is always the unforgettable action of
Judge Davidson in insisting on his own salt-and-pepper program
for Dallas.

The most drastic action a judge can take is to order the board
to admit immediately all Negroes to the public schools on the
same terms as other students. This has been done only in a few
instances—Clinton, Tennessee; Mansfield, Texas; and in some
of the Virginia districts at the high school level where the board
maintained no high schools at all for Negroes, or where the
state's massive resistance laws left no opportunity for local boards
to submit desegregation programs. In each instance the judge
made it perfectly clear that if the authorities presented a desegregation schedule, the court would gladly modify the injunction to
allow for a more gradual approach.

Judge John Paul's handling of the Warren County, Virginia,
suit illustrates how federal judges may, if they are so minded, see
to it that the issues are quickly litigated and decisions swiftly
made. On August 29, 1958, twenty-six Negro students via
NAACP counsel filed a complaint telling Judge Paul that Negroes were not allowed to attend the only high school operated
in the county but instead were transported to a "colored" school
in an adjoining county. After a brief hearing Judge Paul told the
board to cease discriminating against Negroes. He postponed,
but only for a week, the effective date of his order to permit the
board to seek a stay of his injunction from the Court of Appeals

for the Fourth Circuit. Four days later Virginia's Attorney General A. S. Harrison, Jr., went to Baltimore to ask Circuit Judge Sobeloff for a stay of Paul's order. Judge Sobeloff denied the request. In all, it took two weeks between complaint and an enforceable injunction. It can be done if the judge wants to do it.[49]

Since most of the legal battles have been concerned with *when* a district should start to desegregate, there has been less consideration of *how* it should be done. School authorities have the duty of determining the details of integration procedures. Judges have consistently refused to do so. But if authorities fail to come up with an acceptable program, in time the judge may order the immediate integration of all the schools or at least some of the grades.

If school boards come up with a plan, the judges have been willing to approve almost anything submitted. Nashville, New Orleans, Houston, and Knoxville were permitted to begin with the first grade and take twelve years to desegregate, one grade a year. Little Rock was allowed to postpone action for two years, and then start with the selected admission of a few Negroes to one high school, taking six years to complete integration. Judges have allowed, even encouraged, school boards to change attendance districts, to urge white parents who object to having their children attend desegregated schools to transfer their children from these schools, or to screen Negroes assigned to desegregated schools.

In Atlanta a plan has been approved which is about as minimal as it could possibly be. The key man in the Atlanta suit is Judge Frank A. Hooper. Judge Hooper is a native Georgian, born in 1895, who before his appointment to the federal bench in 1949 was a judge of the Georgia Court of Appeals, a member of the Georgia legislature, and an active supporter of Senator Richard Russell.

That a close associate of Senator Russell is a segregationist

[49] *Kilby v. County School Board of Warren County,* 3 RRLR 972 (1958).

is not a very daring inference. But he is a judge. Prior to the actual hearing of the case, Judge Hooper announced: "Even the most ardent segregationists . . . now recognize that racially segregated public schools are not permitted by the law. . . . This court can not at this time make any other ruling except a ruling to the effect that the operation of racially segregated public schools in Atlanta violates the Fourteenth Amendment. . . . To make any other ruling would only add to the confusion which already exists in the minds of so many of our good citizens, and to build up in the breasts of our citizens hopes of escape which would soon be torn into shreds by rulings of our appellate courts on review." [50]

To emphasize that his action was not the caprice of an individual judge, Hooper asked the other district judge assigned to the court, William Boyd Sloan, to sit with him in an advisory capacity. With two native Georgians hearing the case it was hoped that Atlantans would recognize that they did not have a choice of segregation or desegregation, but only as to method and time.

Suggesting he would approve a plan for "token integration," Hooper ordered Atlanta to present a program by December 1, 1959. Actually Atlanta officials were ready if not willing to do so, but under Georgia law, until 1961, if any Negro were admitted to a "white" school all schools in the district would have been automatically closed. The mayor and school authorities in Atlanta accepted Hooper's edict; the governor and rural Georgians at first insisted on an appeal, but when they discovered an appeal would put the matter into the hands of circuit judges, they changed their minds.

The Atlanta School Board filed its plan. It called for the use of a pupil-placement law, but just for the senior year of high school, then moving down one grade every year. In other words, for the first year of the desegregation program Negroes in the twelfth grade could ask for a transfer to "white" schools. In the other grades Negroes could not legally request a transfer.

This plan was acceptable to Judge Hooper. At first he re-

[50] *Calhoun v. Members of Board of Education, City of Atlanta et al.,* 4 RRLR 576 at 577 (1959).

frained from placing any definite date for Atlanta to inaugurate its program in order to give the Georgia legislature an opportunity to enact local option legislation. The 1960 session of the Georgia legislature failed to take any action other than to appoint a commission to survey Georgia opinion. Thereafter Judge Hooper announced that he would give the legislature just one more year. Whatever they decided, Atlanta must begin its program in September 1961.[51] (In 1961 as a result of the University of Georgia case, the legislature finally adopted a local option plan.)

About the only proposed desegregation plan which judges, always excepting Judge Davidson, have rejected, is the voluntary choice, parents' preference, or "salt-and-pepper" plan. In essence these schemes call for the establishment of three kinds of schools: integrated schools, schools for Negroes, and schools for whites. Students are to be assigned in accord with preferences expressed by their parents in a yearly census.

Proponents of these plans cite the words of Judge John Parker that the Supreme Court does not require integration, it merely forbids discrimination, and that "no violation of the Constitution is involved even though the children of different races voluntarily attend different schools, as they attend different churches."

Judge Parker pointed out, however, that a state may not deny a Negro on account of race the right to attend any school it maintains. Voluntary segregation is permissible only so long as there is no requirement of authorities to that effect. But under parents' preference schemes, there would be schools from which Negroes by law would be excluded. A board may encourage transfers and allow students to go where they wish. Perhaps this would result in segregation. A board may even ask parents for their preferences, but it may not refuse to admit a student to a school because of his race. It is for these reasons that Judge William E. Miller held such a program tendered by Nashville authorities "to be unconstitutional on its face." Six months later the Nashville board, under constituent pressures, presented another scheme to

[51] *Calhoun v. Atlanta*, 5 RRLR 374 (1960).

Judge Miller varying only in its details from the one he previously rejected. Again he refused to allow Nashville to use it.[52]

What has been the impact of over two hundred judicial hearings and six years of litigation? Desegregation has been hastened in the border states. By the end of 1960 Atlanta, Chattanooga, Knoxville, and Galveston had been forced to come up with programs. In Miami authorities under court compulsion had introduced token integration as had those of Little Rock, New Orleans, Clinton, Nashville, Houston, and in several cities in Virginia. A few North Carolina schools had admitted a few Negroes to "white" schools in order to forestall court-compelled integration. Yet no Negro had been admitted to a North Carolina school because of a court order. In Arkansas some cities desegregated when legal action was threatened.

The formal position of the judges is that the attitude of the community toward desegregation is irrelevant. A board, and the judge, is supposed to act promptly and completely "uninfluenced by private and public opinion as to the desirability of desegregation." As the Court of Appeals for the Fourth Circuit said: "The fact that the schools might be closed if the order [to desegregate] were enforced is no reason for not enforcing it." [53] Any doubt about the legal rules was put to rest by the Supreme Court: in 1959 in its Little Rock case it held opposition in a community, even violence, does not justify a board in refusing to desegregate the schools under its jurisdiction or authorize a judge to refuse an injunction.

But federal judges do not live in a vacuum. Whatever the formal doctrine may be, community attitudes have been a crucial if unmentionable factor. The administrative obstacles to desegregation are no more difficult to overcome in the Deep South than in the border states, but "the earliest practicable date" has been defined differently in the two regions. The judges' awareness of the unmentionable but nevertheless important factor of local opinion, combined with the NAACP's disinclination to push proceedings in areas of maximum resistance, makes it likely that judicial ac-

[52] *Nashville Banner*, October 8, 1957.
[53] *Allen v. Prince Edward County*, 2 RRLR 1114 at 1120–1121 (1957).

tion will take place first in the big cities but that judges will grasp at technicalities to postpone desegregation elsewhere.

Even within the big-city South there are patterns: the federal judges operating in Texas, Florida, and Arkansas are more inclined to "injunction-dragging" than those in Louisiana, Virginia, and Tennessee. There are exceptions to this generalization. For example, in Louisiana Judge Ben C. Dawkins, Jr., is among the more ardent segregationists serving on the federal bench. Dawkins, though a Democrat, was appointed to the bench in 1953 to succeed his father, who had held the post since 1924. He holds court in Shreveport in northern Louisiana, right in the midst of the strongest segregation area of the state. He is the judge who not only refused to interfere when white citizens councils manipulated the law with the help of Monroe City officials to disfranchise 2500 Negro voters, but accused the Negro plaintiff of "bad faith . . . sheer stubborn vindictiveness." The court of appeals reversed, telling Dawkins: "[It] is no sign of his bad faith or of a spirit of vindictiveness for him [the plaintiff] to seek to redress this wrong in court." [54] Dawkins also, at the request of the Louisiana attorney general, enjoined the United States Commission on Civil Rights from holding hearings into alleged voting discrimination in Shreveport. He admitted his order might be upset, but he said, "It is all part of the game." [55]

It is not surprising that Negroes have decided not to press the Shreveport school case, which will be heard by Judge Dawkins, but to concentrate on the New Orleans case where not only is the white moderate faction stronger, but where a less committed judge is handling the legal aspects.

The refusal of some of the district judges to clamp down on recalcitrant boards has had a cumulatively adverse impact on the other judges. When one judge in one district sanctions the continued operation of segregated schools, his action intensifies the pressures on other judges to do the same. The judge least willing to act serves as a drag, setting limits to how far other judges are willing to get in front.

[54] *Reddix v. Lucky,* 3 RRLR 229 at 235 (1958).
[55] United States Commission on Civil Rights, *Report,* 1959, p. 101.

From 1955 to 1957 lawsuits were marching along. Federal judges forced authorities to produce plans, looked at them with a critical eye, and issued meaningful injunctions. Then the segregation reaction set in. The failure of some federal judges to crack down on Dallas and Houston, and for a time on Virginia, caused a noticeable softening of judicial action all along the line. When Little Rock secured a strong prosegregation decision from Judge Lemley in the summer of 1958, judicial action was brought to a complete halt until the Supreme Court reversed. Then there was a moderate reaction. And as the general tides of public opinion have altered, judicial decrees have responded to these political developments.

The external pressures have also had their impact on the judges' articulated premises. In 1955 few informed observers would have thought that the federal judges would permit a school board to do nothing for six years. But in Dallas, Houston, and New Orleans judges construed "all deliberate speed" to mean that a school district may take six years or longer. In Atlanta, six years after the Supreme Court's 1954 ruling, the judge gave the board two more years before it had to start to desegregate.

In 1955 few observers would have thought that federal judges would construe the Supreme Court's opinions in such a fashion as to permit a school to retain segregation provided it admitted a few Negroes to a few "white" schools. Nor would they have predicted that a school could so stretch out the program of desegregation so that "at the earliest practicable" date has come to mean the next generation.

But the scoreboard must be balanced: judges may not have required much action; still they are the only ones to require any action. Judges have done something, certainly more than the Congress, the President, the state legislatures. Whatever desegregation there has been has come about because a judge has insisted on it. Judges have allowed school authorities to evade and to delay, but at least they have insisted that total segregation must be abandoned eventually.

5 ✳ The Uses and Abuses of Violence

When segregationists call upon all decent men to resist, they do not, of course, advocate violence; they specify "lawful resistance." Senator W. M. Rainach, former Chairman of the Louisiana Legislative Committee on Segregation, has said: "We want to provide an incentive in case [public school officials] decide they want to defy a federal court order to integrate." [1]

Those holding high office, as well as low, have been notably unwilling to condemn public disturbers of the peace. Governor Shivers of Texas described the crowds massed in front of Mansfield High School, calling for the blood of Negro students and preventing the execution of a federal injunction, as "Texas citizens who are making orderly protest against a situation instigated and agitated by the National Association for the Advancement of Colored People." [2] And Garland B. Porter, the segregationist editor of *Southern Advertising and Publishing,* objected to the fact that northern newspapers referred to the demonstrators in front of Central High in Little Rock as a "mob." Admitting they had "roughed up a bit" some northern reporters, Porter nevertheless wrote: "The fact is that these people who are vilified as

[1] *Chicago Tribune,* November 4, 1957.
[2] Statement released August 31, 1956, quoted in 1 RRLR 885 (1956).

135

being a southern mob are parents and Americans and Christians with standards of life and conduct just as high as the reporters who were there to seek the truth." [3] In a similar fashion Van Buren, Arkansas's Chief of Police Voll Russell referred to the fifty-five white students who cursed their superintendent, their principal, and school officials and threw up picket lines to keep Negro students from entering school as "orderly demonstrators." "The strike," he said, "was no more a crime than the Boston Tea Party." [4]

Violence is not new to the southern scene. Nor is racial conflict an exclusively southern phenomenon, as a glance at any northern newspaper will readily demonstrate—there have been more race riots in northern than in southern cities. Although since 1954 Negroes have been the target of bombs, beatings, and economic harassment, except in Mississippi, there have been no murders or lynchings. And despite the mob scenes there have been no head-on clashes. Violence is there but it is under the surface.

White persons have not been spared from pressure. Economic reprisals, social ostracism, even physical violence—the southern version of McCarthyism, as eleven prominent southern clergymen termed it—have been the fate of those dissenting from the segregationist line, especially in the small towns. Most of these terror campaigns are organized *sub rosa,* though Roy Harris, for one, openly urged his supporters to make miserable the lives of Atlanta's moderates. He got a dose of his own medicine—Hamilton Locky, a former legislator, rang Harris's phone at 5:00 A.M. after Locky had been awakened by a call from a Harris lieutenant.[5]

With minor exceptions the violence and the campaigns of harassment have been in one direction. No white councilman's home has been bombed, no white street agitator has been at-

[3] Editorial quoted in full in *Congressional Record,* vol. 104, February 19, 1958, p. 2444.

[4] U.P.I. dispatch, September 9, 1958.

[5] *Southern School News,* March 1960, p. 15.

tacked, no outspoken segregationists have been harassed. No doubt in part the reason is fear. It is also because Negro leaders, men like the Reverend Martin Luther King, have stressed passive resistance. When the president of the NAACP chapter in Union County, North Carolina, advocated that Negroes "meet violence with violence," Roy Wilkins, executive secretary of the national NAACP, immediately suspended him from office. How long Negro leaders will be able to restrain the lawless element among their own people in the face of the provocation of lawless whites no one knows. A Negro in Houston said, as he reflected on the treatment dished out to the nine Negro students attending Little Rock's Central High, "They had better not try that in Houston. Maybe they can get away with it in Arkansas. But they couldn't do that to us; remember we're Texans!"

Segregation-minded governors, state legislators, and other officials do not themselves advocate the use of force. But prior to the opening of schools which are preparing to initiate desegregation, many public officials fill the air with dire warnings of trouble. Whatever their opinion of the findings of sociologists as quoted by the Supreme Court, these segregationists are well aware of, and adept practitioners of, the sociologists' discovery, the self-fulfilling prophecy. The situation becomes tense, and with the threat of violence they intervene and defy the courts. Sometimes the actual rioting is allowed to take place without interference as evidence that the predictions were correct.

These tactics are not new. Alexander Hamilton ironically commented about officials in western Pennsylvania who stood by while insurgents defied tax collectors. "These officials," he wrote in 1794, "are among the loudest in condemning the disorderly conduct of the insurgents. They would agree that it is utterly unjustifiable . . . and of the most dangerous tendency. But they would at the same time, slyly add, that excise laws are pernicious things, very hostile to liberty (or perhaps smoothly lament that the government had been imprudent enough to pass laws so contrary to the genius of a free people), and they would still more cautiously hint that it is enough for those who disapprove of such laws to submit to them—too much to expect their aid in forcing them upon others." [6] Circuit Judge Warren E. Burger of the United States Court of Appeals for the District of Columbia expressed the same thought. He stated: "The desegregation orders have led some reckless and irresponsible men in high places to think they can aid and abet defiance of laws they do not like without seeming to realize that this would encourage others to defy the laws." [7] A Clinton lawyer put it more forcefully when he accused the southern congressmen of creating the disrespect for law which produced so much trouble in his town: "What the hell do you expect these people to do when they have 90 some odd congressmen from the South signing a piece of paper [the Southern Manifesto] that says you're a southern hero if you defy the Supreme Court." [8]

When schools opened in 1954 and 1955, mobs in a few communities were able to frighten authorities into "postponing" voluntarily inaugurated desegregation programs. In none of these districts were boards of education under specific legal injunction to desegregate. The first such incident was the famous Lucy Case, which hit the headlines in February 1955.

It all started in the summer of 1953 when Miss Autherine Lucy and Mrs. Polly Hudson, after being denied admission to the University of Alabama graduate school, filed a complaint in the United States District Court for the Northern District of Alabama. The case was handled by the then newly appointed Judge H. Hobart Grooms. In July 1955 Judge Grooms, a tall, fifty-ish, Kentucky-born Republican, ordered the university to admit Mrs. Hudson, Miss Lucy, and all other qualified Negroes to its graduate school.

The trustees of the university did not expect Judge Grooms's order could be set aside, but they appealed anyway. They wanted

[6] Henry Cabot Lodge (editor), *Works of Alexander Hamilton,* New York: Putnam, 1904, vol. VI, p. 412.

[7] *Washington Post & Times Herald,* November 7, 1958.

[8] Wallace Westfeldt, "Communities in Strife," in *With All Deliberate Speed,* edited by Don Shoemaker. New York: Harper, 1957, p. 38.

to show the people of Alabama that they were doing all they could to keep the university white. The circuit judges of the Court of Appeals for the Fifth Circuit, calling Judge Grooms's opinion "well considered," said they were in complete agreement with him. On October 10, 1955, the Supreme Court affirmed their decision.

The Supreme Court's action came four days after the deadline for the first semester enrollment, so the university refused to admit the two women for that semester. Judge Grooms dismissed a petition for contempt, holding the university had rejected Mrs. Hudson and Miss Lucy because of late registration, not because of their race.

Prior to the second semester Mrs. Hudson was notified she did not meet admission standards because of her "marital record." There is more than a little doubt that white students were subject to the same rigorous scrutiny, but Mrs. Hudson decided not to confuse the issues so she dropped out of the case. University authorities could find no reason for rejecting Miss Lucy that would not expose them to legal contempt; they had no choice but to allow her to enroll.

To that moment Negroes had been admitted without incident to universities throughout the South. But on February 1, when Miss Lucy arrived to register, crowds formed and she attended classes under escort of campus police. During this time she was accused of such sordid crimes as flashing a $100 bill to pay her fees and arriving on campus in a Cadillac, though others claimed it was only a Pontiac.

University officials did not disperse a constantly growing crowd of students and many others which assembled on Monday, February 6, to shout and jeer at Miss Lucy as she went to and from classes. Two women deans were dispatched to escort her, but by noon the crowd was an uncontrollable mob. At 1:15 P.M. it was necessary to spirit her away in a highway patrol car.

Late that night the board of trustees suspended Autherine Lucy until further notice. This was done, it was explained, for her safety. Pre-law student Leonard Wilson, the rioters' ringleader, was expelled, but no further action was taken against the troublemakers.

The Board of Trustees of the University of Alabama and its distinguished president, O. C. Carmichael, were caught between the orders of Judge Grooms and the pressures of the segregationists. Whom would they obey? What should they do?

The board was divided. Some trustees felt they should readmit Miss Lucy and ask the governor to maintain order. Others suggested that Judge Grooms and the Department of Justice be asked for help. Many faculty members and students urged the board to readmit Miss Lucy, insisting the issue was no longer integration or segregation but law or mob rule. Days passed. The board did nothing.

On February 9 Autherine Lucy, through her attorney, asked Judge Grooms to cite university officials for contempt. She charged that these officials failed to prevent the unauthorized assembly from milling about the campus. In addition, her attorneys made the mistake of accusing the university administration of conspiring with the mob to defy the injunction and of lacking good faith in suspending her from classes. These charges were repeated outside the courtroom to members of the press.

Judge Grooms had ample authority to see that his orders were obeyed. Those who ignore court injunctions, whatever the pretext, can be punished for contempt. Or if he felt the trustees had acted in good faith, he could have enjoined the rioters, warning them to stay off the campus or otherwise attempting to keep Miss Lucy from attending classes. If they failed to obey, they could be punished for contempt. Furthermore, Judge Grooms could have called on the Department of Justice for help.

On February 29, the walnut-paneled room in the white-marble post office building was crowded to capacity: there were so many reporters that the judge had to limit the number of seats they could pre-empt.

Since they had no evidence to support their charges, at the outset the NAACP attorneys withdrew the accusation that university authorities had actively conspired with the mob to defy the injunction. The issues were narrowed: did the university's failure to prevent the riot, or to attempt to prevent it, and its subsequent suspension of Autherine Lucy violate Judge Grooms's mandate?

John Caddell, Decatur attorney and member of the board of trustees, was called to the stand. He admitted that the board had taken no action to readmit Miss Lucy. He said, "It is a matter of speculation whether, if ever, she will be readmitted."

Marshall pressed his argument: "We have one person acting in a lawful manner, and the other side in an unlawful manner. The law-abiding person was ordered from the campus. That being true, what did the board do to the unlawful group?"

Caddell: "I'm not at all sure that Autherine Lucy and persons accompanying her were not the very cause of the demonstrations. . . . Autherine Lucy came [to the campus] in a Cadillac automobile, she had a chauffeur [Arthur Shores, her attorney], and walked in such a way as to be obnoxious and objectionable and disagreeable."

Marshall: "Is there anyone else on the campus with a Cadillac automobile?"

Caddell: "I don't know." [9]

University spokesmen told Judge Grooms that they had done what they were supposed to do: admit Autherine Lucy. The university is not a police agency, they contended, and cannot be held accountable for public disturbances. Autherine Lucy had been suspended to maintain order and for her own safety. The university had not committed contempt.

Judge Grooms quickly made his ruling: university officials had not violated his injunction. On the other hand, he told the university it could not continue to deny Miss Lucy the right to attend classes; he ordered her to be readmitted by March 5.

Even as Judge Grooms made his ruling, he knew the board

[9] *Birmingham News,* March 1, 1956.

was going to expell Miss Lucy permanently, ostensibly because of the charges she had made against the university administration.[10] That very evening the board did so.

Once more she returned to Judge Grooms asking him to cite the board for contempt, arguing that her permanent expulsion violated both his original order against denying Negroes admission to the university and his most recent order calling for her reinstatement. The judge did not agree. Since the board had expelled her for disciplinary and not racial reasons, he held, it had not violated his orders. By this time Miss Lucy was mentally and physically exhausted. She did not appeal the decision, and left the state with the battlefield in the victorious hands of the segregationists.

It is possible to construe the actions of Judge Grooms to mean school authorities may expel students, whatever their color, for disciplinary reasons. But few made such refined distinctions. The more obvious conclusion: school authorities ordered by a judge to admit Negroes have no obligation other than to open the doors. If mobs protest, authorities may with impunity remove Negro students. It becomes easy to nullify a desegregation injunction.

Judge Grooms's complacence in the face of the challenge of the mob contrasts sharply with his original handling of the Lucy case. His original injunction not only preserved the constitutional rights of the plaintiffs, but by recognizing the action as a class suit reflected a determination to give full effect to the Supreme Court's desegregation decisions. It has been the last pro-civil rights order Judge Grooms has made.

With the Alabama decision, segregationists lost a lawsuit, but won a battle.

One who watched the Lucy Affair with more than usual inter-

[10] The course of this involved litigation can be followed in *Lucy v. Adams,* 350 U.S. 1 (1954); *Lucy v. Adams,* 1 RRLR 85 (1955); *Lucy v. Adams,* 1 RRLR 88 (1955); *Lucy v. Adams,* 1 RRLR 332 (1955); *Lucy v. Adams,* 1 RRLR 894 (1956); *Lucy v. Adams,* 2 RRLR 350 (1956). For details on incidents in this and other cases, *see Southern School News,* a monthly publication of the Southern Education Reporting Service.

est was Governor Shivers of Texas. Six months later, in the fall of 1956, he used the Lucy precedent to defy not one, but two federal courts. The first of these cases involved Texarkana Junior College, where authorities came close to being held in contempt. Texarkana Junior College was ordered to cease discriminating against Negroes and specifically to admit two named Negro students. In September 1956, just before schools were to open, the president of the college, Dr. W. H. Stilwell, told an audience of protesting citizens that integration would lower educational standards. He said, "It is not only your right but your duty to resist it." The next day these citizens, including a member of the school's board of trustees, "did their duty." [11] They massed in front of the school and shouted "kill the niggers." Governor Shivers sent Texas Rangers to quell the riot, but the ranger in charge refused to escort the students through the mob.[12]

An NAACP attorney, the same one who had represented the students in the original proceedings, filed a motion for a contempt citation against the president and trustees. Prior to the hearing, however, agents from the Texas attorney general's office interrogated the two teen-age students, securing an admission from them that they did not know the lawyer who claimed to represent them. Their parents had instructed the president of the local NAACP to do everything legally possible to get their children into the college. He in turn had authorized the attorney to take the case, but no one had specifically instructed the attorney to file a motion for contempt. For this reason, Federal Judge Joe W. Sheehy dismissed the motion; Texarkana Junior College's officials went unpunished; Texarkana Junior College remained white.[13]

Trouble erupted also in Mansfield, Texas. Mansfield, fourteen miles from Fort Worth, is a town of 1500 people, including 350 Negroes. Its white citizens were proud of their record for peaceful race relations. But the Negroes were not so satisfied. Until 1954 their only school was a one-room building which lacked

---

[11] *Dallas Morning News,* September 8, 1956.
[12] *Dallas Morning News,* September 8, 1956.
[13] *Arkansas Gazette,* September 28, 1956.

indoor toilets and running water. The playgrounds were dangerous, and, as many of the Negroes pointed out, "There was not
even a flag on the flagpole."

In 1954 a four-room grade school for Negroes was built, but
high school students still had to ride public buses into Fort
Worth. Although dismissed from school at 3:30 P.M. they
could not get a bus back to Mansfield until 5:30 P.M. Not only
did they arrive home late, but their parents worried about allowing these young teen-agers to remain without supervision in Fort
Worth for two hours every afternoon.

In April 1955 Negro parents retained an NAACP attorney
from Fort Worth. Undoubtedly many of them had no intention
of pressing for integration. They just wanted better schools. Despite petitions to the school board they secured no satisfaction.
Finally, in October 1955, the more aggressive among them
agreed to sue to force admission of Negroes to Mansfield High.

A month later Judge Joe E. Estes, a Fort Worth Republican,
appointed to the bench by Eisenhower a few months earlier, dismissed the petition as "premature and precipitate." In the summer of 1956 the court of appeals reversed Estes, telling him that
in the absence of any high school for Negroes, not only was the
suit not premature, but Negroes were entitled to admission to
Mansfield High when schools opened the next fall. Judge Estes
reluctantly issued the necessary order.

Here was a valid, final, order of a federal court directing the
Mansfield School Board to admit Negroes to the high school.
The segregationists were undismayed. The town's only newspaper, taking a straight councilman line, published editorials and
letters to the editor charging that the suit was communist-inspired, and the judge's injunction unconstitutional. The city was
flooded with all kinds of antisemitic and other hate literature.
Mobs began to form.

Many who protested did not contemplate violence. Perhaps
most of the people of Mansfield did not approve of mob rule,
but they did approve of the cause the mob was championing.

The situation was quickly out of control. The mayor and the chief of police left town, and extremists took charge.

The school board was frightened. Their attorney went to Fort Worth to ask Judge Estes to stay his order. He told the judge that if Negroes tried to enroll there would be trouble, serious trouble. Judge Estes refused to stay his injunction, explaining he had no choice because of the court of appeals' mandate.

When schools opened on August 29, over two hundred persons were milling about in front of the high school. Some carried signs, "A Dead Nigger is the Best Nigger." Vigilantes stopped cars on the edge of town and escorted out any who might be sympathetic toward integration. The superintendent of schools, R. L. Huffman, told the crowd, "Now you guys know I'm with you, but I've got this mandate hanging over my head."

Labor Day intervened, but when schools opened again the crowd was there. Some ministers tried to persuade the people to disperse, to no avail, stimulating an editorial in the local newspaper about "pin-head preachers who preach the brotherhood of man." There was no violence—no Negroes appeared to exercise the rights supposedly conferred by Judge Estes' injunction.

At this juncture Governor Shivers sent in the Rangers, ordering them to arrest anyone who "represents a threat to the peace." He made it clear he meant the Negro students. He instructed local officials to "transfer out of the district any scholastics, white or colored, whose attendance or attempts to attend Mansfield High School would reasonably be calculated to incite violence"—that is, the Negro students.[14] "This action," said Shivers, "would be in line with the U. S. Supreme Court decision in the Lucy Case in Alabama. . . . Personally I hope that the U. S. Supreme Court will be given an opportunity to view the effect of its desegregation decision on a typical law-abiding Texas community. . . . Should the resulting actions . . . be construed as contempt of the federal courts, I respectfully suggest that the

[14] Statement by the Governor, August 31, 1956, quoted in full in 1 RRLR 885 (1956).

charge should be laid against the Governor and not the local people." [15]

The Mansfield Negroes were too terrified to take any further action—in fact they even withdrew from the NAACP. The federal judge assumed no initiative to defend his injunction, and President Eisenhower, in a press conference a few days later, said Mansfield's troubles were a local responsibility.[16] Shivers said that he had demonstrated that racial controversies could be settled without violence.[17]

The credit for pioneering the legal doctrine to support the claim that the need to maintain order excuses officials from obeying desegregation decrees must be given to the Supreme Court of Florida. The Florida Supreme Court believes in segregation. As one of the Florida jurists explained: "When God created man, he allotted each race to his own continent according to color, Europe to the white man, Asia to the yellow man, Africa to the black man, and America to the red man." [18]

Back in 1949 one Virgil Hawkins, a middle-aged Negro postal carrier, asked the Florida Supreme Court to help him secure admission to the University of Florida Law School. The court refused to do so. Even after the Brown decision the Florida Supreme Court refused. The United States Supreme Court told the Florida Supreme Court three times there was no reason for delay; still the court refused to act.

On what grounds could the Florida Supreme Court justify its refusal to follow the United State's Supreme Court's directions? The Florida jurists conceded that segregation is unconstitutional. But they contended Florida retained the power to maintain order. If Hawkins were to attend the University of Florida there would

---

[15] *Ibid.*

[16] The description of events in Mansfield is taken from an unpublished report by John Howard Griffin of Mansfield and Theodore Freedman of Houston, "What Happened in Mansfield," which is based on tape-recorded interviews of the participants.

[17] *Dallas Morning News,* September 25, 1956.

[18] Judge Glenn Terrell concurring in *Florida ex rel Virgil D. Hawkins v. Board of Control,* 1 RRLR 89 at 95 (1955).

be "violence in university communities" and a "critical disruption of the University system." [19] Under such circumstances, whatever the Supreme Court of the United States said, they would not mandamus the university to admit Hawkins.

Since the Florida Supreme Court was of no help, Hawkins asked the United States Supreme Court itself to issue the needed order. The United States justices refused, telling Hawkins to go to the United States district court for further relief. Hawkins petitioned the United States District Court for the Northern District of Florida.

This court was presided over by seventy-four-year-old Dozier A. DeVane, about ready to retire. Judge DeVane, a native of Florida, had returned to Florida after serving as solicitor for the Federal Power Commission; in 1943 he was placed on the federal bench by President Roosevelt. Judge DeVane, a staunch believer in states' rights, has said that his years on the bench had not "changed to any extent my views as to the rights of the states under the United States Constitution." [20]

Prior to his handling of Hawkins's case Judge DeVane had demonstrated his preference for segregation by sustaining a Tallahassee bus-driver assignment law. The Tallahassee City Council adopted this ordinance after the Supreme Court had ruled that segregated seating on public buses is unconstitutional. This ordinance gives bus drivers authority to tell passengers where to sit: they were not to consider race but such factors as promoting public health, maintaining order, and providing for the proper distribution of weight on the buses. Judge DeVane

[19] *Florida ex rel Hawkins v. Board of Control,* 2 RRLR 358 at 362 (1957). The Florida court based its prediction of turmoil on a study conducted by the Board of Control. This study showed that 72 per cent of the students at the University of Florida were *in favor of admitting Negroes.* Twenty per cent said they would leave. Their parents were less enthusiastic; only 6 per cent approved the admission of Negroes. Yet only a small fraction of parents or students indicated they would do more than refuse to associate with Negro students. Board of Control, *Study of Desegregation,* Parts I and II, May 1956.

[20] *Florida Times-Union,* December 17, 1957.

told Negroes challenging this law, clearly designed to circumvent the Supreme Court's decisions, that they should not destroy the bus system. He urged them to give the problem some "Christian thinking." [21]

This was the judge before whom Hawkins, via his attorney, appeared in January 1958 to ask for an injunction, not only in his own behalf, but for all Negroes being denied the right to attend Florida's public universities because of their race. Judge DeVane was in no more of a hurry to act than his fellow Floridians serving on the state supreme court. Finally, the Court of Appeals for the Fifth Circuit in a terse ruling told Judge DeVane, in effect, to get moving. The court of appeals, indicating its disapproval of his handling of the case, ordered that its own mandate issue forthwith.

In June 1958, more than nine years after Hawkins first went to court, DeVane instructed the University of Florida not to exclude qualified Negroes. But Judge DeVane, showing his reluctance, carefully restricted his order to cover only graduate and graduate professional schools and only at the one institution, the University of Florida.[22] Moreover, Judge DeVane's ruling excluded Hawkins, for he had failed to meet the entrance standards. Finally, Judge DeVane made a point of saying that he recognized the university's right "to act in emergencies to avoid mischief and to take such normal, reasonable and neces-

---

[21] *Florida Times-Union,* December 17, 1957.

Judge DeVane also refused to hear a damage suit brought by a Jamaican minister and his wife who on a trip through Florida had been beaten by a passenger for sitting in seats in the front of the bus. The assailant had boarded the bus solely to attack them after he overheard the bus driver at a coffee stop report that the minister refused to sit in the rear. The court of appeals reversed Judge DeVane. *Bullock v. Tamiami,* 4 RRLR 361 (1959).

[22] The Board of Control has jurisdiction over all public universities in Florida. On March 21, 1956, it raised admission standards for all white universities and threatened to apply these same standards to Florida A. & M., the Negro school, if a court required integration of a "white" university. If this threat had been carried out, it would have drastically reduced the number of students eligible for study at Florida A. & M. See Minutes of Special Meeting, March 21, 1956.

sary steps as will provide for the orderly and peaceable administration of said University. . . ." [23]

Judge DeVane's order was an invitation to university officials to use the possibility of disturbances on campus as an excuse for the continued exclusion of Negroes. His mandate was not much stronger than that of the Florida Supreme Court. However, under the leadership of Governor Collins, Florida decided to litigate no longer. In the fall of 1958 a Negro, but not Hawkins, was admitted to the law school. There were no disturbances, no incidents.

Most school boards, after losing their lawsuits, do their best to comply with the ensuing injunctions. The resistance, the refusal to accept the finality of the judge's instructions, most frequently comes not from the authorities to which the order is directed but from those who are called "strangers" to the proceedings. In 1960 Congress made it a federal crime to conspire by intimidation, organized boycotts, and other illegal means to interfere with a school board attempt to carry out a federal desegregation injunction. Even without such a law federal judges have authority to prevent "strangers" from thwarting the effectiveness of a desegregation plan.

A school board attempting to carry out a program of desegregation has a constitutional right to be free from illegal interference. They merely have to petition the judge, and, if he is convinced that certain persons are conspiring to interfere, he may order such persons to cease and desist. If they refuse to do so, they may be punished for criminal contempt. School authorities and the judge need not stand idly by while segregationists make the Constitution meaningless and render the federal judiciary ineffective. This is the lesson of the Hoxie case.

On June 25, 1955, the five-man school board of Hoxie, Arkansas, without waiting for the local federal district judge to order it to act, announced it would allow twenty-five Negro

[23] *Florida ex rel Hawkins v. Board of Control,* 3 RRLR 657 at 660 (1958). Thomas Miller Jenkins, "Judicial Discretion in Desegregation: The Hawkins Case," *Howard Law Journal,* vol. 4, 1958, pp. 193–202.

students to attend classes with one thousand white pupils because "Integration is right in the sight of God, obedience to the Supreme Court . . . and it's cheaper." [24] When schools opened there was no trouble until Herbert Brewer, a local farmer, with the help of Amis Guthridge, a Little Rock attorney, and head of the Capital Citizens Council, organized the opposition. Meetings were held, inflammatory speeches made, petitions circulated, and literature distributed. Parents were urged to withdraw their children from the schools, members of the board were threatened, and attendance fell off so sharply the board closed the summer session a week early.

When schools opened in the fall, the board asked the district judge to issue a restraining order calling upon Brewer and those working with him to cease interfering with the free operation of schools by acts of trespass, boycott, or picketing; from in any manner deterring the attendance of children at school; "from in any manner threatening or intimidating" the board of education.[25]

After a full hearing the order was issued and made permanent. Brewer and his associates appealed to the court of appeals. They contended that the injunction deprived them of their rights of speech, assembly, petition, and peaceful picketing and exposed them to prosecution for such innocent activities as campaigning against the re-election of school board members. The attorney general of Georgia came to their defense.

The Hoxie board was not without its friends. For the United States Attorney General filed a brief in support of the board, the first intervention by the Department of Justice in any school suit. In an exhaustive opinion the court of appeals sustained the injunction. The court held that school officials have a duty to desegregate, even in the absence of specific court instructions. As a necessary corollary, they have a federal right to be free from direct and deliberate interference with the performance of their constitutionally imposed duty. This is a right which the

[24] *Southern School News,* August 1955, p. 15.
[25] *Hoxie School District v. Brewer,* 1 RRLR 43 (1955).

federal government may protect against abridgment by state officials or private persons. This would suggest that governors and state legislators who directly and deliberately interfere with school desegregation programs are guilty of violating federal civil rights statutes.

What about Brewer's constitutional rights? The court of appeals pointed out that the injunction was aimed at acts and speech "calculated and intended, at the time and under the circumstances in which they were made, to incite disobedience of the law and to coerce . . . the school board to cease and desist from the performance of its sworn and lawful duty and to engage in unlawful conduct." The Constitution does not protect the right to advocate disobedience of the courts when there is a clear and present danger that disobedient conduct will result.[26]

The Hoxie precedent makes available to school authorities the injunctive protection of a federal court. This precedent was confirmed and extended by Judge Robert L. Taylor and the Clinton, Tennessee, School Board who refused to be intimidated by the then unknown but since famous, perhaps infamous, John Kasper.

On January 4, 1956, after four years of litigation, Judge Taylor ordered the Anderson County School Board to admit pupils to Clinton High School on a racially nondiscriminatory basis beginning with the 1956 fall term.[27] When schools opened, twelve Negroes joined 750 white classmates. There was some grumbling, but that was all.

On August 25 John Kasper, executive secretary of the Seaboard Citizens Council of Washington, D.C., came to Clinton and announced he intended to "get the niggers out of Clinton High School." Kasper is often charged with the sole responsibility for the trouble that resulted. He did furnish the spark, but there was much discontented local sentiment to be ignited. Within two days there were picket lines around the school, and parents, white and black, were threatened by telephone. A mob attacked one of the Negro pupils.

[26] *Hoxie School District v. Brewer,* 1 RRLR 299 and 1027 (1956).
[27] *McSwain v. Board of Education,* 1 RRLR 872 at 876 (1956).

On August 29, Judge Taylor, on petition of school officials, ordered Kasper and certain other individuals and "all other persons who are acting or may act in concert with them" to cease "hindering, obstructing, or any wise interfering with the carrying out of the aforesaid order of this Court, or from picketing Clinton High School, either by words or acts or otherwise." It was further ordered that Kasper and the others named appear before Judge Taylor at 1:00 P.M. the next day to show cause why a preliminary injunction should not be issued.

That evening a United States marshal served these orders on Kasper as he was about to speak in front of the local courthouse. Kasper read the restraining order but was not restrained. He told his audience they need obey neither the order nor the desegregation ruling. He lashed out at school officials and Judge Taylor. The next morning Kasper was back at his old stand in front of the high school somewhat more circumspect, but still encouraging his cohorts to continue boycotting and picketing.

School officials reported to Judge Taylor about Kasper's speech and they asked that he be arrested and tried for contempt. At the request of the court, the United States district attorney participated at the hearing of Kasper. After trial, Judge Taylor held that the restraining order had properly been issued, that the evidence justified its continuance as a preliminary injunction, and that Kasper had willfully violated the restraining order. Kasper was sentenced to a year in jail, but allowed his freedom on bail, pending appeal.[28]

On appeal Kasper argued that Judge Taylor's injunction— broader than the one issued in the Hoxie case—infringed on First Amendment freedoms by prohibiting peaceful picketing, lawful assembly, and free speech. The American Civil Liberties Union, although seeing no civil liberties issue in the contempt punishment, supported Kasper's contention that the injunction was too sweeping. The words "any wise interfering with the court order," the ACLU argued, were too vague to meet due process

[28] *McSwain v. Board of Education,* 1 RRLR 872 (1956).

standards and the blanket prohibition against picketing was unconstitutional. Furthermore, the ACLU contended, persons have
a constitutional right to advocate the flouting of judicial orders
except where there is a clear and present danger of illegal conduct.[29]

However, the court of appeals held: "The speech here enjoined was clearly calculated to cause a violation of law and
speech of that character is not within the protection of the First
Amendment."[30] The clear and present danger test was met by
the mob violence resulting from Kasper's speeches. The court
ruled, on the basis of Supreme Court precedents, that picketing
may be enjoined when it becomes enmeshed with violence and
even peaceful picketing may be banned when it is for an unlawful purpose, such as coercing a school board to violate a court
order.

It was hoped Judge Taylor's action against Kasper would
place a damper upon the activities of the rioters. However, pending his appeal, Kasper was free and remained in Clinton. To the
uninformed, it appeared that Kasper was going unpunished even
though he had deliberately flouted the court's authority. The
immediate impact of the injunction had little deterring effect.
On the day of Kasper's first trial, Clinton's six-man police force
was unable to maintain order. The governor sent the National
Guard, order was restored, and by Labor Day the Negro students
were back in class and student attendance was normal. Although
there were sporadic incidents, tension gradually subsided.

Then, on November 17, Kasper and his ringleaders were
brought to trial by county authorities for inciting riots. A local
jury acquitted them. Thus encouraged, the extremists renewed
their efforts, there was a reactivation of picketing, and a flurry
of violence followed. By the end of the month Negro students
were again forced to withdraw from school.

[29] American Civil Liberties Union, "Nor Speak With Double Tongue,"
37th *Annual Report,* pp. 80–81.
[30] Before the court of appeals the case was styled *Kasper v. Brittain,*
2 RRLR 792 (1957).

The harassed school authorities and local officials appealed to the federal government for help. At first they secured none. After additional violence, including an attack on a popular minister, the board closed Clinton High School, again urged the Attorney General to intervene, and finally the Department of Justice acted. The district attorney petitioned Judge Taylor to order the arrest of Kasper and seventeen other persons who it was alleged had conspired with him to violate the injunction first issued in September and made permanent in January. The court issued the necessary orders. The persons named were taken into custody. This, combined with an overwhelming defeat for citizens council candidates in the local city election, led to a restoration of order. Schools were opened and the county attorney warned students that misconduct on their part would lead to expulsion and might be in violation of Judge Taylor's injunction.

Trial of Kasper and his companions was postponed until July 1957, by which time the number of persons charged with contempt had been reduced to twelve and the federal government assumed full responsibility for their prosecution before a jury. The defendants had the support of the attorneys general of several southern states. They received financial aid from the Governor of Georgia and other prominent segregationists.

For ten days, eighteen defense attorneys challenged the proceedings, but after four hours the jury brought in a verdict of guilty against seven of the defendants, including Kasper. Judge Taylor sentenced the culprits, but they were released on bail pending appeal. Kasper was to have one other brush with the injunctive power of federal judges before he finally landed in a federal penitentiary.

Despite setbacks in Hoxie and Clinton, segregationists believed they had a one-two punch to knock out judicial integration decrees: one, encourage violence or at least do not discourage it; two, use the violence as an excuse to keep Negroes out of "white" schools. When schools opened in 1957 segregationists brought these tactics into play in Little Rock and Nashville. In Nashville they did not work; in Little Rock they did.

The two cities make an interesting comparison. They have much in common. Both are middle-sized state capitals standing just outside the upper Mississippi River country. Until 1957 both were, and Nashville is still today, open cities: a man could publicly stand up as an integrationist without suffering more than a few crank calls and poison-pen letters. A Negro could be active in the affairs of the NAACP without jeopardizing his job or family.

Although Negroes and whites lived under the terms of the traditional segregated pattern, they had a long history of peaceful race relations, more peaceful than most northern cities. Buses in both communities were desegregated in 1956 without difficulty. Negroes serve on the Nashville City Council and on the school board, and in Little Rock, except for a brief interlude, moderates have always been in charge of city affairs.

Obviously most white citizens prefer to send their children to schools from which Negroes are excluded, but prior to the late summer of 1957, by all the signs they had accepted the necessity of making minor adjustments. There seemed to be wide community support behind the six-man Little Rock School Board which just six days after the Supreme Court's 1954 decision stated: "It is our responsibility to comply with Federal Constitutional Requirements and we intend to do so when the Supreme Court of the United States outlines the method to be followed." [31] In Nashville a similar pronouncement was made.

In 1955 the Little Rock board announced its program of gradual integration: there was to be no action for two years while a high school for Negroes was being finished. Then in September 1957 a few selected Negro students were to be admitted to Central High School, one of the three such schools for white students. Over the next six years there was to be a gradual and limited extension of this policy covering other grades. A liberal transfer provision was adopted to minimize the actual number of mixed classrooms and schools. It was frankly ad-

[31] *Aaron v. Cooper,* 1 RRLR 851 at 853 (1956).

mitted that this plan, known after the Superintendent of Education, Virgil Blossom, as the "Blossom Plan," was designed to reduce integration to the minimum amount acceptable to the courts.

In Nashville the board of education elected to start desegregation in 1957 with just the first grade, moving up one year at a time. A liberal transfer program was also established so that any white parent who wished to have his child transferred out of a school to which Negroes had been assigned could do so. The school district lines were redrawn to reduce the number of schools with mixed classes. This plan was also acknowledged as an attempt to provide the least amount of desegregation over the longest period of time.

In both cities Negroes sued, complaining that the proposed programs failed to meet constitutional standards. In 1955 Judge William E. Miller approved the Nashville Plan and Judge John E. Miller (no relation) approved the Little Rock Plan. After their decisions were sustained by the courts of appeals for their respective circuits, the Negro plaintiffs decided to litigate no more and pledged their support to make the programs successful.

School officials now set about preparing the community to accept integration. In Nashville Superintendent Bass and in Little Rock Superintendent Blossom each explained to more than two hundred civic and religious groups that the planned programs would make no significant change in the segregated pattern of schools, and pointed out that whatever one felt personally, some desegregation was inevitable. They reported they received, if not an enthusiastic, at least a sympathetic response. Local civic leaders assured their respective school boards of support. In each city one of the major newspapers—*The Banner* in Nashville and the *Arkansas Democrat* in Little Rock—was lukewarm or even resentful of the coming of desegregation, but the other major newspaper—*The Tennessean* in Nashville and the *Arkansas Gazette* in Little Rock—added strong editorial support.

Segregationists in Nashville and Little Rock seemed unable to

organize much opposition. In the spring of 1957 two segregationists were defeated by a two-to-one majority when they tried
to unseat incumbent members of the Little Rock Board of
Education. Fifty per cent of the voters of Little Rock refused to
support even a mild anti-desegregation referendum calling for
an amendment to the national Constitution to legitimatize segregation.

At the state level, outside of Nashville, in western Tennessee,
and outside of Little Rock, in eastern Arkansas, segregationists
were considerably stronger. They had forced segregation laws
through their respective state legislatures. But the governors of
the two states gave no sign of using these laws to interfere with
their capital cities' programs. Governor Frank Clement of Tennessee was a moderate who had called out the National Guard to
prevent a Kasper-inspired mob from creating riots in Clinton.
Governor Orval Faubus of Arkansas was also thought to be a
moderate. In the 1956 gubernatorial campaign, he had defeated
an ardent segregationist, Senator Jim Johnson, later elected to
the Arkansas Supreme Court. Moreover, Faubus had refused to
interfere with desegregation programs previously carried out in
other Arkansas cities, despite the considerable urgings of segregationists. In his election campaigns Faubus had had the support of the state's liberals and had refrained from inflammatory
comments. He had appointed Negroes to important positions
within state and party. All looked well in both cities for the
peaceful passing of the old order.

In both cities segregationists continued to agitate. In Nashville the Tennessee Federation of Constitutional Government, a
"gentleman's-type" organization, created a front group—the
Parents' Preference Committee—to collect six thousand signatures on a petition stipulating that the signers preferred segregation. No petition was needed to demonstrate that Nashville's
white parents preferred segregation, but it was used by the
Tennessee federation to urge the board to invoke the Tennessee
preference law. This law authorized local boards to establish
three kinds of schools: white only, colored only, and integrated.

Three days before schools were to open and after Negro children had already registered, the Nashville board weakened. It petitioned Judge William E. Miller for permission to postpone desegregation and to use the preference plan. Judge Miller, a handsome, forty-nine-year-old graduate of the Yale Law School, had been appointed to the bench by President Eisenhower in March 1955. Before that time he had been active in Republican politics, an unsuccessful candidate for Congress and delegate to the 1953 Constitutional Convention, and a law partner of Judge Taylor.[32]

Judge Miller promptly ruled against the Tennessee preference law and told the board to proceed as planned. School officials trusted that Judge Miller's decision would finally dispel any hopes that the community might harbor that there was any way it could squirm out of desegregation. The board still had to reckon with the troublemakers.

While free, pending appeal on his Clinton convictions, John Kasper transferred his attention to Nashville. Late in August he came to town and started his usual routine. He attracted small audiences at first, less than fifty, and most of these were city detectives. He accused Mayor Ben West, Judge Miller, the Supreme Court, and Nashville newspapers, of being part of a "Jewish-Communist conspiracy." [33] He told his avid followers he was against dynamiting public schools, but hinted it might get to that point. He was joined in his rabble-rousing by another Nashville visitor, one John Mercurio, a self-styled preacher, and by a local minister, the Reverend Fred Stroud, who had been previously expelled from the Presbyterian Church and who had

[32] *Nashville Tennessean,* September 13, 1957.

[33] See statements of James B. Bridgers, Detective, Metropolitan Police Force, August 25, 1957, in the files of *Kelly v. Nashville.* Kasper said: "We are not going to have these Negroes in our school regardless. . . . I hope Bennie Boy upstairs will stick out his head and listen to this. He can hear you if he wanted to. . . . On the Board of Education they have a Jew on that. It is hand picked." "As to Judges Miller and Taylor," Kasper said, "they look like niggers."

long been active "exposing" the "communist influence" in the major Protestant denominations. Few paid much attention to these three apostles of hate. It is highly questionable if Kasper and his associates would have been able to whip up any sizable following if they had not been vicariously supported by the Governor of Arkansas. Over in Little Rock Faubus was making international news. His intervention had a "backlash" impact on Nashville; it helped make resistance respectable and it encouraged the segregationists, who intensified their work. More mass meetings were called.

On September 8 Nashville's schools opened. Nineteen six-year-old Negro children appeared at seven previously "white" schools. The entire Nashville police force of 115 was on duty. Pickets appeared at each of the schools, but police were under orders to make no arrests and to let the pickets alone so long as there were no overt acts of violence. There were catcalls, speeches, and scuffling. All the white parents had been telephoned the night before and told there would be danger if they brought their children to school. Many of the parents reached school authorities to explain they were keeping their children at home, not to protest the admission of the Negroes, but out of fear for their own children's safety. Within the schoolrooms the teachers did their best to ignore the crowds outside.

Many Nashville citizens who to that moment were strong supporters of segregation were now so appalled at the intensity of human hate that henceforth they became active "moderates." But for the moment Kasper and his followers were left undisturbed. Encouraged by their success in disrupting the first day of school, they organized more rallies that night. *The Tennessean* received an anonymous call late that night warning that the Fehris school would be bombed within an hour. The police were notified but they found nothing. At 12:36 A.M. Hattie Cotton School was bombed.

The next morning Chief of Police Douglas E. Hosse faced his police detachments. "This has gone beyond a matter of integration," he told his men. "These people have ignored the laws and they have shown no regard for you or any citizen." [34] When the demonstrators tried to throw up their picket lines around the schools, they found police barricades. Any adult who could not explain his presence was ordered to leave. Those who refused were arrested. Kasper and his lieutenants were picked up by the police. After Kasper posted bond on one charge, he was re-arrested on another, once because of illegal parking while in police headquarters. He posted more bond. He was arrested again. Finally his supporters ran out of money. Professional bondsmen refused to put up the money. A city magistrate gave Kasper a stern lecture and sent him off to the workhouse. As one veteran Nashville newspaperman put it: "In southern cities there are three types of justice, white man's justice, poor white trash justice, and nigger justice. For the first time in history, a white man was given nigger justice."

A few days later, Mayor West, after a day-long conference with the United States district attorney, decided to petition Judge Miller for a restraining order to forbid Kasper, Mercurio, Stroud, and eight other individuals and all who acted in concert with them from picketing or in any other manner attempting to interfere with the orderly desegregation of the schools. Judge Miller granted the order, copies were mimeographed and distributed to each policeman, and a hearing was set in which those named would have a chance to show cause why the order should not be made permanent.

The "get-tough" policy worked. By the day of the hearing the schools were back in business. Kasper played a new role at the proceeding, that of the abject, injured innocent. For four hours his attorney read the Constitution and quoted the Bible, but it did Kasper and his supporters little good. The silence which his martyr's role imposed on him was hard to bear. He tugged constantly at his attorney's coat and passed notes to his fellow conspirators.

[34] *Southern School News,* October 1957, p. 6.

Of those named in the injunction only Kasper, Stroud, and Mercurio appeared to know what was going on. Stroud, an older version of Kasper, with the same deep-set, intense eyes and the same compulsion to make speeches, was represented by the Tennessee Federation of Constitutional Government, which incidentally had refused to defend Kasper. Like many fanatics they argued their cause rather than their case. When they did get down to the issues at hand they contended that to enjoin Stroud from interfering with school integration would abridge his religious freedom since Stroud believed that integration is sinful and that he had a religious duty to preach against sin. Stroud took the stand to insist he was a man of peace; his calls for a holy war against integration were not intended to create violence. Mercurio made long, disconnected speeches on various topics having no pertinence to the hearing but the substance of which was that everybody in the United States, with few exceptions, was a Communist. Of the others, only two still defended their cause. These two were under investigation in connection with school bombing. Under questioning as to why they were present on the school grounds, one responded, "To keep the niggers from shooting children." The other persons named in the order were a confused and frightened lot who had little idea of what was going on and were obviously tools in the hands of Kasper, Mercurio, and Stroud.

At the end of the long hearing, Judge Miller issued the injunction. Kasper was returned to jail so he had no opportunity to violate this court order. Eventually he was released on bail and left the city. At a later date, he returned and was convicted by local authorities of stirring up a riot. The combined weight of city, school, and federal authorities had been too much for the segregationist forces. Gradually enrollments returned to normal. Each year a new grade has been desegregated. There have been only minor difficulties.

In Arkansas things were going less smoothly. Little Rock had the misfortune of facing a showdown without effective leadership. Whereas Nashville had a strong mayor, a determined police

chief, and a vigorous judge, in Little Rock Mayor Woodrow
Wilson Mann had just been repudiated by the voters, who over
his protest in November 1956 had voted in the city-manager
form of government, to be installed in November 1957. The city
was operating with a lame-duck mayor and city council. Chief of
Police Marvin Potts was opposed to integration and he did not
have much heart for his assignment. Under the best circumstances
he was not what one would call a tough cop. He resigned soon
after schools were opened. Osro Cobb, the United States district
attorney in Little Rock, was a mild-mannered, everybody's-friend
type, a former state Republican chairman who did not have political stature in heavily Democratic Arkansas. It was rumored
that he hoped to become a federal judge, but failed to get backing from any local bar association.

Nor was there any resident district judge. Judge Thomas C.
Trimble had retired in 1955 and Judge John Miller, a native
Arkansan from Arkansas's other judicial district, had originally
issued the Little Rock injunction. He disliked this assignment
and arranged that the Little Rock suit be transferred to the
docket of a visiting judge from North Dakota, Judge Ronald N.
Davies, who was sitting in Little Rock on a temporary basis.
Judge Davies, small in appearance and decisive in action, was
to show his mettle, but as an outsider he was an easy target and
lacked political standing in Arkansas.[35]

Superintendent Virgil Blossom and his school board tried to
step into the vacuum and take charge of the forces of moderation. Until 1957 Blossom was considered the most popular man
in Little Rock, and he had the silent support of many civic and
business leaders, but they were at first afraid to help him. A
rather sizable proportion of Little Rock's leading businessmen
are Jewish and many of them were fearful of taking a promi-

[35] Judge Davies had been appointed to the bench in August 1955 by
President Eisenhower with the support of Senator William Langer of
North Dakota. Davies went to Georgetown University Law School in
Washington and had managed Langer's successful campaign for governor
in 1932.

nent role for fear of being caught in the cross fire—for the anti-semitic character of the segregationist was just beneath the surface.

The events of Little Rock during the fall of 1957 are so well known that detailed account is unnecessary. During the summer Little Rock authorities had assigned nine Negro students to Central High. About sixty had asked to go; permission was refused to all but seventeen carefully selected pupils, eight of whom removed themselves from the list.

During August Little Rock's segregationists, assisted by supporters from the eastern part of the state and under the leadership of Amis Guthridge and several local ministers, stepped up their campaign. Unlike Nashville, Little Rock had the dubious distinction of having home-grown agitators. They put advertisements in local newspapers, held mass meetings, and charged the school board with being tools of Mrs. L. C. Bates, head of the Arkansas NAACP. But their biggest effort was a giant rally featuring Governor Marvin Griffin of Georgia and Roy V. Harris, executive director of the States' Rights Council of Georgia.

The meeting was held on the night of August 22. It was widely noted that Governor Faubus was absent from this $10-a-plate dinner, but he had asked Griffin and Harris to be his guests. Since Faubus was still thought to be a moderate, Harris had to explain to "our people" that he and "Marve" were staying at the Executive Mansion because they felt it would have been too rude to refuse. Griffin told his audience that whatever federal judges might say, he would never allow integration in Georgia. Harris urged the people of Arkansas to join Georgia in resisting federal encroachment to the last man. He told them that in Georgia they would use the highway patrol if necessary, just the way Governor Shivers had done; he suggested that Governor Faubus should be urged to do the same thing.

All observers—segregationists, moderates, integrationists—agree that this visit by the emissaries from Georgia had an electrifying impact on Little Rock. Faubus had long been bombarded with messages by segregationists warning him of violence and urging him to intercede, but the speeches of Griffin and Harris, he later said, "triggered a charge." Soon messages were pouring into the Executive Mansion. Superintendent Blossom stated: "Griffin and Harris had a tremendous amount of effect on this community. People kept saying to me, 'We don't have to do this when the Governor of Georgia says nobody else has to do it. . . .'"

By the end of August Governor Faubus's role, it was clear to all, would be crucial. Segregationists knew that without his support they could not stop integration. The school officials continued to be confident they could handle the situation, provided Faubus would let them. It would ease their minds considerably if they could get Faubus to make a simple public statement to the effect that he would tolerate no violence and would preserve law and order in the event he was needed, but failing to get that, all they wanted was for Faubus to leave them alone.

Right up to the moment Faubus called out the National Guard, the Little Rock authorities tried to persuade the governor to make the statement. They were in constant touch with him and made one desperate effort through the good offices of Winthrop Rockefeller, chairman of the Arkansas Industrial Development Commission and political associate of the governor. Rockefeller flew back to Little Rock and had a secret conference with Faubus who "did not say 'yes,' but he did not say 'no.'" The night before schools were to open Faubus told Blossom that he could not make any public statement supporting the board—he was under too much pressure—but after he had gone through the motions, he would not stand in the board's way. Personally, he told Blossom, he felt the Little Rock plan was the best solution that had been offered in the United States and would become the model followed in other cities.[36]

At Faubus's request, A. B. Caldwell, head of the Civil Rights Section of the Department of Justice, a native and former resi-

[36] V. T. Blossom's sworn statement to the FBI, September 7, 1957; released by school authorities, June 18, 1958; *Arkansas Gazette,* June 19, 1958.

dent of Arkansas, was sent to Little Rock on August 28. He conferred privately with the governor. The conference consisted for the most part of questions put to Caldwell by Faubus as to what action the Department of Justice would take in event of disturbances.

Caldwell told Faubus that the federal government was not a party to the litigation that had resulted in the desegregation decree and disturbances in the city would not of themselves furnish a basis of federal intervention. "What about Clinton, Tennessee?" the governor inquired. Caldwell explained that federal officials became involved there only after the school board had asked for an injunction against Kasper and the judge had requested the help of the department in making his order effective.

As Warren Olney III, then head of the Criminal Division, said later: "The governor's subsequent action has given [the conference] a significance which was not appreciated at the time." [37] Faubus, thus assured that he need not fear federal intervention, was free to proceed with his own plans. On the other hand, Caldwell, who also talked with Blossom and Little Rock officials, could give them no promise of protection.

On August 27, just five days before schools were to open, Mrs. Clyde A. Thomason, secretary of the Mothers League of Central High, a recently created organization, went before State Chancellor Murray O. Reed to request an injunction forbidding the board to allow Negroes to enroll at Central High. This suit was undertaken by the Mothers League at Governor Faubus's suggestion after he had failed to persuade the school board to do so. Faubus testified in favor of the injunction, saying there was danger of bloodshed. Chancellor Reed issued the injunction "not to impair the basic principle announced in *Brown v. Board of Education*," he said, but "solely to preserve peace." [28] No one knew it at the time, but the very day he testified in chancery

[37] See Warren Olney III, "A Government Lawyer Looks at Little Rock," address to Conference of Barristers of the State Bar of California, *Congressional Record*, vol. 104, March 24, 1958, p. 4532.
[38] *Thomason v. Cooper*, 2 RRLR 931 at 933 (1957).

court, Governor Faubus was in touch with Major General Sherman T. Clinger, commander of the Arkansas Guard, giving him secret orders to prepare for action.[39]

The state chancellor's injunction did not relieve educational authorities of their obligation to comply with the mandate of the United States district court. Nonetheless, the board wanted to play it safe. On August 30 they went before Judge Davies for instructions. He told the board he would "neither hesitate nor equivocate" and reminded them of their legal duties. Furthermore, he himself enjoined Mrs. Thomason and "all other persons . . . from in any manner, directly and indirectly, interfering with or hindering the actions of petitioners in carrying out the Decrees of this Court entered herein on August 15, 1956." [40] Although this injunction warned Faubus and anyone else not to interfere, because of its sweeping nature there are serious doubts it would afford the basis of contempt citations against any person other than Mrs. Thomason and for any action other than the continued prosecution of the state court proceedings. Judge Davies dashed any hope that Faubus might have had that he could use the state courts to prevent integration. Schools were scheduled to open on Monday, September 3. Segregationists were desperate.

Blossom had a talk with the nine Negro students scheduled to take the long walk to Central High. Their parents were naturally concerned. Blossom asked the parents not to accompany their children to school for fear that their presence might provoke trouble. He assured them that steps had been taken to assure the safety of their children. And so, as one parent said, "We turned our children over to the white people."

Blossom still had not given up hope that Faubus might come around and publicly back Little Rock officials. On September 2 he had a long talk with Faubus, but at the conclusion of his

---

[39] Fletcher Knebel, "The Real Little Rock Story," *Look,* November 12, 1957, p. 32.

[40] *Aaron v. Cooper,* 2 RRLR 934 (1957).

conversation he turned to Lieutenant Jackson of the Little Rock Police Force and said, "I am afraid Governor Faubus himself is behind this program of intimidation." [41]

Even as he talked with Blossom, Governor Faubus had already decided to call out the National Guard. That night he made Central High "the most famous high school in the world." [42] Two hundred guardsmen quietly took up positions surrounding the school. The school board was in special session making last-minute preparations when word came that the governor was making a television address. For the first time they and the other citizens learned what the governor had done. He told them that he had been forced to act to prevent massive violence. He did not tell them that he had secretly instructed the National Guard commander to exclude Negroes from the school premises, a deliberate frustration of the orders of the district court. [43]

The board issued a statement calling on the Negro students to stay away from school the next morning. When school opened the Negro pupils made no attempt to enter. About two or three hundred people stood quietly to watch the white students file into Central High.

Meanwhile the school board's attorney had gone to the third floor of the United States Post Office, where Judge Davies held court, to ask for instructions. After a four-minute hearing, including the testimony of Mayor Mann that there was no evidence of massive uprising or trouble which the Little Rock police could not handle, Judge Davies said: "An order will be issued tonight, directing you to put into effect forthwith the plan of integration which you presented to a judge of this court and which was approved by him and by the Court of Appeals." The

[41] Statement by Virgil T. Blossom to FBI, September 7, 1957, released by school board June 12, 1958; reported by *Arkansas Gazette,* June 19, 1958.

[42] A Faubus boast made later in a campaign speech in Mount Nebo, Arkansas, June 18, 1958, *Arkansas Gazette,* June 19, 1958.

[43] This was the evidence, documentary in nature, uncovered later by the FBI, as reported by Warren Olney. *See op. cit.,* p. 4533.

board announced, "The plan of desegregation ordered by the federal court is still in force and effect." [44]

On September 4, before the eyes of the world, the nine Negro students walked down the long street. In front of them were the National Guard. To the other side a jeering crowd. Guardsmen blocked the way and the Negro students were forced back through the howling mob. Although they were spat upon and names were hurled at them, there was no other violence. They were forced to leave the scene. Central High was still segregated.

In Washington President Eisenhower commented: "We are going to whip this thing in the long run by Americans being true to themselves and not merely by law." This offered little immediate help to school officials and provided little comfort to Judge Davies, who was confronted with a condition that could hardly wait to allow Americans to ignore the law until they learned to be "true to themselves." Somewhat more encouraging was Eisenhower's public response to Faubus's complaint about the presence of so many FBI agents in Little Rock. The President said: "When I became President, I took an oath to support and defend the Constitution of the United States. The only assurance I can give you is that the federal Constitution will be upheld by me, by every legal means at my command." [45]

In Little Rock the school board asked Judge Davies to suspend the integration decree. The board pointed out that the governor's action had made it impossible for them to proceed. Privately they asked Judge Davies to order the United States marshal to assist them in carrying out the order, but the judge refused, perhaps feeling that it was not his responsibility to precipitate such a head-on clash between the marshal and the Arkansas National Guard. [46]

For three days Little Rock's Central High operated without the Negro students. Behind the scenes the Department of Justice was considering what line to take. On Saturday morning, Sep-

[44] *Arkansas Gazette,* September 4, 1957.
[45] *Southern School News,* October 1957, p. 2.
[46] Testimony of Virgil Blossom hearing, *Aaron v. Cooper, op. cit.,* p. 356.

tember 7, Judge Davies held a brief open hearing on the board's petition to delay desegregation. Blossom spoke for the board. Judge Davies asked Blossom if the plan of integration had been discussed before civic groups and whether the plan appeared to be acceptable to them. Blossom said he had spoken before 125 groups when the plan was first adopted, and about fifty more since. The plan "was accepted. . . . The people did not want integration but they accepted it as the best solution to a difficult problem."

Judge Davies declared a forty-five-minute recess. At eleven o'clock he returned and read his decision slowly. He pointed out that the integration plan had originated and was conceived by the citizens of Little Rock. He said that Mayor Mann had reported not a single case of interracial violence and that there was no indication that there would be violence. He added he had given careful consideration to the problem, but: "It must never be forgotten that I have a constitutional duty and obligation from which I shall not shrink." He called the board's petition for delay "anemic" and rejected it. "In organized society there can be nothing but ultimate confusion and chaos," he said, "if the court decrees are flouted, whatever the pretext. . . . " [47]

Even more significant, Davies instructed Osro Cobb, the United States district attorney, and Herbert Brownell, the Attorney General of the United States, to investigate the events leading to the governor's intervention and to report to the court as soon as possible. For the first time, the Department of Justice was drawn into the fray.

Even prior to this formal request the FBI had been gathering data—there were so many FBI agents in Little Rock that newsmen had difficulty in finding hotel rooms. The FBI had documentary evidence that Faubus had originally instructed the Guard to exclude Negroes, that there was not, as Faubus had charged, any unusual sale of knives, guns, or other weapons, and that there had been no request, as Faubus had charged, by local

[47] *New York Times,* September 8, 1957; *Aaron v. Cooper,* 2 RRLR 940 (1957).

authorities for his intervention. Two days after requested, Cobb turned the detailed FBI report over to Judge Davies. An hour after he received this report showing that Faubus had deliberately frustrated the orders of his court, Davies ordered the Department of Justice to appear as *amicus curiae*. He instructed them to file a petition against the governor and his Guard commanders seeking such relief "as may be appropriate to prevent the existing interferences with and obstructions to the carrying out of the orders heretofore entered by the court in this case."

Judge Davies' important move was unusual, but not unprecedented.[48] Normally the plaintiffs, in this case, the parents of the Negro children, must initiate moves to secure enforcement of orders issued in their behalf. Here was an unusual situation calling for unusual action. A governor was challenging the authority of the federal government; this was no longer an ordinary lawsuit. A federal judge has the right to call on the law officers of the United States for assistance. What had been heretofore a nominal case between Negro school patrons on one side and the school board on the other had turned into a conflict between the state of Arkansas and the national government. The case was still to be styled *Aaron v. Cooper* but from here on it was really the *Department of Justice v. Orval Faubus*.

Judge Davies' order to the Department of Justice came as no surprise. Since early September the local district attorney had been in constant contact with Washington conferring about the various legal moves which might be made. Although there is no evidence of prior consultations between Judge Davies and the district attorney's office, the offices of the judge's staff and the district attorney's staff were only steps away from each other. Their respective staffs frequently had coffee and meals together. It would not have been unusual or unethical to talk over tactics.

What kind of legal action should be taken? There were several choices. The Department of Justice could have moved for an immediate contempt citation against Governor Faubus alleging

[48] *See,* for example, *Universal Oil Company v. Root Refining Co.,* 328 U.S. 575 (1956).

a violation of the August 30 injunction against "any person" who in any manner "directly and indirectly" interfered with the plans of integration. Or they could have asked Judge Davies to issue a restraining order which would have forced Faubus either to admit the Negro pupils immediately or risk contempt. However, Judge Davies privately instructed the Department to limit their petition to a request for a preliminary injunction.[49] This choice allowed for a ten-day delay prior to a hearing giving Faubus a chance to conform with the requirements of the Constitution as he had promised to do when he met with President Eisenhower in Newport, Rhode Island. But on September 20 the Guard was still on duty, still with orders to turn away Negro pupils.

At precisely 9:00 A.M. on the morning of September 20 Judge Davies called his court to order. The attention of the world was focused on this small room. Sitting on the judge's right were the nine Negro children against whom the governor had called out his National Guard. They were dressed in their best, talking quietly and nervously among themselves. To his left, in the jury box, were the reporters of the national and international press. Each seat in the room was occupied; on the left side were many of those who had felt compelled to spend the last several weeks maintaining guard around Central High to be sure no "niggers" got in. One of these ladies announced to all, "Let me in; I am a segregationist from the top of my head to the tip of my toes." The right side of the aisle was occupied mostly by Negroes. They sat very quietly. Thousands jammed the narrow corridors outside, hoping to get a chance to see this climactic legal struggle. Crowded into the various small rooms leading off the narrow corridor were over two hundred witnesses whom the Department of Justice had called to be available if needed.

The governor did not attend the hearing, but he was represented by three attorneys who had filed various motions asking for dismissal of the petition. They argued that Judge Davies should disqualify himself since he had a personal prejudice

[49] See Olney, *op. cit.*

against the governor and a personal bias in favor of the plaintiffs. They challenged the right of the United States to petition the court for the injunction and to make the governor a party to the case. They made much of the fact that in the recently enacted Civil Rights Act of 1957, Congress had specifically refused to authorize the Attorney General to participate in the school-entry cases.

Wiley A. Branton, the attorney who had represented the Negro students, was there. So was Thurgood Marshall. But they did not speak. They left it up to the attorneys for the Department of Justice.

The major issue raised by Faubus's lawyers was that the federal court lacked jurisdiction to restrain the operations of the chief executive of a sovereign state. They cited a 1909 Supreme Court decision (*Moyer v. Peabody*) in which the Court had ruled that a governor is the final judge of when the militia should be used to suppress violence within his state.

The Department of Justice answered that in the Moyer case the governor had not interfered with the operation of a federal court. Moreover, in 1932 the Supreme Court had ruled (*Sterling v. Constantin*) that federal courts do have the authority to review the calling out of the militia "where there is a substantial showing that the exertion of state power has overridden private rights secured by the Constitution."

Preliminary motions took the better part of the morning. When the argument was finished Judge Davies held that all the dismissal motions lacked substance. "Any further preliminary matters?" he asked.

Faubus's chief counsel rose: "The Governor of the State of Arkansas cannot and will not concede that the United States in this court or anywhere else can question his discretion and judgment as chief executive of a sovereign state. . . . In view of that, if the court please, may counsel for respondents be excused?"

"You may be excused," said Judge Davies.

The governor's attorneys walked out of the courtroom, sparing themselves the embarrassment of having to present evidence to support Faubus's contention that he had acted to prevent violence, not to prevent integration. Over in the state house, the governor, using what appears to be a somewhat sacrilegious but nonetheless favorite analogy of demagogues, commented, "Now begins the crucifixion."

The rest of the hearing was concerned with the question, "Did the governor have evidence that violence was imminent?" Federal authorities made a strategical mistake by joining the argument on this largely irrelevant question. Even if there had been such evidence, it would in no way have legally justified Faubus's using troops to prevent Negroes from attending Central High. This strategy played right into Faubus's hands and itself indirectly encouraged violence. After the Guard was withdrawn, Faubus and his supporters could claim vindication only if riots did develop. It was naive on the part of the federal authorities to fail to recognize that their insistence that Faubus had been lying would practically force the segregationists to produce the violence so they could say "we told you so."

Finally, if the Department of Justice was going to try to undermine Faubus's contention that he had acted because he knew that otherwise there would be massive violence, they should have gone all out to prove their point. They could have released the FBI report, called all their witnesses, piling it on so convincingly that Faubus would be thoroughly discredited. However, they did not do so. They called to the stand only eight persons: Superintendent Blossom, Mayor Mann, Chief of Police Potts, Jesse Mathews, principal of Central High, the president of the school board, and three of the nine Negro students. All testified they had been fully prepared to handle any incidents, had not asked Faubus to intervene, had no evidence indicating they could not have proceeded with desegregation without serious public disturbances.

At the conclusion of the hearing Judge Davies announced: "It is . . . demonstrable from the testimony here today that there would have been no violence in carrying out the plan of integration, and that there has been no violence." The judge then enjoined Faubus "from obstructing or preventing by use of the National Guard or otherwise attendance of Negro students at Little Rock High School . . . and from otherwise obstructing or interfering with orders of this court in connection with the plan of integration." [50]

Judge Davies's order did not require Faubus to withdraw the National Guard, but merely to refrain from using the Guard to prevent Negroes from entering the school. At no time did the judge or any federal authority deny that Faubus had the right to use the Guard to preserve the peace. But as Judge Davies wrote in his formal opinion released the following day: "If it be assumed that the Governor was entitled to bring military force to the aid of civil authority, the proper use of that power in this instance was to maintain the Federal Court in the exercise of its jurisdiction, to aid in making its process effective, and not to nullify it, to remove, and not create, obstructions to the exercise by the Negro children of their rights as judicially declared." [51]

That night every television set in Little Rock was channeled to hear Faubus. It was a speech cleverly contrived. He accused Judge Davies of "unwarranted and biased" action; he lashed out at newsmen, naming six of them; he called on the Negro pupils to exercise restraint; and he iterated and reiterated his contention that if and when they tried to enter Central High there would be bloodshed. Nonetheless, he said, he would call off his troops. Having made this contribution to peace and good order, Faubus left the city to attend the Governors' Conference at Seaford, Georgia, and to receive the plaudits of segregationists for his determined stand. The man they thought was a moderate had turned out to be their hero.

Sometime over the weekend the decision was made that the Negro students should enter Central High the next Monday morning. Chief Potts made his preparations. Segregationists had big advertisements in Little Rock newspapers calling for a "big demonstration" to show the people that they were behind the

[50] 2 RRLR 958 (1957).
[51] *Ibid.,* 962.

governor. There were wild rumors going throughout the city of
carloads of men coming into town from eastern Arkansas to
"keep the niggers out." Potts decided that his police would not
disperse the crowd but keep them behind barricades and otherwise leave them alone. The state police were called and it was
thought they would lend a hand if needed.

What happened on Monday morning when the nine Negro
students started to Central High School is history. Mob violence
was triumphant. The nine students were able to slip through a
screaming, hysterical mob of over one thousand, but the Little
Rock police, who had failed to disperse this unlawful assembly
—and who did not receive any help from state police—were
forced to accede to the demands of the rioters: the nine teen-age
Negro students were hustled out of the building.

Word of the riot was flashed to the President. To this moment
the President had taken no direct hand in the Little Rock affair.
Maxwell Rabb, the President's special assistant on minority matters, had been in close touch with Mayor Mann and that morning
the President issued a proclamation calling on "all persons engaged in such obstruction of justice to cease and desist there-
from, and to disperse forthwith. . . . " During the afternoon Mann
called Rabb to ask for help. He reported that unless the President
sent in federal troops the Little Rock police could not break the
mob rule. The President decided to wait and see.

On Tuesday morning, September 24, two hundred and fifty
people gathered in front of Central High, Presidential proclamation to the contrary notwithstanding. Negro students made
no attempt to enter. Mann called Rabb and they decided the
mayor should send a telegram to the President formally requesting help.

At 10:22 A.M. Little Rock time the President ordered the
Arkansas National Guard into federal service and instructed parts
of the famed 101st Airborne Division stationed at nearby Fort
Campbell to surround Central High and to enforce the court's
order. By that evening the troops were in position.

On Wednesday morning, September 25, an army station

wagon delivered the Negro students to school and troops escorted them into the building. A crowd gathered, but the troops, using standard riot-prevention procedures, refused to allow them to assemble and forced them to disperse. Eight persons were taken into custody. From then on a token force of federalized guardsmen maintained order outside the high school.

Did the President have the constitutional authority to send the troops to Little Rock? Faubus argued that Congress in 1957 had repealed the provision authorizing the Chief Executive to use military force to protect civil rights. And he cited a provision of the United States Criminal Code making it a crime for any person to use willfully any part of the Army or Air Force to execute the laws, "except in cases and under circumstances expressly authorized by the Constitution or Act of Congress." [52] The President, charged the governor, had no authority to use troops in Arkansas without the consent of state officials.

The governor was wrong. Congress did repeal statutory language authorizing the President to use troops to enforce civil rights laws, but this language was superfluous. For Congress also reaffirmed two laws adopted in 1782 and 1861 authorizing the President to use the militia and armed forces "whenever it is impracticable to enforce the laws of the United States . . . by the ordinary course of judicial proceedings." [53] The prohibition against using the armed forces applies only where there is no authorization and was passed by Congress to limit United States marshals calling out the armed forces as part of their posses.[54]

Furthermore, even in the absence of specific congressional authorization, the President has the constitutional duty "to take care that the laws be faithfully executed" and, said the Supreme Court in 1890, this includes the authority to enforce "the rights, duties, and obligations growing out of the Constitution itself . . .

[52] Sec. 1385, Title 18, U.S.C.

[53] Sec. 332, 333, Title 10, U.S.C.

[54] Daniel H. Pollitt, "A Dissenting View: The Executive Enforcement of Judicial Decrees," *American Bar Association Journal,* vol. 45, 1959, p. 606.

and all the protection implied by the nature of the government under the Constitution. . . . " [55] No President need wait for an invitation from state authorities to enforce federal laws. The government of the United States does not operate within a state by the grace of state authorities.

On September 24 President Eisenhower issued a statement of principles emphasizing that the duty to formulate desegregation plans belongs to state authorities. Governors, he said, do have the responsibility for maintaining domestic order. "However, under the pretext of maintaining order, a Governor may not interpose military force or permit mob violence to occur so as to prevent the final order of a Federal court from being carried out." And the President warned, "When an obstruction of justice has been interposed or mob violence is permitted to exist so that it is impracticable to enforce the laws by the ordinary course of judicial proceedings, the obligation of the President under the Constitution and laws is inescapable. He is obliged to use whatever means may be required by the particular situation." [56] So it was that those who insisted that the mobs in the street shout with the voices of the people were not allowed to have their way.

Orval Faubus made a major contribution to the cause of desegregation. He made it impossible for President Eisenhower to continue to ignore those persons in high authority who had been using the threat of violence to justify their frustration of federal judicial decrees. Before Faubus's clumsiness compelled the President to intervene, the University of Alabama, Governor Shivers, and the Florida Supreme Court had been allowed to get away with their tactics. Faubus only did more openly what others had done before him. But Faubus so bluntly used these preserver-of-peace tactics that even Eisenhower had to meet the challenge.

After Faubus and Little Rock, it was no longer possible to use violence to justify the continuation of segregation in the face of contrary federal court orders. In January 1961, after an outbreak of violence on the campus, the University of Georgia suspended

[55] *In re Neagle,* 135 U.S. 1 (1890).
[56] Quoted in full, 2 RRLR 929 (1957).

two Negro students who had been admitted a few days before under an order issued by Judge Bootle. Judge Bootle immediately ordered their reinstatement. He made it clear that he would call on the President for federal forces if state authorities could not or would not keep order. He quoted from a decision of the Supreme Court and added, "Nor can the lawful orders of this court be frustrated by violence and disorder." [57] Others may try, but the enthronement of lawlessness no longer provides a technique to circumvent federal desegregation decrees.

[57] *Southern School News,* February 1961, p. 10.

6 * The Battle of Little Rock: Round II

Deprived by Judge Davies of the legal right to use the National Guard to keep Negroes out of Central High; deprived by President Eisenhower of the opportunity to use mob rule to keep Central High white, segregationists turned to new tactics: indirect aggression.

If they could harass the Negro students, make their life so miserable that one morning they would just decide not to go to Central High any more, segregationists could have their way. And there would be nothing the President or the entire United States Army could do about it.

But would the segregationists be allowed to intimidate the students? At first it looked as though they would be kept in check. Seventy-four students active in the riots were suspended from Central High. St. John Barret, from the Civil Rights Section of the Department of Justice, came to Little Rock. FBI agents identified those who were trying to encourage white students to harass the Negroes and to bully any white student who showed any sign of friendliness.

School officials pressed the Department of Justice to prosecute, warning that unless the adults who were egging the students on were brought in line there would be little hope of maintaining discipline within the school. The Attorney General agreed that a prosecution would have a healthy restraining impact not only in Little Rock but throughout the South, and some members of the local United States attorney's office thought they had enough evidence to make a conviction stick.

Attorneys in the Department of Justice had two choices. They could have asked Judge Davies to order the ringleaders to stop organizing boycotts, to cease coercing school authorities, and not to interfere with Negro pupils attending Central High. Such an injunction had been successfully used in Hoxie, Clinton, and Nashville. Or the lawyers for the United States could have tried to use the Civil Rights Act of 1870, which makes it a crime for two or more persons to conspire to deprive a citizen of rights secured by the Constitution. The Negro pupils had a constitutional right to attend Central High; the school board had a constitutional right to obey the court's mandate without direct interference.

Judge Davies was vacationing in his Fargo, North Dakota, home, but with his return, federal prosecution was expected. As long as federal action was expected segregationists, although they tried, were unable to create much trouble. A strike at Central High failed when fewer than sixty students participated. A segregationists' slate for the city council was defeated in the November elections.

Then on November 21, the newly appointed Attorney General, William Rogers, announced that the United States had dropped plans to prosecute agitators. Department of Justice officials in Washington were afraid they could not persuade a grand jury to indict the troublemakers or a trial jury to convict them. To fail would be taken as "proof" that a conspiracy to intimidate Negro pupils did not exist and a sign of the impotence of the federal government.[1] Nor would the Department of Justice initiate action for an injunction. Such a move, the federal lawyers said, was up to the school board. The FBI withdrew in force from Little Rock.

On the same day that Attorney General Rogers announced there would be no federal prosecutions, thirteen white persons

[1] *New York Times,* October 19, 1957, May 30, 1958.

arrested for their part in the rioting during the opening days of Central High were cleared of the charges against them by Little Rock Municipal Court Judge Harry C. Robinson. The only person fined was a Negro student attending a Negro school who had been picked up for carrying a gun.[2] As for state officials, they refused to prosecute anybody except two NAACP officials charged with violating a recently enacted anti-NAACP law.[3]

Little Rock was defenseless. The city would not prosecute agitators, the state would not prosecute, the federal government would not prosecute. The school board even refrained from disciplining unruly students.

Federalized guardsmen were on duty in the halls of Central High, but there were miles of corridors. Furthermore, the guardsmen were not allowed to testify against any student. Inside the classrooms teachers kept order and there was not a single incident during the entire stormy school year in the classrooms themselves. But during the brief period between classes the Negro students were exposed to their tormentors. Of the more than 1200 students at Central High, about 150 participated in these activities, and only two dozen were active. But they were very active! During the year there were forty-three bomb threats, thirty fires, innumerable firecracker explosions. The Negro pupils were shoved, their lockers rifled, and their books destroyed.[4]

---

[2] *Arkansas Gazette,* November 22, 1957.

[3] *Dallas Morning News,* November 2, 1957.

Mrs. Lucius Christopher Bates, better known as Daisy Bates, was president of the Arkansas Branch of the NAACP and it was she who was the major adviser to the students. Her home was their headquarters and after several fiery crosses were burned in front of the Bates's home and bullets had been shot through the window, floodlights were installed and friends took turns guarding the house. Faubus's state police arrested some of the Negroes guarding the Bates's home, charging them with carrying deadly weapons. Mrs. Bates and her husband published the *Arkansas State Press,* a Negro weekly, until forced out of business because of a boycott by local advertisers. But the Bateses stayed. "We believe," said Mrs. Bates, "that it will be easier for other Negro children everywhere to break the color line if we win here." *See New York Times,* September 24, 1957, for a personality sketch.

[4] Testimony of J. O. Powell, vice principal for boys, before Judge Lemley, Transcript, *Aaron v. Cooper,* June 3, 1958, p. 43 ff.

Troublemakers were suspended for three or four days and then allowed to return to school. Two students were expelled; one a white student. She then made a television address, sponsored by segregationists, accusing school authorities of "coddling the Nigras." Later she was readmitted. The other, a Negro girl, was expelled permanently for calling one of her tormentors "white trash."

Toward the end of the school year, Police Chief Eugene G. Smith, who had taken over from Potts, took a more determined stand. But the local magistrates refused to back him up. For example, on May 25, during the Baccalaureate service, Curtis E. Stover, an eighteen-year-old white youth, spat in the face of one of the Negro girls. The police intervened, and Stover cursed the police. He was arrested for disorderly conduct and brought before Traffic Judge Robert W. Laster. Laster was one of Little Rock's most prominent segregationists. So was young Stover's mother. When the deputy city attorney tried to question Stover, Judge Laster ordered him to stop. "This boy," he said, "just gave way to an emotion he couldn't control. There is no insult worse than spitting in someone's face, but if anyone is to be blamed, it should be Dwight D. Eisenhower." [5]

J. O. Powell, vice principal for boys in Central High, testified that if he had been allowed to crack down on the five or ten of the student leaders who were tools of outside adults, "we would have had a much smoother disciplinary problem." [6] But the school board felt they lacked the power to make their action stick. Furthermore, they argued that a "tough policy" would have merely aroused more opposition.

During most of the school year there was no resident federal judge. Judge Davies returned to his home district and the vacancy was still unfilled. Ministers held days of prayer and the *Arkansas Gazette* tried to rally moderate support behind the school board. But no one took any action against the troublemakers, and in the churches they attended the ministers were praying to preserve the whiteness of Central High.

[5] *Arkansas Gazette*, June 14, 1958.
[6] Powell, *op. cit.*, p. 71.

Many have questioned the wisdom of Little Rock's initiation of its desegregation program at the high school level. Superintendent W. H. Oliver in Nashville has pointed out: "There is lots of difference in mixing five-year-olds and fifteen-year-olds." [7] There are no worries about school dances to contend with, no fears of interracial dating, and if two five-year-olds bump into each other in the hall, they are not likely to precipitate a riot.

Little Rock authorities rejected a proposal to start integration with the first grade because it would have required mixed classes in several schools, while by beginning at the high school, they could restrict integration to a single school. They had hoped this would diminish opposition. They were wrong. Instead it was possible for segregationists to concentrate their attentions; it made Central High a battlefield.

With first graders there might have been less intimidation. One has to be pretty mean to threaten a six-year-old, even if he is black. On the other hand, would any parent have been willing to expose a small child to what the Little Rock nine had to go through? Could a six-year-old be expected to understand the stakes involved?

The miracle of Little Rock is that the Negro students refused to give in. The Little Rock nine were old enough to know what they were fighting for, mature enough to stand the day-by-day pressures, secure in the knowledge that outside of Central High they had the moral backing of people from all over the world. When the year ended, eight of the nine were still in Central High. Ernest Green received his diploma with 601 classmates; Carlotta Weeks, sixteen, was on the class honor roll.

The segregationists, nevertheless, were making some progress. On February 20, 1958, the Little Rock School Board filed a motion asking the district court to allow them to suspend desegregation for two and one-half years, and transfer the Negro pupils back to the "colored" school.

The motion was assigned to the docket of Judge Harry J. Lemley, a seventy-two-year-old jurist, who normally held court

[7] *New York Times,* March 15, 1959.

in the eastern part of Arkansas, a man who said, "The South is almost a religion with me." [8] The board did not think they had much chance of getting court sanction for resegregation; nonetheless, they told Judge Lemley of their problems, of the emotional strain on teachers and students. They conceded that none of their difficulties had been caused by the Negro students.

Judge Lemley several times kept pressing the attorney for the school board about the impact of the presence of federal troops on the educational program, a point which the school board attorneys had given little emphasis. But upon questioning by Judge Lemley they said the presence of the troops had been "distracting."

Why did the authorities think conditions might be improved in two and one-half years? Wayne Upton, president of the board, told Lemley that by February 1961 Governor Faubus might no longer be in office. Blossom testified that by then the courts could have passed on the various segregation laws being turned out by the Arkansas General Assembly. Perhaps by then the citizens would finally come to recognize that they must desegregate. However, at the present time, said Blossom, because of the pronouncements of state officers, many citizens in Little Rock were completely confused about the law; they had come to feel that there was no constitutional or legal compulsion to give up segregation.

The burden of the NAACP's argument was that the rights of Negro students should not be forfeited because of the violence of others, and that if the judge were to suspend the desegregation program, segregationists in every other school district would be encouraged to render court injunctions impotent.

The NAACP produced witnesses from outside Little Rock—Dr. Virgil M. Rogers of Syracuse University, and Dr. David G. Salten, superintendent of schools in Long Beach, Long Island—who criticized Little Rock authorities for not dealing more severely with troublemakers. In fact, the school board's own wit-

[8] *Arkansas Gazette,* June 22, 1958.

nesses had admitted they could have maintained order if allowed to do so. But the NAACP's expert witnesses admitted they were not familiar with the local situation; the political and legal consequences of using these "outsiders and Yankees" to question procedures used by the local board did not help the NAACP.

Although Judge Lemley invited United States District Attorney Osro Cobb to participate in the proceedings, he refused. Then on June 21, 1958, to the surprise of all, Judge Lemley granted the Board's petition. He wrote:

It is important to realize . . . that the racial incidents and vandalism which occurred . . . did not stem from mere lawlessness on the part of the white students in the school or on the part of the people of Little Rock. . . . Rather, the source of the trouble was the deep-seated popular opposition in Little Rock to the principle of integration. . . . To this opposition was added the conviction of many of the people of Little Rock, that the Brown decisions do not truly represent the law. . . .

It is not denied that . . . the Negro students . . . have a constitutional right not to be excluded from any of the public schools on account of race; but the board has convincingly shown that the time for the enjoyment of that right has not yet come. . . .

[We] do not think that its [the board's] failure to commence criminal action or to seek injunctive relief [against the vandals] should militate against its present position. . . . [By] reason of the nature, source and extent of the opposition to integration in Little Rock, action by the board . . . might have aggravated rather than eased the situation.[9]

Judge Lemley's ruling was a major victory for the segregationists. Three days later Judge Lemley refused to stay his order pending review. The NAACP went directly to the Supreme Court asking that it exercise its discretionary authority and hear the case immediately without waiting for the court of appeals. On June 29 the Supreme Court declined, but the justices stated: "We

[9] *Aaron v. Cooper,* 3 RRLR 621 at 632 ff. (1958).

have no doubt that the Court of Appeals will recognize the vital importance of the time element in this litigation, and that it will act upon the application for a stay or the appeal in ample time to permit arrangements to be made for the next school year." [10]

Ten days later Chief Judge Archibald Gardner of the Court of Appeals for the Eighth Circuit assigned three circuit judges, but then, deciding that the case was of such importance that it should be heard by all seven members of the court of appeals, called them all into special session. At this stage the Department of Justice entered the proceedings, urging the court of appeals to reverse Judge Lemley.

On August 18, by a six-to-one vote (the one dissenter was ninety-year-old Chief Judge Gardner), the court of appeals reversed Lemley. Judge Marion C. Matthes, speaking for the majority, wrote: *We say the time has not yet come in these United States when an order of a federal court must be whittled away, watered down, or shamefully withdrawn in the face of violent and unlawful acts of individual citizens in opposition thereto.* He pointed out that if Lemley's order were affirmed every school district in which integration has been opposed would have "justifiable" excuses to petition the courts for delay. "An affirmance of 'temporary delay' in Little Rock," said Judge Matthes, "would amount to an open invitation to elements in other districts to overtly act out public opposition through violent and unlawful means." [11]

Lemley had been wrong, but in the normal course of events, the court of appeals' mandate would not be served on Judge Lemley in time for it to have any impact before Central High would open on September 2. Furthermore, at the request of the school board's attorneys, the court of appeals had agreed to stay its instructions to Judge Lemley until their own ruling could be carried to the Supreme Court.

Here was the situation: the court of appeals agreed Negro

[10] *Aaron v. Cooper,* 3 RRLR 619 (1958).
[11] *Ibid.,* p. 648.

students should be allowed to attend Central High. Nonetheless, Judge Lemley's decree would stay in effect until the Supreme Court considered the issues. Since the high court was not due to convene until October 6, Faubus would have an opportunity to force the board to reopen Central High, transfer the Negro students back to their "colored" school, and score a notable psychological victory.

Perhaps the court of appeals wanted to compel the Supreme Court to re-enter the fight. Since 1955 the Supreme Court had left the enforcement of the Brown decision to the district and circuit judges. If the court of appeals had immediately reversed Judge Lemley, the Supreme Court could have taken its time, eventually affirmed without opinion the decision of the court of appeals. However, by staying its order, the court of appeals gave the Supreme Court the option of allowing Faubus to resegregate Central High or convoking a special session. The Supreme Court chose the latter. On August 28 it met in special session, for only the fifth time in thirty-eight years, to consider the NAACP motion to vacate the court of appeals stay order.

Faubus, whose hand had been strengthened by his victorious bid for a third term, called the Arkansas General Assembly into special session. He told the legislators that they must pass six bills to give him, among other things, the power to close the public schools and lease the buildings to private institutions. Otherwise, he charged, the school board would integrate more schools. They were about ready, he said, to integrate "Eastside Junior High with approximately 50 per cent Negro students and 50 per cent white students," [12] an unsubstantiated charge which helped to spur the legislature into doing Faubus's bidding.

The spotlight shifted to Washington. On August 28 more than a thousand persons lined up in front of the Supreme Court building. Normally 180 seats are reserved for the public, but there were so many lawyers and guests of the court and newsmen that

[12] *New York Times,* August 27, 1958.

there was room for only fifty others. At noon the marshal's gavel banged. The preliminaries were disposed of and then Chief Justice Warren said, "Mr. Marshall."

Thurgood Marshall began his argument. He talked quietly and quickly for forty-five minutes. The justices interrupted frequently with questions. Then it was the turn of Richard C. Butler, attorney for the school board. Wayne Upton, the board president and a lawyer himself, sat with Butler at the counsel table, supplying information requested by the justices. Chief Justice Warren asked Butler what would happen to the Negro students if the Supreme Court should leave in effect the stay granted by the court of appeals. "They would be sent back to segregated schools." Warren reminded Butler that the Court had previously ruled that "the vitality of these constitutional principles cannot be allowed to yield simply because of disagreement with them." He asked why the Court should defer the enforcement of constitutional rights because "some elements in the community would commit violence." Butler did not answer directly, but he said that it would be unfair to force the Little Rock board, which had made a good faith attempt to desegregate, to go through another year of "trying circumstances" while officials in other districts who had refused to act were being allowed to defer desegregation for years.

Solicitor General J. Lee Rankin had his turn. "Opposition to the Brown decision expressed in violence cannot," he said, "justify the abandonment or modification of the plan." He urged the Court to vacate the stay. He said that in Virginia and elsewhere district judges were waiting to see what the Supreme Court would do, and if the Court should allow Lemley's decision to stand it would bring to a complete halt all school-entry litigation. It would be taken as a sign that community opposition justified the postponement of desegregation; it would be an invitation to all school authorities to delay.

The justices recessed. The audience waited. Just after 5:00 P.M., five hours after the session began, the Chief Justice announced the Court would delay any ruling on vacating the court of appeals' stay order until September 11, by which time all could present briefs dealing with the full merits of the case.[13] The Little Rock School Board, braving Faubus's wrath, announced that Little Rock schools would await the Supreme Court's ruling and would not open until September 15.

On September 11 the courtroom drama was repeated. It was another crowded session. Butler spoke more than half the session. He argued that the school board was caught between state and federal governments, "helpless" to resolve the conflict, unable to put its integration program into effect because "of the total opposition of the people and the State Government of Arkansas." The opposition was so strong, he said, that it would require federal troops to integrate and "you can't teach if you are going to have troops in the classroom." It is far better "to defer certain intangible constitutional rights of a few [Negro] students than to destroy the full educational opportunities of two thousand students. . . ." But with a reasonable period of time "perhaps the extreme opposition could be overcome."

The justices questioned Butler closely. Said Justice Tom C. Clark: "What does the school board propose to do [if it wins a two-and-a-half-year delay] with reference to trying to effect a program [to carry out desegregation]?"

Butler: ". . . It has not made any particular plans. . . ."

The Chief Justice inquired if after the expiration of two and one-half years the climate of opinion had not changed, would the board ask for another two and one-half years?

Answered Butler: ". . . We don't know. . . ."

Warren inquired further: "The [first] decision was in 1954. This is 1958. Two years and a half will bring it up almost to 1961. Now if all those [Negro] children are denied the right to go to [integrated] schools, aren't they being denied permanently and finally a right to get equal protection under the laws?"

Butler had no answer.

Thurgood Marshall and Solicitor General Rankin took little

[13] *New York Times*, August 29, 1958; *Washington Post & Times Herald*, August 29, 1958.

time to present their position, reiterating their contentions: "This case involves the question of the maintenance of law and order not only in this community . . . but throughout this country. . . . There can be no equality of justice for our people if the law steps aside even for a moment, at the command of force and violence," said Rankin.

When it was his turn Marshall said: "I am not worried about the Negro children. . . . I worry about the white children . . . who are told, as young people, that the way to get your rights is to violate the law and defy the lawful authorities." Marshall attacked Butler's argument that the board was caught between federal and state sovereignties. Such a conflict, he pointed out, had been resolved by the Constitution itself; Article VI proclaimed the supremacy of the national government.[14]

On September 12 the Supreme Court, recognizing the urgency of the situation, announced without waiting for the preparation of its formal opinion: "The Court . . . is unanimously"—and when the Chief Justice read out these words he paused and looked up to emphasize the Court's unanimity—"of the opinion that the judgment of the Court of Appeals . . . must be affirmed. . . . The expression of the views supporting our judgment will be prepared and announced in due course. . . . The judgment of this Court shall be effective immediately, and shall be communicated forthwith to the District Court for the Eastern District of Arkansas." Little Rock's desegregation program was in effect once more.

Two weeks later the Supreme Court released its supporting opinion. The Court reaffirmed its decision against segregation in a blunt, forceful, and powerfully written opinion. The Court mentioned no psychologists or sociologists, but based its rulings squarely on judicial precedents. Many civil rights advocates wished that the Court had been as forceful in 1954.

This opinion was signed individually by each member of the Court, an unprecedented move designed to accentuate the

14 *New York Times,* September 12, 1958; *Cooper v. Aaron,* 3 RRLR 855 at 856 (1958).

justices' unanimity and determination. The Court emphasized: "Since the first Brown opinion, three new Justices have come to the Court. They are at one with the Justices still on the Court who participated in that basic decision as to its correctness, and that decision is now unanimously reaffirmed."

The Court minced no words in accusing Faubus and the Arkansas legislature of causing the disorder at Central High. "The constitutional rights of respondents," said the Court, "are not to be sacrificed or yielded to the violence and disorder which have followed upon the actions of the Governor and Legislature. . . . Law and order are not here to be preserved by depriving the Negro children of their constitutional rights."

The Supreme Court recalled some elementary constitutional propositions in order to answer Faubus, who had been contending that he had no obligation to obey the Brown decision. "The federal judiciary," said the Supreme Court, citing the 1803 precedent of *Marbury v. Madison,* "is supreme in the exposition of the law of the Constitution. . . . The interpretation of the Fourteenth Amendment enunciated by this Court in the Brown case is the supreme law of the land. . . . Every state legislator and executive and judicial officer is solemnly committed by oath . . . to support this Constitution. . . . No state . . . officer can war against the Constitution without violating his undertaking to support it. . . . A governor who asserts a power to nullify a federal court order is similarly restrained."

The Court commented that a state could not avoid its constitutional duty to operate desegregated public schools by operating them behind the façade of "private institutions." "The constitutional rights of children not to be discriminated against in school admission on grounds of race or color . . . can neither be nullified openly and directly by state legislators or state executives or judicial officers, nor nullified indirectly by them through evasive schemes for segregation attempted 'ingeniously or ingenuously.' " [15]

[15] *Cooper v. Aaron,* 3 RRLR 855 (1958).

Justice Frankfurter filed a concurring opinion in which he pointed out even more bluntly that to have granted the request for delay would have meant the "law should bow to force. To yield to such a claim would be to enthrone official lawlessness. . . . For those in authority thus to defy the law of the land is profoundly subversive not only of our constitutional system but to the presuppositions of a democratic society."

The Supreme Court's words contrast with its more gentle tone of 1954 and 1955. Earlier the Court had tried to soften the blow, to tender to southerners the right to desegregate gradually, to indicate that they could decide for themselves how to accomplish the abolition of segregation. By its moderateness the Court hoped to encourage the co-operation of southern leaders. By 1958 the Court was no longer so soft-spoken.

The Supreme Court's more aggressive tone apparently prompted the Department of Justice to take a more positive role than it had in 1957; when schools opened then federal authorities had no plans to deal with persons, public or private, who defied the federal courts. But by the time Little Rock's schools were scheduled to open in 1958, Attorney General Rogers had his plans ready. Early in September he publicly promised to help the board. More than one hundred deputy marshals would be assigned if they were needed. And in Little Rock itself civic officials strengthened their police force and prepared to prevent disorder.[16]

With city and national authorities united, and faced by a determined judiciary, Faubus had to play his cards differently. He had one final card to play.

[16] *St. Louis Post-Dispatch,* September 9, 1958; Press Release, Department of Justice.

7 * The Retreat to Private Schools

Even before the Supreme Court's decision in the Brown case, South Carolina's constitution had been amended to allow the legislature to abolish public schools if integration were imminent. Other states enacted similar measures. Details of these plans vary: some cut off funds to schools which desegregate; some automatically close any "white" school to which a Negro has been assigned; in North Carolina, and in Virginia since 1959, the closing of public schools in districts where a court has called for integration is a local option; in Alabama and South Carolina there is no such choice—the legislature is in control.

As far as the national Constitution is concerned, no state has an obligation to provide public schools. All the Constitution requires, as presently construed, is that a state operate its public schools without respect to race.

The more ardent segregationists are prepared to take the drastic step of abolishing public schools altogether, but except in the Black Belt this is a higher price than most citizens are willing to pay, especially since all they have to do in order to comply with judicial decrees is to admit a few selected Negro students to "white" institutions.

To avoid the political pressures generated by a complete shut-down of schools, segregationists had hoped to operate public schools but to pretend they were "private." When this prospect failed, they sought to close only those schools to which Negroes were admitted. In some states the plans called for a closing not only of the "white" schools to which Negroes are assigned, but also the "colored" schools from which they had come. Segregationists knew that such a threat, especially to shut down the "colored" schools, would have particular meaning to Negro public school teachers, since teaching is one of the few professions open to middle-class Negroes.

Segregationists also felt that "only a few school closings [would] be needed to show the country at large the depth of their determination to stand for a principle." [1] The *Richmond News Leader* editorialized: "With ingenuity and determination on the part of parents, such closings could be kept to a minimum and educational opportunities could be provided for affected children." [2]

The Constitution does not obligate private schools to desegregate; however, any form of governmental aid to such schools makes them subject to the prohibition against segregation. Nor can a state close just a few schools while others remain in operation if the purpose is to avoid desegregation. Students, white or black, shut out of a school that a judge has ordered to desegregate are being denied their constitutional rights.

Many segregation leaders knew that these programs to operate "public-private" schools or to close down institutions to avoid integration were unconstitutional, but they had counted on being able to force time-consuming legal tests. As soon as one scheme was declared unconstitutional, others differing only in details were to be put into operation, and another delaying lawsuit would be underway.

But the Supreme Court's Little Rock decision had caused a stiffening of judicial attitudes up and down the line. It had taken

---

[1] Virginius Dabney, "Virginia's Peacable, Honorable Stand," *Life,* September 23, 1958, p. 56.
[2] October 22, 1957.

three years for federal judges to call a halt to the use of the
pretext of violence to avoid judicial decrees; nevertheless, these
judges aggressively and quickly set aside "public-private" school
schemes and school-closing programs. By 1961 when Governor
S. Ernest Vandiver of Georgia tried to close the University of
Georgia to avoid its desegregation, Judge Bootle issued a restraining order even before the governor could sign the proclamation.

Segregationists also guessed wrong about the political consequences of their programs. Not content with forcing rural schools
to close, they also tried to compel city schools to do so, and
thereby generated the first major political force in support of
token integration. Instead of putting pressure on the moderates,
the threat of schools closing intensified the conflict between city
moderates and rural segregationists, to the disadvantage of the
latter.

Many citizens remained silent until faced with the loss of
their schools. But when the alternative clearly became token integration or no schools, leaders discovered it was no longer politically dangerous to champion token integration. Every city in
which the segregationists forced a showdown produced for the
first time a moderate organization—the Committee on Public
Education in Virginia, the Stop This Outrageous Purge Committee in Little Rock, the Help Our Public Education in Atlanta,
the Save Our Schools in New Orleans.

On the day on which the Supreme Court reinstated Little
Rock's desegregation program, Governor Faubus, invoking laws
rushed through the legislature, issued a proclamation closing all
the city's high schools: "I have determined that domestic violence
within the Little Rock School District is impending." A special
election was called in which the citizens were to vote for or
against integration of all the city's schools. Faubus promised the
voters that if they would reject integration, he would arrange for
the Little Rock Private School Corporation, which had just been
chartered, to take over the public school buildings and operate
them on a segregated basis. He had pledged state funds for these

"private" schools, and the citizens could have tax-supported segregated schools, Faubus said.

Sixty-three of the city's most prominent attorneys pointed out in full-page advertisements that this scheme was patently unconstitutional. Faubus was aware that his subterfuge would be put to a court test, but it might take months, perhaps years, before a final judgment could be rendered. Judge Davies had returned to North Dakota and there was still no resident district judge. The initial challenge would be before Judge John Miller, whose past performances inspired confidence among segregationists.

If the state could convert the public schools into private schools before the Negro plaintiffs secured a judicial hearing, it could open the schools and present the judge with a *fait accompli*. If the schools were placed under private operation prior to the referendum a more convincing case could be made that the scheme would work.

Faubus publicly called on the School Board "to demonstrate their good faith" by handing over immediate control of the schools to the Private School Corporation. The board, much to Faubus's anger, refused to do so without first asking the federal court for instructions. It went before Judge John Miller stating frankly that they would lease the public schools to the corporation if they would not be subjecting themselves to charges of contempt. Miller denied the petition for instructions on the ground it would be improper to render an advisory opinion, but nothing he said suggested to the board that it would get in trouble if it turned over schools to the segregationists.[3]

Two days before the referendum, Negro students who had been closed out of Central High asked Judge Miller for an immediate restraining order to keep the board from co-operating with the Private School Corporation. Attorneys for the Negro students and the Department of Justice, which supported their petition, argued that unless Judge Miller issued a restraining order, the leases would be executed, private schools would be

[3] *Chicago Tribune,* September 26, 1958.

opened, Negro students would be left out in the cold, and the court's own mandates would be rendered useless.

Judge Miller, who heard these arguments, had been appointed to the bench in 1941. He had been a member of Congress from 1931 to 1939 and had been elected to the Senate to fill the vacancy caused by the death of Senator Joseph T. Robinson. A favorite of Senator McClellan, Judge Miller made no secret of his own feelings. He told the Sebastian County Bar Association, "Judges must speak for the will of the people," and he criticized "some of the appellate courts" for an "inclination . . . to arrogate unto themselves the power to declare for us certain standards contrary to the mores . . . which have existed for centuries in this country." [4] Earlier in September 1958 Judge Miller had refused to give the NAACP any help in putting down a student strike keeping Negroes out of Van Buren High School. Judge Miller had said he was not going to be "rushed off my feet in this matter. Suppose a person is denied a right for a few days. He wouldn't be the first person whose rights have been denied for a few days, and if ultimately those rights are restored there is no great harm done." [5]

It was not surprising, therefore, that Judge Miller denied the NAACP's and the Department of Justice's request to restrain the school board from handing over schools to the corporation. "I have always been opposed to precipitant action by a court," he said.[6] He explained that the three-judge court would be required to issue such a restraining order; he refused to issue an order to maintain the *status quo* until a three-judge court could be convened for a hearing.

Even if a three-judge court were required, which it was not, Judge Miller could have issued a restraining order until such a court could have been assembled. The plaintiffs were not asking him to enjoin the enforcement of state laws, which does require

[4] *Southern School News,* March 1959, p. 2.
[5] *Chicago Tribune,* September 9, 1958.
[6] Oral opinion of Judge John E. Miller, *Aaron v. Cooper,* 3 RRLR 882 (1958).

three judges. They were asking only that he keep the school board from co-operating in an unconstitutional maneuver. As the Court of Appeals for the Eighth Circuit subsequently said: "They [the school authorities] were simply yielding to the local desire or clamor and to the importuning of the Governor . . . to try to thwart integration—the thing which [board members] were under judicial mandate to use their efforts and powers to achieve." [7]

At the moment, however, Judge Miller's ruling left the board free to proceed. It helped to convince the citizens of Little Rock that Faubus could carry his program into effect without judicial interference. It stripped the school board of any excuse for not co-operating with Faubus.

On September 27 the citizens of Little Rock went to the polls. They were given a ballot worded in such a way as to give them a choice between complete segregation or complete integration of *all* schools in the district. A majority of all registered voters, not merely a majority of those voting, was required before public schools could be opened—an almost certain guarantee of a segregationist victory. Yet Faubus's precautions were unnecessary; the vote was 19,470 to 7,561 against integration.

That evening the Private School Corporation opened negotiations with the school board. The NAACP had to act quickly if it were going to appeal Judge Miller's ruling. It decided to seek help from the court of appeals. Under the rules of the Eighth Circuit, two judges are required to hear applications for restraining orders. The court of appeals was in recess, but there were two circuit justices resident in Omaha, Nebraska. The first opportunity the NAACP attorneys would have to secure a hearing would be at 10 o'clock on Monday morning, September 29. They intended to be at the judges' doors when they opened.

The corporation, with Faubus's full backing, went into all-night session with the school board, which at 1:30 A.M. on Sep-

[7] *Aaron v. Cooper,* 3 RRLR 1135 at 1140 (1958).

tember 29 capitulated and agreed to lease the buildings before the NAACP could present its case to the circuit judges. The formal signing took place at 8:30 A.M., an hour and a half before court opened in Omaha. It was announced that high schools would open immediately. They would be "private" schools and they would be segregated.

The strategy failed. In Washington, D.C., at the very hour when the circuit judges were convening in Omaha, the Supreme Court released its opinion in the Little Rock case. The Supreme Court stated: "State support of segregated schools through any arrangement, management, funds, or property cannot be squared with the Amendment's [the Fourteenth] command." Government lawyers in Washington dashed to the phone and read the Supreme Court's words to a stenographer in Omaha, who rushed them to the chambers of the circuit judges.

It did not take the circuit judges long to issue a restraining order. The order was wired to Little Rock. More than one hundred marshals immediately served it on all members of the school board, all teachers, and all staff officials. A state trooper refused to allow Faubus to be served personally. The next morning the high schools stayed closed.

The Court's critics were quick to point out that the issue of publicly supported private schools had not been presented to the Supreme Court by the Little Rock ruling of Judge Lemley. Therefore, the Supreme Court's dictum that the use of public funds to operate segregated private schools is unconstitutional, was itself a violation of the taboo against advisory opinion. The Supreme Court's defenders responded that the Court's boldness conformed to long-established practice and that a more timid judicial attitude would have played right into the hands of those trying to evade the Constitution.

The court of appeals told Judge Miller that he should insist on the board's taking "affirmative steps" toward carrying out the previously planned program of integration. The school board, the circuit judges pointed out, had a legal duty to act positively.

Judge Miller was on his vacation when these instructions were issued in November 1958. "I won't be back home for a week," he said, "and I can't do anything about it until I get home." [8]

It was not until January 1959 that Miller finally acted. He gave the board—newly reconstituted after the fall elections and evenly divided between three moderates and three segregationists—thirty days to report to him on what it "had done and was planning to do" to desegregate. Eleven days later the board returned to Miller. They had no plan. They told Judge Miller, "With some schools closed and with the air of tenseness encompassing the whole school district . . . it is impossible . . . to carry into effect the so-called 'Blossom Plan.' " The only thing they could do would be to reopen the high schools on a segregated basis. If the judge would permit them to do this, they promised to hire experts and to develop new desegregation plans.

Attorneys for the plaintiffs objected strongly. "The relief now sought by the defendants," they said, "raises the same issues which were disposed of" when the board sought a "temporary delay" in 1958. Government lawyers, still participating in the case, pointed out that board members, instead of taking affirmative action to carry out the integration plan as they had been ordered to do, were acting "in bad faith" to avoid their obligation. They should be cited for contempt unless they immediately proceeded with the approved plan.[9]

Judge Miller, cautious as always, refused to act. He denied the board permission to open segregated schools, but he ruled board members had acted in good faith. He said that as long as Faubus kept the schools closed, the board's only duty was to sit tight. In short the court of appeals' mandate that the board should take affirmative steps was construed by Judge Miller to mean that the board take no negative steps.[10]

Clearly Judge Miller was going to be of little help to the

---

[8] *New York Times,* November 11, 1958.

[9] *Aaron v. Cooper,* 4 RRLR 17 (1959); *see* A.P. dispatch, January 21, 1959.

[10] *Ibid.*

moderates. If they were going to regain control of their schools they would have to do so by political rather than legal victories. This was to take time. In the fall it seemed as if Faubus would be able to provide a substitute for the public high schools. For a while most of the people appeared content with the substitute minimal education being provided for white students. Faubus continued to find overwhelming support in Little Rock. Schools were closed by his own proclamation, but he had convinced most of the people that it was the federal judges who had deprived them of their high schools. Back in November 1958, after the only segregationist member of the school board, Dr. Dale Alford, a dentist, defeated the nationally respected Brooks Hays in an upset write-in campaign for Congress, the five other members of the school board had resigned.

Faubus seemed invincible. He had won an unprecedented third term. Jim Johnson, a bitter-end segregationist, was elected to the Arkansas Supreme Court. The members of the school board felt they had tried to do their job but without support from the community, the district court, or the President. Because they were afraid that the board to be elected in December would not treat Blossom fairly, as their last act the resigning board members paid up Blossom's contract.

This was the high point of Faubus's influence in Little Rock. From then on, slowly but gradually, moderates began to pick up political support. In December three candidates backed by the citizens council were elected to the school board, but so were three moderates.

The Private School Corporation, after being blocked from taking over the public schools, leased other buildings and operated a private school; so did various churches. Faubus's plan to divert public funds to the Private School Corporation was blocked by a three-judge federal court (Sanborn, Beck, and Miller) which ordered Arkansas to cease paying tuition for students attending private segregated schools.[11] Deprived of public school buildings

[11] *Aaron v. Cooper*, 4 RRLR 543 (1959).

and unable to use publicly paid teachers or state funds, the Private School Corporation had to depend on private contributions. Faubus did his best to help—on official stationery he sent a letter to thousands of people requesting contributions. But the inadequacy of these makeshift educational arrangements became more and more obvious as the school year progressed. By the end of the term, the corporation was bankrupt.[12]

Little Rock's economy was suffering. Home building had declined since 1957 by 20 per cent; between 1950 and September 1957 forty new plants had come to Little Rock, but since then there had been none; in 1959 the city was threatened with a decline in population—one among every five professional persons wanted to or was planning to leave the city.[13]

One Arkansas businessman complained: "The rest of the South tells us, 'Fight to the last ditch . . .' but their high schools are not closed. I say to hell with it." [14] The Little Rock Chamber of Commerce polled its members on February 23: they voted 819 to 245 in favor of reopening the high schools "on a controlled minimum plan of integration acceptable to the Federal Courts." In large advertisements the Chamber of Commerce told Little Rock citizens: "The decision of the Supreme Court of the United States, however much we dislike it, is the declared law and it is binding upon us. We think the decision was erroneous . . . but we must in honesty recognize that, because the Supreme Court is the court of last resort in this country, what it has said must stand until there is a correcting constitutional amendment or until the Court corrects its own error. We must live and act now under the decision of that Court. We should not delude ourselves about that." [15]

---

[12] *Arkansas Gazette,* October 30, 1959.
[13] *Southern School News,* October 1959, p. 2.
[14] *Texas Observer,* August 21, 1959.
[15] *Arkansas Gazette,* March 25, 1959.

The Little Rock Chapter of the American Association of University Women in January 1959 asked eighty-five businessmen if their business had been hurt by the school dispute; forty-four said their business had

Earlier, in the December 1958 school board elections, Faubus had come close to capturing control of the board when three of his men were elected. But because moderates held the other three positions, in the 1959 session of the Arkansas General Assembly Faubus proposed that he be empowered to appoint three additional members of the Little Rock board. The legislature refused; it was Faubus's first defeat. To that moment the Arkansas General Assembly had docilely passed any law Faubus had wanted, it didn't matter how extreme or unconstitutional, so long as it promised to keep segregation.

Early in May the three moderate members of the board walked out of a meeting in an attempt to dissolve a quorum. The three Faubus men seized the opportunity. They fired forty-four teachers, including some veterans of more than thirty-five years' service. They proceeded to hire as superintendent T. H. Alford, father of Congressman Alford.

This purge gave the moderates just the kind of issue they needed. Up to that moment they had been unable to rally much support behind token integration, but now they could counter-attack against this arbitrary dismissal of teachers. That very night the Little Rock PTA Council, which had tried to stay on the fence, issued a fighting statement calling for the recall of the three segregationist board members. A recall election was possible because of a 1957 law, sponsored by Faubus, and passed as a threat to the moderates who then controlled the board.

During the week there was one PTA meeting after another. One hundred and seventy-nine of Little Rock's most prominent business and civic leaders organized a Committee to Stop This

---

been hurt; thirty-five said they had noticed no effect; six said their business had improved.

One company president said, "Anyone who doesn't think the school situation will affect his business adversely has rocks in his head." Seven of the eight real estate dealers said their business had been hurt. Others who said that business had declined were pharmacists, manufacturers, and variety store owners. Retail store owners, insurance men, and bankers said they could see no impact.

Two of the three moving-van owners said their business had improved. Governor Faubus disputed the significance of these findings.

Outrageous Purge (STOP). Although STOP deliberately avoided taking a stand on integration, the issue was clearly joined. Everett Tucker, Jr., vice president of the board and spokesman for the moderates, told crowds jammed into school auditoriums: "We are faced with two alternatives—some degree of integration in the public schools, or segregation and no public schools at all." He advocated the former. He drew applause—for the first time since Faubus had intervened a white audience in Little Rock cheered a moderate who advocated token integration.[16]

Segregationists counterattacked with the Committee to Regain Our Segregated Schools (CROSS); they filed petitions to recall the moderates. During the next thirty days each side was engaged in a battle for public opinion—radio, TV, mass meetings, and speeches. STOP insisted the issue was the firing of forty-four teachers without notice or hearing; CROSS insisted the issue was segregation versus integration. Faubus threw his support to CROSS and took to television.

STOP deliberately refrained from co-operating with the Negroes of Little Rock. Yet segregationists circulated invitations purportedly put out by STOP which invited Negroes to a rally. CROSS then made its worst tactical error: it accused the forty-four dismissed teachers of "teaching alien doctrines, incompetence, intimidation of students, and immorality."

On May 25 there was a heavy vote in the recall election. Faubus lost for the first time since 1957. The margin was close but all three of the segregationist board members were recalled; all three of the moderates were retained. Faubus termed it a temporary skirmish, but at the next school board election, December 1959, moderates trounced the segregationists.

The political winds were shifting. Judge Miller, joined by two other federal judges, in June 1959 ruled: "The proclamation of the Governor of Arkansas closing the public high schools in Little Rock was and is void." The judges reminded the board: "defendants are permanently enjoined from engaging in any acts

---

[16] *New York Times,* May 19, 1959.

which will, directly or indirectly, impede, thwart, delay, or frustrate the execution of the approved plans for the gradual integration of the schools of Little Rock." [17] The Faubus program had been declared unconstitutional. The Supreme Court of Arkansas had been of little help. By four to three in April 1959 it had sustained Faubus's closing of the schools. The decision of the Arkansas court had no legal significance in the face of the contrary federal decisions, but politically it served to confuse the situation. Perhaps of greatest significance, however, was the fact that even three Arkansas Supreme Court jurists had ruled against Faubus.

With the increased political backing, the Little Rock board prepared to reopen high schools when the 1959 fall semester began. The board used the pupil-assignment law to limit the number of Negroes, originally assigning a single Negro student to Central High School, three to Hall High, and none to the Technical High. After eighteen other Negroes asked for reassignment, one more was assigned to Central High and three to Hall. Under the board's original assignment a lone teen-age Negro student would have had to face a year in isolation in Central High; most of those Negro students who had gone through the 1957–58 year at Central were assigned to the "colored" school. It was prudent of the board, however, to avoid sending Negro students to Technical High, where segregation strength could be expected to be especially strong since Technical enrolled noncollege-bound students, and it was wise to send some Negroes to Hall High, which served a predominantly middle-class neighborhood. If there were to have been only one integrated high, Hall—more than Central—would have been a better choice; it served more economically prosperous constituents, among whom segregationist sentiment was less widespread and less virulent. Negroes assigned to Hall High have had much more pleasant experience than those who attend Central.

Little Rock Chief of Police Smith, supported by civic leaders,

[17] *Aaron v. Cooper,* 4 RRLR 543 at 550 (1959).

was determined to keep segregationists from creating a turmoil, so that the governor would not have an excuse to intervene; Smith let it be known that he had the force ready and would tolerate no demonstrations.

Faubus continued to predict violence and to describe Little Rock officials as tools of the NAACP, but before he could interfere, the school board abruptly reopened schools a month early. The night before schools opened the governor, in a television address, criticized the "integrationist federal puppets" and the Little Rock police. He warned that he would move in the State Police and the National Guard if the Little Rock police could not control the situation. But he told his followers, "I see nothing to be gained . . . by disorder and violence." [18] The next morning, before schools opened, he advised one thousand segregationists who rallied on the capitol steps (in the forefront were Mrs. Alford, the wife of the Congressman, and her children): "I see no reasons for you to be beaten over the head today or to be jailed. That should be faced only as a last resort, and when there is much to be gained." [19]

Several hundred of the most determined segregationists, many from out of town, marched on to Central High. As they approached Central High, Chief Smith, using a portable electric megaphone, told them: "Your behavior is a disgraceful matter . . . let's get out of the streets." [20] But on they marched. Fire hoses were turned on; the police arrested twenty-one persons and the demonstrators were dispersed. The riot was over. Faubus accused the Little Rock police of using Gestapo tactics. He compared Chief Smith to Janos Kadar, the Hungarian puppet, and he charged that Smith "went out and arrested and beat people." [21]

At Central High School officials were dealing more severely with troublemakers. Any student taking overt hostile action

[18] *Southern School News,* September 1959, p. 2.
[19] *Southern School News,* September 1959, p. 2.
[20] *Southern School News,* September 1959, p. 2.
[21] *Southern School News,* October 1959, p. 15.

against the Negro students was punished. Within a brief period, the school year was underway. The two Negro students still had to walk to school in fear; their parents still wondered whether their children would return safely. But at least the community was no longer standing idly by. Law, order, and ordinary school operations were gradually restored.

Faubusism was still strong in Arkansas, as the fourth-term gubernatorial victory of 1960 demonstrated, but the magic was gone; Little Rock authorities were no longer afraid of their governor. Senator J. W. Fulbright, who to that moment had said nothing about the Little Rock school crisis (his timidity had much to do with President Kennedy's decision not to offer him a position as Secretary of State), finally declared that Faubus had mishandled the situation. Even the Arkansas Supreme Court responded to the changing climate; in September 1959, it unanimously made its first antisegregation ruling when it struck down the State Sovereignty Commission, a commission established to investigate the NAACP.

Desegregation is underway in Little Rock, but not because of the federal district judges. The judges followed the path of least resistance and provided no leadership; except for Judge Davies they consistently backed down in the face of pressure.

In Virginia it was a different story. Virginia's federal judges were slower than their brethren in Arkansas to crack down on segregation, but after the decisions were made, the Virginia jurists insisted on compliance.

At first it appeared that the federal judges would have the widespread backing of the political forces in Virginia and that the Commonwealth would place itself in the camp of the moderates. Following the 1954 Brown decision, Governor Stanley appointed a commission, which in the fall of 1955 recommended a program, based primarily upon local option. The Gray Plan,[22] named for the commission's chairman,

---

[22] Public Education, Report of the Commission to the Governor of Virginia, Senate Document No. 1, Commonwealth of Virginia, Richmond, 1955.

Senator Garland Gray, took into account the fact that in northern Virginia many cities could and would easily desegregate, that in Southside Virginia it would be difficult to do so, and that the Piedmont and Southeast sections would fall somewhere in between. Each school board was to be given authority to design its own desegregation program. Tuition grants were to be made available to send to private schools children whose parents objected to sending them to integrated public schools. Governor Stanley called the Virginia legislature into emergency session. By narrow vote the legislature proposed an amendment to the Constitution to permit the tuition grants.

Virginia moderates opposed this amendment, charging that the tuition program was a device to undermine the public schools. "Our school system," they wrote, "cannot stand half public and half private." [23] Despite their support for a pupil-assignment law as the best plan to keep integration under control, they emphasized that total segregation in all parts of Virginia could not be secured forever.

Early in 1956 the Gray Plan was endorsed by the voters, two to one. The votes had hardly been counted when there was a noticeable lessening of enthusiasm by state officials for the plan. Southside segregationists, flushed by their victory in defeating the moderates, were demanding that Governor Stanley repudiate the Gray Plan in favor of total resistance. By the end of the summer they had their way.

Virginia is dominated by a single political organization. The Democrats win all the state-wide elections and the Byrd organization wins most of the primaries. When Senator Harry Flood Byrd came out for "massive resistance," the Gray Plan was dead. Governor Stanley repudiated it. So did Senatòr Gray himself. By a slim margin, a special session of the Virginia General Assembly adopted thirteen laws to rivet segregation on all communities. The power to assign pupils to schools was taken from the local school boards and vested in a state-wide three-man

[23] Information Sheet published by the Virginia Society for Preservation of Public Schools, 1955, p. 6.

Pupil Placement Board. The board's instructions and the governor's control over its personnel assured that no Negro would ever be assigned to a "white" school. Furthermore, if any judge should order a Negro admitted to a "white" school, it was to be closed automatically with control over the school taken from the board of education and vested in the governor.

In 1957 the Democratic candidate for governor was Lindsay Almond, Jr., the attorney general who had taken a prominent part in helping school districts resist school-entry suits. He was opposed by Ted Dalton, who in 1953 had come close to defeating Stanley by garnering 45 per cent of the popular vote. The major issue in the 1957 Dalton-Almond campaign was massive resistance. Dalton predicted massive resistance would not withstand legal assault, and argued for local option. In the midst of the campaign Judge Walter Hoffman declared Virginia's pupil-placement law unconstitutional. Dalton called for an emergency session of the legislature, contending that the court's decision marked the beginning of the end for massive resistance. The Byrd organization went down the line for Almond and massive resistance and, after President Eisenhower's dispatch of federal troops to Little Rock, Dalton's defeat was sealed. "The shock of that incident, which was exploited to the full by Democratic campaigners, had a devastating effect upon the Republican effort in Virginia." [24]

The NAACP now mounted a massive legal attack; more lawsuits were filed in Virginia and pushed with greater vigor than in any other state. Virginia's lack of guile and its open defiance made the task relatively easy; for there was only the slightest pretense that state officials were acting in good faith.

The only hope segregationists had was that the United States district judges would refuse to take judicial notice of the purpose and impact of the several anti-integration laws, considering each law in isolation and taking each at its face value. Segrega-

---

[24] Benjamin Muse, *Virginia's Massive Resistance,* Bloomington: Indiana University Press, 1961, p. 44; *Richmond News Leader,* October 23, 1957.

tionists wanted the judges to assume, for example, that the placement board would not discriminate against Negroes, and that the threat to close integrated schools was not designed to keep them segregated. Virginia's leaders said they were preparing to desegregate but needed more time, lots of it. But with one exception, the district judges were unwilling to ignore the obvious purpose, design, and intentions of the massive resistance laws.

Judge John Paul of the Western District of Virginia, holding court in Harrisonburg, handled the Charlottesville and Warren County cases. Judge Paul (he has since retired to be replaced by Ted Dalton) is a seventy-five-year-old, alert, quick-moving, snap-jawed, and decisive man. The son of a distinguished Republican, he had followed his father's steps through service in the Virginia Senate, the United States House of Representatives, and to the same federal court.

Judge Paul's appointment to the bench by President Hoover in 1931 did not affect his willingness to speak frankly. He opposed prohibition. Months before Pearl Harbor he urged American intervention to prevent the Axis powers from consolidating their strength. In 1937 he told the Richmond Bar Association:

The States . . . have allowed their water power and other natural resources to be exploited until it was necessary for the national government to step in. . . . We may say the same regarding child labor, lynching and other evils. . . . The states would not legislate. . . . Many governors lack the courage to call their sheriffs and other responsible officers to account when there is a lynching or a similar outrage.[25]

In July 1956, Judge Paul directed Charlottesville to admit Negroes to white schools. He indicated he would çonsider any plan that might be presented, but he left no doubt about what he expected. "I am accustomed to being perfectly frank," he said. "Maybe sometimes too frank for a judge on the bench. But I would close my eyes to the obvious facts if I did not

[25] *Richmond Times-Dispatch,* November 14, 1956; *New York Times,* September 9, 1958.

realize that the state has been pursuing a deliberate and well-conceived policy of delaying these cases. . . . I absolve you from any participation in that policy, Mr. Attorney General [Almond] . . . but I am not willing that this Court should be a knowing and conscious accessary to a program which has for its purpose delay and evasion of the decree of the Supreme Court of the United States." [26]

Judge Paul's fellow judge, Walter E. Hoffman, of the Eastern District, who presides over the Norfolk and Newport News cases, is no less forthright. Hoffman became a federal judge in September 1954, a year after he had unsuccessfully challenged Almond for attorney general. Judge Hoffman, a big man nicknamed "Beef," was one of Eisenhower's first boosters. He was supported for his position by the Republican Virginia Patronage Committee and the then Republican national committeeman, Dalton. Senator Byrd pointed out he had nothing to do with the recommendation but said "I had no reason to object to his confirmation."

On the day Attorney General Almond announced his candidacy for governor, he was arguing the Norfolk case before Judge Hoffman. When the Virginia laws requiring closing of schools were referred to, Judge Hoffman said, "What the legislature of Virginia did in Richmond was not too much to the credit of good judgment. It may have been politically wise." [27]

Judge Hoffman's bluntness and his open criticism of Virginia Democratic leaders have made him one of the major verbal targets of segregationists. Senator Byrd charged Judge Hoffman with "ungoverned prejudice." Hoffman refused to yield. "When I took this job," he said, "I had the Seashore State Park Case [suit to prevent segregated operation of a public park]—and when you get the volume of mail you get after one of those decisions, you wonder whether you are going to live another day." [28] The political leaders "excite the interest of the people

[26] *Richmond Times-Dispatch,* June 30, July 3, 1954.
[27] *Beckett v. Norfolk,* transcript of Record, November 17, 1956, p. 30.
[28] Transcript of pre-trial *Beckett v. Norfolk,* p. 23.

and get them greatly aroused and I get all the telephone calls," but if what happened in Clinton should happen in Norfolk, "I will handle it. I will be here until I die." [29] On another occasion he said: "I understand some of the leaders of Virginia have said they would like to see whether a federal judge has the nerve enough to punish for contempt, and I can assure you that the order will have to be complied with." [30]

Judge Albert V. Bryan, who presides over the United States District Court for Northern Virginia sitting in Alexandria, has heard both the Arlington and Alexandria cases. Judge Bryan was nominated in 1947 by President Truman from a list of names presented by Senators Byrd and A. Willis Robertson and was heartily endorsed by Congressman Howard W. Smith. Judge Smith, as he is known, is chairman of the Rules Committee of the House of Representatives, a determined foe of civil rights legislation, and leader of the southern Democrats in the House. It was he with whom Speaker of the House Sam Rayburn duelled and won, in the contest in early 1961 to enlarge the Rules Committee to prevent further obstruction of liberal legislation by the Committee's former coalition of southern Democrats and conservative Republicans.

Judge Bryan is an old-fashioned-looking judge with steel-rimmed glasses, who has a reputation for being meticulously just. He permitted Arlington to delay for six months in September 1958, and, until reversed by the court of appeals, allowed school officials to subject Negroes to special tests; nevertheless, the general thrust of his work has been toward compliance. A former member of the Byrd organization and more guarded in his comments than his two Republican colleagues, Paul and Hoffman, Judge Bryan has been less exposed to political criticism.

The fourth district judge to become deeply involved in desegregation litigation was sixty-six-year-old Sterling Hutcheson, the senior judge for the Eastern District until his retirement on September 1, 1959. Judge Hutcheson comes from Southside Vir-

---

[29] *Beckett v. Norfolk,* transcript, p. 103, February 12, 1957.
[30] *Ibid.,* p. 55.

ginia. For eleven years he served as United States district attorney, upon the recommendation of Senators Byrd and Carter Glass, and was promoted to the bench in 1944. He is the son of a prominent Democratic leader and cousin of Circuit Judge Joseph C. Hutcheson, Jr., of the Court of Appeals for the Fifth Circuit. Judge Sterling Hutcheson sticks pretty close to his business and seldom comments on any subjects outside of his court.

In 1948 Judge Hutcheson fined the Gloucester County School Board and its superintendent $250 for contempt after he found they had failed to carry out an order to equalize the Negro public schools.[31] In 1956 and 1958, however, he refused to require Prince Edward County to desegregate. He criticized his judicial superiors mildly for failing to understand properly the special situation of rural Black Belt communities.

By the time schools opened in 1958 Virginia had worn out the last strand of its legal rope. Norfolk, Newport News, Arlington, Charlottesville, Alexandria, and Warren County all were under court order to admit Negroes to "white" schools. In some of these cities the litigation had taken three years. Although Arlington, Alexandria, and Newport News were able to delay once again the effective date of their respective orders, in the other cities the judges refused to back down.

As a final resort Governor Almond closed the schools to keep Negroes from being assigned. By the end of September about thirteen thousand children were locked out of nine schools in Norfolk, Charlottesville, and Warren County. Various substitute educational arrangements were made. In Warren County and Charlottesville private educational foundations operated classes for white students. In Norfolk the teachers, led by Superintendent H. E. Brewbaker, refused to participate in these *ad hoc* programs for fear that the parents would be misled into thinking their children were getting an adequate education.

Battle lines were quickly drawn. Committees to Preserve the Public Schools took over the leadership of the moderate forces.

[31] *Richmond Times-Dispatch,* November 14, 1956.

These committees drew the bulk of their membership from the city and suburban middle class, with their strength centered in the northern part of the state. Persons in urban communities knew that through judicious juggling of school lines and through use of pupil placement, they could contain integration so that it would make little difference to the actual operation of their schools. Though they favored segregation they were not prepared to give up so much to gain so little.

The Defenders of State Sovereignty and Individual Liberties headed the segregation forces, with the bulk of their strength coming from the southern part of the state. In rural areas where there is but a single high school and where the white-Negro ratio approaches 50 per cent, desegregation of the high school would make a much more significant change. But the Defenders were fighting to prevent integration not only in rural communities but in the cities as well.

The Virginia PTA Convention held in Richmond early in October provided the first battleground. Governor Almond made a fighting, uncompromising speech. He called on the people to rally behind the massive resistance program and to show their determination to avoid integration. He drew strong and loud applause. However, the moderates turned back an attempt by William I. McKendree, president of the Norfolk PTA Council and a charter member of the Defenders, to take over the state PTA organization. A resolution, endorsing the state's stand, was defeated by a tie vote and another, supporting local option, was carried 515 to 513.[32] (As an indication of how rapidly the political situation can change, the PTA a year later snowed under a segregation resolution.[33])

Six thousand Norfolk parents asked the governor to reopen the schools.[34] So did Superintendent Brewbaker and the teachers.[35]

---

[32] *Washington Post & Times Herald,* October 23, 1958.
[33] *Southern School News,* November 1959, p. 9.
[34] *New York Times,* October 18, 1958.
[35] *Washington Post & Times Herald,* October 23, 1958.

And so did many business leaders, concerned that the city might lose its major industry, the United States Naval installation, and the federal 1.3 million dollar annual subsidy to help educate the children of federal employees. The same kind of counterpressures were generated in Charlottesville and Arlington.

The pressure on the governor was not all one-sided. Senator Byrd himself called on the governor to stand fast. Southside Virginia reminded Almond of his campaign promises to stand by massive resistance. The Norfolk City Council, taking issue with the Norfolk School Board, called for a public referendum in which the voters were asked if they wanted the high schools to be reopened without state aid, with parents paying "a substantial tuition." By 3 to 2 the voters in the referendum advised against the opening of the schools under these terms. Each side hailed the vote as a victory: moderates charged the ballot had misled the voters, that many of the young parents recently arrived in the city had not been qualified to vote, and that even under these adverse circumstances the referendum indicated considerable community opposition to closing the schools. The segregationists claimed the referendum proved that the citizens of Norfolk were willing to do without public schools if necessary to stand up for their principles.

Governor Almond was in a tight spot. He had the strong backing of the Byrd organization, of Virginia's Fourth and Fifth Congressional Districts, embracing Southside, and had championed massive resistance in his campaign. On the other hand, though a convinced segregationist, he was an excellent lawyer with a profound respect for law and order. Segregationists pressed him to close the Negro high schools; under Virginia's laws the only schools shut were the "white" high schools. Almond refused.[36] At no time did he give the slightest encouragement to street agitators. He and all of Virginia's leaders, except for a few from the Southside, were determined to avoid violence. By the

[36] *Washington Post & Times Herald,* November 21, 1958.

fall of 1959 it was clear to the governor that further obstruction could only lead to chaos, yet to abandon massive resistance required some advanced political and legal preparations.

On November 11 a trial balloon was launched. James J. Kilpatrick, editor of the *Richmond News Leader,* confidant of the governor, and the most articulate defender of states' rights, told the Richmond Rotary Club: "I believe the time has come for new weapons and new tactics. I believe the laws we now have on the books have outlived their usefulness, and I believe that new laws must be devised—speedily devised—if educational opportunities are to be preserved and social calamity is to be avoided." Kilpatrick predicted that the courts would soon strike down the massive resistance and proposed that each community be given a free choice.

Senator Byrd insisted that the people of Virginia would never accept integrated schools anywhere in the state. But within a week every major metropolitan newspaper in Virginia was calling for a change in tactics. All had shifted their editorial policy to an endorsement of local option.[37]

The pressures on Almond intensified. Twenty-five of the top Virginia industrial leaders warned him of the damaging economic effect of massive resistance and threatened to withdraw their support if he continued to insist upon it.[38] Almond needed a graceful way to abandon the program he had so strongly supported in the recent campaign. The courts could give it to him.

The day after Kilpatrick made his speech, Governor Almond announced the appointment of a commission to study the anti-integration laws in the event they were declared illegal. He instructed the attorney general to arrange a test case before the Virginia Supreme Court of Appeals. "I fully realize," said Almond, "I am in the jaws of a vise, but I'm going to stay with the statutes of Virginia as long as they are vital." [39] Clearly, here

[37] *New York Times,* November 16, 1958.
[38] Paul Duke in *Wall Street Journal,* February 16, 1960.
[39] *New York Times,* November 13, 1958.

was an invitation to the judges to help Virginia get out of the vise, and incidentally to extricate Almond.

While the governor was arranging for the massive resistance laws to be challenged before the state supreme court, numerous white children and their parents filed suit in the federal district court attacking the massive resistance program.

By a "coincidence," the Virginia Supreme Court of Appeals and the United States special three-man district court (Circuit Judges Sobeloff and Haynsworth and District Judge Hoffman) handed down their decisions on January 19. Both declared Virginia's school-closing laws unconstitutional.

The governor had his "out," but he found it emotionally difficult nonetheless to jettison massive resistance. The day after the courts declared the Commonwealth's massive resistance program unconstitutional, Almond made a state-wide radio address, still talking the language of defiance. But Almond explained later: "I was tired, harassed, and under strain, and I wanted to reassure the people that I was doing all that I could, consistent with honor and law, to avoid that which I then considered, and now consider, a calamity. My words inadvertently gave the impression that I knew of some way to prevent any mixing of the races in the public schools, when nothing of the sort was possible." [40]

The governor called the General Assembly into emergency session. He proposed that the state repeal its massive resistance program, that compulsory attendance laws be abolished, that $250 tuition grants be made to any parent who wished to transfer his child from a public integrated school to a private one, and that a forty-man commission be created to study future policy.

The embittered core of segregationists fought back with nothing to offer except outright defiance of federal courts and complete abandonment of public schools. The legislature, however, supported Almond. In Norfolk, with its large sprinkling of northerners, and in Arlington and Alexandria in the shadow of the

[40] Quoted by Virginius Dabney, "Next in the South's Schools," *U. S. News & World Report*, January 18, 1960, p. 93.

nation's capitol, the old order passed quickly and quietly. A few mopping-up injunctions were required to prevent the Norfolk City Council from cutting off funds for the about-to-be-integrated high schools, but an era of token integration had begun.

Only in Prince Edward County have Virginians chosen to abandon public education rather than to comply with a court desegregation order. This rural county, of which the county seat is appropriately called Farmville, consists of fifteen thousand Negroes and fifteen thousand whites, including Robert B. Crawford, president of the Virginia Defenders.

Prince Edward was one of the original cases heard by the Supreme Court. In 1955, immediately after the Supreme Court ruled that segregation is unconstitutional, the county fathers created a private school system ready to be activated if integration could not be avoided. The board of supervisors, which supplies the funds for local schools, started to finance schools on a month-to-month basis; public school teachers were signed up by the private Prince Edward Educational Corporation; textbooks and desks were purchased; lodge halls and churches were made ready to be converted into classrooms; and $300,000 was pledged to support these schools.

The chance that Prince Edward would be compelled to desegregate had seemed remote in 1955, for Prince Edward "stood behind the barricade of a state-wide massive resistance." Judge Hutcheson, who had jurisdiction over the school suit, appeared to believe that the time had not yet arrived for integration to begin and that it would not arrive soon. It seemed unlikely, moreover, that the NAACP would force a showdown in Prince Edward County. But in the spring of 1956, five years after the suit had been started, the Negroes of Prince Edward, speaking through the plaintiffs who represented them, asked Judge Hutcheson to fix a date by which Prince Edward should begin to desegregate. Nine months later Judge Hutcheson ruled that "in the present state of unrest and racial tension in the county it would be unwise to attempt to force a change. . . . The passage of time with apparent inaction on the part of the defendants of itself does not necessarily show non-compliance. . . . [By] submitting the usual budget . . . [they] have done all that reasonably could be required of them." [41]

Judge Hutcheson's language forced the NAACP to appeal, for it would be a dangerous precedent that unrest and racial tension justified a school board in doing no more than submitting budgets to continue segregation. The court of appeals reversed Judge Hutcheson and ordered him to set a time limit. On August 4, 1958, he did—1965, ten years from the 1955 Brown decision, fourteen years after the original complaint, seven more years from the time of the hearing. His ruling, furthermore, left the way open for the date to be extended beyond 1965. [42]

In the spring of 1959 the court of appeals (Soper, Haynsworth, and Roby C. Thompson) again reversed Judge Hutcheson. It said: "The proceedings of the District Court . . . and the total inaction of the School Board speak so loudly that no argument is needed to show that the last delaying order of the District Judge cannot be approved, and that it has become necessary for this Court to give specific directions as to what must be done." [43] The court directed Hutcheson to order the school board to permit—immediately—the entrance of qualified Negroes into the "white" high schools in the school term beginning September 1959. Applications for grade schools were to be considered, but the court of appeals did not order integration at this level to begin, other than "at the earliest practical date."

The court of appeals' determined stand left Prince Edward with little choice. Though they might have used pupil placement to gain additional time, it was clear from the tone of the court of appeals' opinion that the circuit judges were in no mood for delay. Prince Edward closed its public schools.

Some white citizens of Prince Edward were deeply opposed to

[41] *Davis v. School Board of Prince Edward County*, 2 RRLR 341 at 347 (1957). See also Paul Duke, *The Wall Street Journal*, December 1, 1959, and Walter F. Murphy, "Private Education with Public Funds," *Journal of Politics*, vol. 20, 1958, pp. 635-654.

[42] *Allen v. Prince Edward*, 3 RRLR 964 (1958).

[43] *Allen v. Prince Edward*, 4 RRLR 298 at 300 (1959).

the closing of their public schools. Even a member of the school board admitted privately that the two high and six elementary schools operated by the private foundation cannot give students an education comparable to that of the public schools.[44] He dares not speak out publicly even now. He hopes that in time the crippling of the community which will result from the lack of educated citizenry will generate the same support for token integration in Prince Edward that it has in other more metropolitan communities. It seems unlikely, despite his hope, that Prince Edward's citizens will respond to the closing of their public schools as have those in the larger cities. Prince Edward can do what a larger city cannot do. The number of white children to be educated is relatively small, only around 1500. Since the public schools which Prince Edward formerly operated were modest in their educational standards, its private schools suffer only slightly by comparison. In the setting of urban communities, these private schools might be considered makeshift, but not so in Prince Edward.[45]

In Prince Edward, segregationist political pressure is so strong that unless the federal judiciary intervenes it is unlikely that the public school system will be restored. There is a serious constitutional doubt that Virginia can permit one of its counties to abandon public education while students in other counties are provided with tax-supported institutions. Even if the federal judges support the contentions of the Negro paintiffs, there is such a wide gulf in Prince Edward between the requirements of the law and the balance of political forces that it is doubtful whether antisegregation judicial decrees could have any major impact.

Judges can do much to speed desegregation, but they need political support from the White House, the State House, or the City Hall. Unless they have this backing they will not, perhaps cannot, desegregate the schools. This is the lesson of Prince Edward.

[44] Private Interview.
[45] *Richmond News Leader,* February 8, 1960.

8 ✳ Louisiana — The Last Step Before Secession

By the spring of 1960, after eight years of litigation, Judge J. Skelly Wright realized that it was up to him to take the Orleans Parish School Board off the spot.[1] He ordered the board to desegregate the first grade in the fall of 1960. But he did not face the crisis alone: New Orleans was not to be another Little Rock with a lonely judge, a few Negro school children, and an embattled school board forced to face angry segregationists without civic support or federal assistance.

"Several years ago," said Judge Wright, "I was almost like a voice crying in the wilderness. Today we have support, substantial support, among the responsible people here in the city. Lots of people don't like what I have done, but more and more are willing to understand that it is something we must do."[2] He was right. No school board had fought more determinedly to retain segregation than had the Orleans Parish board: they had filed thirty-six delaying motions. But after the judge's integration order became final, four of the five elected members recognized, as Board Chairman Lloyd J. Rittiner said, "We must yield as gracefully as is possible."[3] Only one member, Emile A. Wagner,

[1] *Wall Street Journal*, November 16, 1960.
[2] *Ibid.*
[3] *New York Times*, August 24, 1960.

221

Jr., an arch-segregationist, continued to argue "integration as required by Judge Wright would be an evil far worse than closing the schools." [4]

The school board was not alone in accepting defeat. Mayor de Lesseps S. Morrison and the responsible citizenry backed the board, as was convincingly demonstrated just a few days before desegregation was inaugurated. Matthew R. Sutherland, a moderate member of the school board, decisively defeated three other candidates, one of whom Wagner endorsed. Sutherland made no effort to hide his position: he promised to comply with Judge Wright's order.[5]

Unlike those in Little Rock, moderates in New Orleans had federal support. President Eisenhower had remained aloof, even when the entire state legislature and governor defied the federal courts, but moderates were convinced that when President Kennedy took office this failure of Presidential leadership would be remedied. And from the very outset of the New Orleans crisis, President Eisenhower's Attorney General had been an active participant. This time Attorney General Rogers did not give segregationists a chance to use violence as an excuse for interfering with desegregation or any encouragement that the Department of Justice would remain passive. He warned: "Any resistance, or obstruction or interference with federal court orders will be in violation of federal law." [6] And he deployed a large force of federal marshals "ready to co-operate fully with city police." [7]

Moderates also had the support of the Roman Catholic Church, the Church to which more than half of the white citizens of the city belong. At the time of the crisis Archbishop Joseph Francis Rummel was ill and parochial schools did not integrate as expected, but there was no doubt of the Archbishop's position. For a majority of the white citizens of New Orleans to insist on segregation was to insist, not merely on illegal conduct,

[4] *New York Times,* August 30, 1960.
[5] *Southern School News,* December 1960, p. 9.
[6] *New Orleans Times-Picayune,* November 13, 1960.
[7] *Ibid.*

but also on behavior condemned by their church. Backed by the mayor, the responsible citizens, the Department of Justice, and the federal courts, the school authorities prepared to make the transition from total segregation to token integration, the first city to do so in the Deep South.

Moderates may have controlled New Orleans, but they did not control the state government. In Baton Rouge, Governor Jimmie H. Davis, of ballad-singing fame, who had defeated New Orleans Mayor Morrison in a run-off primary in January 1960, had yet to make his move. Davis had opposed Louisiana's most extreme segregationists in the first primary, but he had done so on a platform promise of keeping public schools open and segregated, even if he had to go to jail for doing so. Attorney General Jack P. F. Gremillion, who was fond of saying that he was a descendant of General Stonewall Jackson, announced he was prepared "to stand like a stone wall" to defend segregation.[8] State Superintendent of Education Shelby M. Jackson insisted that the Orleans Parish School Board had no legal obligation to obey Judge Wright. Legislative leaders from rural northern Louisiana segregation country demanded that the governor and other state officials act to prevent New Orleans from desegregating.

Segregationists elsewhere had already used every known device to circumvent injunctions and none of them had been able to prevent a city from complying with a judicial decree. Judge Wright was ready to counter any move they might make and he had the support of two other federal judges. Chief Judge Rives of the court of appeals and Chief Judge Christenberry of the district court were standing by in the event a three-judge court might be needed to counter an attempt to enforce segregation laws. The intervention of state authorities might cause disorder, and perhaps frustrate desegregation momentarily, but it did not have the slightest chance of forcing reversal of Judge Wright's

---

[8] *New Orleans Times-Picayune,* December 19, 1960. *See also* Statement by Governor, August 17, 1960; Open Letter from Attorney General; *Louisiana v. Orleans Parish,* all cited in 5 RRLR 659–666 (1960).

decree or of keeping the Orleans Parish School Board from complying with it.

The hopelessness of the cause was apparent to all except the segregationists themselves. They were so opposed to integration, so convinced of the rightness of their crusade, and so isolated from the countercurrents that they fought on undeterred by the inevitability of defeat. The Second Battle of New Orleans, like the First, in 1815, was fought after the War was over. Nonetheless, it was to be a hard-fought battle.

The governor's first move was easily countered. Just before schools opened, Davis invoked a recently enacted state law to take control of the schools of Orleans Parish. He directed the Superintendent of the Orleans Parish Schools, James F. Redmond, to ignore Judge Wright's order and open schools without desegregating the first grade. Davis had in reserve another law authorizing him to close the schools, but he later admitted that closing schools would not preserve segregation. Attorney General Gremillion secured from a Louisiana state judge an injunction which ordered the Orleans Parish board, despite Judge Wright's injunction, to comply with the segregation laws.

At the request of the NAACP, Judge Wright ordered Governor Davis and other state officials "to show cause" why they should not be enjoined from interfering with the Orleans Parish School Board. The NAACP's request was seconded by thirty-one white parents who, although objecting to integration, objected even more to state interference with the opening and operation of their public schools.

Late in August a three-judge court, Rives, Christenberry, and Wright, assembled to hear the arguments. Attorney General Gremillion and his assistants were present; Governor Davis was not. Two deputy United States marshals reported they had delivered summonses to various employees of the governor, but the governor himself had eluded them. Gremillion contended that the governor had no obligation to appear; Chief Judge Rives cut off the discussion of the matter by ruling that Governor Davis was "in default," but that his personal presence was not needed.

The court put aside for the moment Gremillion's dismissal motions, and instructed Charles Richards, attorney for the thirty-one white parents, to proceed. To save time, Chief Judge Rives told Richards to place certain facts in the record by affidavit rather than call witnesses and Gremillion protested—he had not received a copy of the affidavit and, since he was entitled to notice, he said, he asked for a five-day postponement. Judge Rives read quietly from the rules of federal procedure, which gave the court discretion to dispense with calling of witnesses, and then overruled Gremillion's motion.

"You may proceed, Mr. Richards," Chief Judge Rives said.

Gremillion would not be silenced; he declared loudly, "I don't consider this justice. I demand my constitutional rights. This court is running roughshod over us."

"You may reserve your objections and I hope you will do it in a manner respectful to this court," said Chief Judge Rives, mildly, but with obvious irritation.

Gremillion sat down, muttering in an audible tone about "justice," "the Constitution," and "den of iniquity."

As Richards started to read Gremillion jumped to his feet, strode down the aisle and out of the door, shouting as he went: "This is a kangaroo court."

For a moment there was silence in the courtroom. Then Gremillion's chief assistant got to his feet: "Since I cannot proceed in the absence of my principal, I respectfully ask the court's permission to withdraw."

Judge Rives assented. The attorney general's aides picked up their papers and left. The commotion in the courtroom quieted down while Richards introduced his affidavit and made a brief speech for his clients. His clients, he said, were asking the court either to suspend or modify Judge Wright's ruling. If the court would not do this, then his clients felt the court should prevent state officials from closing schools or from otherwise interfering with the school board.

Thurgood Marshall, who during the New Orleans crisis kept a standing airline reservation so he could attend all judicial proceedings, was there to present the arguments: "This is no longer a case of Negro children seeking their constitutional right. This is now a challenge of the officials of the State of Louisiana to the sovereignty of the United States. The duty of this court is clear."

Judge Rives asked, "Is there any other evidence to be introduced?"

There was no answer.

"Let the record show," Judge Rives said, "that the court has called for evidence from the defense in open court and none is offered." [9]

Five days later the court handed down its ruling. Not only did the judges order Davis to return control of the schools to the school board, but they declared seven state laws unconstitutional, including laws purporting to authorize the governor to close schools. Further, the judges ordered Davis and other state officials not to take "any action which would deny school books, school lunches and school funds to any school because of desegregation." [10]

The federal jurists had checkmated every technique segregationists had employed in the six years since the Brown decision. What had taken two years for Little Rock moderates to litigate, was accomplished in New Orleans in ten days.

There was nothing left to decide—so it seemed. Judge Wright had told the Orleans Parish board to desegregate. He and his fellow jurists, in effect, had ordered state officials, as one might say in New Orleans, to keep their "cotton-picking hands" off the New Orleans schools. Among those restrained by this and subsequent federal injunctions were: the governor, the lieutenant governor, the attorney general, the state superintendent of education,

[9] *New York Times,* August 27, 1960.
[10] *Bush v. Orleans Parish School Board,* and *Williams v. Davis,* 5 RRLR 666 (1960).

the state board of education, the Orleans Parish School Board, the state treasurer, the state adjutant general, the superintendent of the state police, the district attorneys of all judicial districts of Louisiana, all the sheriffs, all chiefs of police, all mayors, and eventually even the state legislature.

And this was not all. Judges Rives, Christenberry, and Wright cited Gremillion for his contemptuous conduct. A few weeks later Federal District Judge Edwin F. Hunter heard the evidence and told Gremillion he was entitled to fight hard but not "out of bounds." [11] He sentenced Gremillion to sixty days, but waived the sentence and put him on eighteen months' probation. Gremillion sobbed with joy at his close escape from prison.

Attorney General Gremillion announced that Louisiana had reached the end of its legal strategy. Governor Davis was silent. He had insisted that the federal injunction was not binding on him, yet he seemed unwilling to challenge it and to take advantage of the opportunity to live up to his campaign promise of going to jail. He continued to elude federal marshals. By the time the New Orleans crisis was over, Davis's office was decorated with plastic-covered federal subpoenas, restraining orders, and injunctions. Federal marshals, denied admission to see the governor, had left their orders with state employees, who refused to touch but neatly covered them with clear plastic.

By this time schools were to open. The four moderate members of the school board went to see Judge Wright in his chambers. They told him that they were prepared to desegregate, but because of the state's interference they had not been able to make preparations. They asked the judge if he would postpone the effective date of his decree until November 14, the beginning of the second quarter. Judge Wright, convinced the board members were acting in good faith, consulted with the attorneys for the negro plaintiffs, and over their objections granted the board's request.[12]

[11] *New York Times,* October 8, 1960. Contempt citation, 5 RRLR 668 (1960).

[12] *Bush v. Orleans,* 5 RRLR 669 (1960).

Judge Wright and the school board had made a strategic error. Governor Davis had saved face by going through the motions of interfering with Orleans Parish. If Judge Wright had insisted on immediate desegregation, the deed would have been done before the segregationists reorganized. But at the time, another short postponement seemed unimportant. The segregationist attorney for the school board resigned in disgust, a more moderate lawyer was chosen, and Superintendent Redmond made quiet preparations.

The delay in the execution of the New Orleans desegregation program had exposed Governor Davis to relentless segregationist pressures. For a while he resisted, and then ten days before the second quarter, the governor called the Louisiana legislature into special session.

One hundred and forty lawmakers converged on Baton Rouge; their mission, to prevent New Orleans from complying with Judge Wright's integration order; their tactics, to "interpose" the legislature between the federal courts and the school board; their hope, that Judge Wright would not dare to move against the entire legislature.

The legislators adopted a package of twenty-nine segregation laws that purported to strip the Orleans Parish board of all authority over New Orleans schools and to transfer control to an eight-man legislative committee. State police were instructed to arrest any federal marshal or federal judge who tried to prevent the committee from operating segregated schools.

Four days before desegregation was to begin, the legislative committee assembled in the school board's offices and went through the formality of taking charge of New Orleans' 121 schools. The committee rehired Superintendent Redmond and instructed him to open schools in compliance with the newly enacted segregation laws. Representative Risley C. Triche, chairman of the committee, announced: "We're going to operate the schools the same on Monday as they are operating today, with the same students assigned to the same schools with the same teachers. There will be no change. . . . We know of no transfer of students nor requests for transfer which have been approved." [13]

To this moment the Department of Justice had refrained from actively entering the case. Minutes after the legislative committee adjourned, United States Attorney M. Hepburn Many filed the first of his many motions "to maintain and preserve the due administration of justice and integrity of the judicial process of the United States." Many was retained in his position by Attorney General Robert F. Kennedy over the protest of Senator Allen J. Ellender of Louisiana. Senator Ellender acknowledged that he had voted to confirm Many in 1957. He said, "He came highly recommended. I didn't know he was going to turn coattail." [14] After Attorney General Kennedy took charge of the Department of Justice, the Attorney General himself, via the long-distance telephone, participated in the legal strategy. [15]

Many's first move was to ask Judge Wright for an order restraining Louisiana police from interfering with the federal marshals assigned to carry out the court's orders. At the same time Attorney Richards, speaking in behalf of the white parents, asked Judge Wright to prevent state officials from enforcing the recently enacted segregation laws. The NAACP did not file its motion for an injunction until several days later.

Ordinarily, federal judges will not restrain the enforcement of state laws until there is time for a hearing before a three-judge court. But this was an emergency. Before a three-judge court could have held a hearing, November 14 would have passed and segregationists would be able, by passing new unconstitutional laws, to postpone desegregation once again.

Judge Wright was just as bold in behalf of the Constitution as his opponents were in behalf of segregation. He issued immediate orders restraining the governor, the state superintendent of education, all state police, sheriffs, and local officials, the legislative

[13] *New York Times,* November 11, 1960.
[14] *Southern School News,* March 1961, p. 9.
[15] *Wall Street Journal,* March 6, 1961.

committee, and, for good measure, any others who might act in concert with them. He told them to cease enforcing state segregation laws and to cease interfering with the Orleans Parish board until a three-judge court could be assembled to determine if these restraining orders should be rescinded or made permanent.

That night the school board, all but Wagner, met. Their new attorney, Samuel I. Rosenberg, told them, "You have absolutely no alternative except to comply," [16] and Board President Rittiner announced that five of the 137 Negro children who had applied for a transfer to schools nearest their homes would be allowed to attend two schools heretofore reserved for white children. Judge Wright's order had left room for the board to apply pupil-placement procedures. Segregationists were unable to prevent token integration, but for the time being their intense opposition forestalled litigation on the question whether the board had properly applied pupil placement. Rittiner refused to make public the names of the children or of the schools to which they were assigned.

The angry legislators returned to Baton Rouge next day for an emergency Sunday session. Despite the pleas of Mayor Morrison and most of the New Orleans delegation, the aroused lawmakers, in the name of the state's rights, and squarely in the face of federal authority, once again seized control of the New Orleans schools. In six hours, three new segregation bills were introduced, adopted, and signed into law. Some of the legislators did not even have time to read the bills they voted for. As Senator French Jordan said at a later date with respect to other segregation legislation, "I don't know what we are fixing to do, but we *are* fixing to do something and I'm going to be for it." [17]

What the legislature was fixing to do, since Judge Wright had ordered its committee to leave the Orleans Parish schools alone, was to have the entire legislature serve as the school board for Orleans Parish. Legislative sergeants-at-arms were instructed "to

[16] *New Orleans Times-Picayune*, November 13, 1960.
[17] *New Orleans Times-Picayune*, December 1, 1960.

repair to all public schools in the parish of Orleans where intruders have ordered the unlawful transfer of pupils from one school to another" and to arrest these intruders if they tried to carry out Judge Wright's instructions. For good measure, the legislature "fired" Superintendent Redmond and Attorney Rosenberg and declared Monday a state-wide holiday. By declaring Monday a school holiday the legislature sought both to prevent the Orleans Parish board from executing its desegregation program and to support State Superintendent Jackson. The day before, Jackson was served a copy of Judge Wright's order not to interfere, and had declared Monday a holiday. For this he was subsequently cited for contempt. His trial was postponed until after the crisis.

At 9:00 P.M., twelve hours before desegregation was scheduled to take place under Judge Wright's injunction, the legislators adjourned. Judge Wright had moved against the eight-man legislative committee. Would he move against the entire legislature? It did not take long to find out.

At 9:45 P.M. Sunday night, on motion of the Department of Justice and the Orleans Parish board, Judge Wright ordered "the Legislature of the State of Louisiana, and the individual members thereof, and their agents" to make no attempt to enforce the laws passed that day and not to take "any other action interfering with or circumventing the orders of this court." [18]

The legislature had done its best; Judge Wright had done more. For the first time a federal judge had addressed a restraining order to an entire state legislature. But then never before, at least not since the Civil War, had any legislature ever so defied a federal judge.

On Monday morning four little girls—the parents of the fifth decided at the last moment to keep their child in her segregated school—under escort of United States marshals, transferred to their new schools; three to McDonogh Number 19,[19] and one to

[18] *New Orleans Times-Picayune,* November 14, 1960.
[19] There are over twenty New Orleans schools named after John McDonogh, an early nineteenth-century philanthropist who gave much of

Frantz. Since segregationists did not know which schools were
to be desegregated, they were only able to assemble a small
jeering crowd of white mothers to greet the children. There was
relatively little commotion.

Desegregation had come to New Orleans and to the Deep
South. There had been little trouble. Mayor Morrison, school
authorities, Judge Wright, and the nation relaxed. The moment
of action had come and gone. The worst appeared to be over.

The worst would have been over if the Louisiana lawmakers
had gone home. But they would not. Judge Wright had ordered
them to "make no attempt" and not to take "any other action
interfering with or circumventing" the orders of his court. The
legislators proceeded as if such an order had never been issued.
Since they refused to question their first premise—segregation
laws are constitutional—to the legislators the federal judges who
ordered desegregation were obviously usurpers whose orders
were not entitled to respect. The legislators considered themselves courageous and dedicated defenders of home and hearth,
champions of "the people" against "atheistic Communists" and
their "dupes."

During the next several weeks the lawmakers adopted one
plan after another, each openly designed to preserve segregation,
each in clear conflict with the Constitution of the United States,
each a violation of Judge Wright's restraining order, each quickly
set aside by the federal courts.

The legislature made seven attempts to oust the four moderate
school board members; it created substitute school boards for
Orleans Parish; it again "fired" Superintendent Redmond and
Attorney Rosenberg, substituting Gremillion as the attorney for
the Orleans Parish schools, a move the federal jurists tagged as
"one of the Legislature's less sophisticated attempts to preserve
racial discrimination in the public schools of New Orleans"; [20] it

---

his fortune to establish schools and who freed his slaves early in the
century.

[20] *Orleans Parish v. Bush; United States v. Louisiana,* 5 RRLR 1026
(1960).

withheld funds from Orleans Parish; it ordered banks to refuse to honor checks drawn by the school board; it withheld the paychecks of the teachers and employees in the two desegregated schools. The Louisiana legislature enacted over forty laws, all set aside as unconstitutional by the federal jurists.

In order to preclude a federal suit, the legislators tried to take advantage of the fact that ordinarily federal district judges will not take jurisdiction over a case once it has been initiated in a state court. Such a case could be carried to the federal courts only if it were appealed up through the Louisiana judicial hierarchy to the Supreme Court of the United States. If both the plaintiff and the defendant were segregationists, and neither appealed, the decision of the Louisiana jurists would be final.

To effect this, the legislature created a new school board of five members for Orleans Parish. The governor was to appoint the board members to serve until 1962 elections. Before he could act, George L. Singelmann, an official of the Citizens Council of Greater New Orleans and an associate of Leander H. Perez, the state's leading segregationist, asked State Judge Fred S. LeBlanc to enjoin the governor from appointing the board members. Judge LeBlanc issued the order. An appeal was hurriedly arranged to carry the issue to the Louisiana Supreme Court, a court almost as much under the control of segregationists as the Louisiana legislature. The Louisiana Supreme Court sustained the law.[21]

The strategy did not work. The Department of Justice and the regularly elected school board challenged it before the federal courts, pointing out that the Louisiana suit was not a new proceeding; it was merely the thirty-eighth round in the eight-year-old Bush Case which had long been within the jurisdiction of the federal district court. Furthermore, under established precedents federal courts have full authority to preserve their jurisdiction and to prevent state judges from undermining federal injunctions.

[21] *New Orleans Times-Picayune,* December 16, 1960.

Once again Judges Rives, Christenberry, and Wright refused to allow the evasion of the purpose of law behind a procedural maze.

Chief Judge Rives, writing for the court, said that ordinarily the creation of a new school board would be insulated from federal judicial review. But "the present acts . . . are no different in kind, or in purpose, from [the others already declared unconstitutional.] . . . The plain object of the measures is to frustrate the Orleans Parish School Board in its effort to comply with this court's orders. . . . For obeying the constitutional mandate and the orders of this Court, the board brought on itself the official wrath of Louisiana. Despite reiterated injunctions expressly prohibiting them from interfering . . . the members of the Legislature, already called into special, now apparently continuous session, took every conceivable step to subvert the announced intention of the local School Board and defy the orders of this court. . . . Every law or resolution of the Legislature, every act of the Executive, which seeks to subvert the enjoyment of this right [equality of opportunity for education through access to nonsegregated public schools] is unconstitutional and null and void." [22]

The Louisiana legislature based its stand squarely on the doctrine of "interposition," on the view that the legislature had interposed its authority between the usurping federal courts and the "people" and by so doing had relieved any person from any obligation to obey the offending federal injunctions. In fact, the Louisiana lawmakers contended that all persons in the state had a positive obligation to refuse to obey Judge Wright's integration decree or any of the other desegregation orders issued by the district court.

Not since the days of John C. Calhoun and the Civil War have many taken seriously the doctrine of "interposition." Southern segregationists had been talking about "interposition" since the 1954 Supreme Court decision, but federal judges con-

[22] *Orleans Parish v. Bush; United States v. Louisiana,* 5 RRLR 1023 (1960).

sidered such resolutions as "escape valves through which the legislators blew off steam to relieve their tensions." [23]

In the face of the Louisiana legislators' insistence that interposition justified their conduct, Judges Rives, Christenberry, and Wright in a strongly worded opinion stated: "Interposition is not a constitutional doctrine. If taken seriously, it is illegal defiance of constitutional authority." Quoting from Chief Justice John Marshall, the federal jurists said: "If the legislature of the several states may, at will, annul the judgments of the courts of the United States, and destroy the right acquired under these judgments, the Constitution itself becomes a solemn mockery and the Nation is deprived of its own tribunals." [24]

The Supreme Court could not be expected to repudiate the district court and endorse "interposition," a doctrine completely destructive of the federal union. Gremillion, nevertheless, appealed for a stay. At the request of Solicitor General Rankin, a prompt, brief, but unequivocal opinion of the Court endorsed the ruling of the district judge. Interposition is "without substance," it said, and never has been a legal doctrine.[25]

The complete repudiation of the doctrine of interposition, and the total rejection of their schemes, did not daunt the Louisiana lawmakers. Representative Ford E. Stinson, a fervid segregationist, called the Court's ruling "claptrap." "We are only saved," he said, "from the hands of these demagogues by the hand of the Lord when he takes them." He called for "full steam ahead, let's keep going." [26]

And so the legislature went ahead in the face of the federal judges' injunctions. They courted contempt citations joyfully. Some of the more extreme and politically ambitious wanted to go to jail. Judge Wright and his fellow jurists refused to be provoked. The Department of Justice did bring contempt charges

[23] *Shuttlesworth v. Birmingham,* 3 RRLR 425 at 431 (1958).
[24] *Orleans Parish v. Bush; United States v. Louisiana,* 5 RRLR 1008 (1960).
[25] *Bush v. New Orleans,* 364 U.S. 500 (1960).
[26] *New Orleans Times-Picayune,* December 1, 1960.

against the presiding officers of the two chambers, and Superintendent Jackson, who had refused to sign paychecks for
teachers and employees of the two desegregated schools. And in
its first public civil rights move the Kennedy Administration ex-
panded these charges.[27] Despite deliberate disobedience of the
orders of the court, however, the judges refrained from moving
against the legislators.

Why did the Department of Justice and the federal judges
allow the Louisiana legislators to go unpunished? In part because of the questionable legality of such a move. Federal judges
may prevent the enforcement of unconstitutional state laws and
restrain those who try to enforce such laws, but whether judges
have the authority to punish legislators for passing laws, however unconstitutional, is a question of a different order. Even if
the authority to do so were unquestioned, politically it would
have been undesirable. Moreover, it was unnecessary. Judge
Wright and his brethren calmly set aside each segregation law
the legislature adopted, and restrained the agents from trying to
enforce these laws.

United States Congressman Otto Passman came home from
Washington to address the Louisiana legislature about the "outrageous" action of the federal judges. He indignantly told the
lawmakers: "My friends, it is not pleasant to contemplate, but
it appears to be true that at least some federal judges take their
orders directly from the United States Supreme Court. . . ." [28]
No one could quarrel with the accuracy of Congressman Passman's statement.

Frustrated by federal judges, the angry legislators gave vent
to their feelings with strong accusations against the government
of the United States. Judge Wright was their primàry target, but
Mayor Morrison and the Orleans Parish school officials were
not far behind.

The legislators condemned the New Orleans police; the Methodist Church and "integrationists ministers"; "un-American"

[27] *New York Times,* February 17, 1961.
[28] *New Orleans Times-Picayune,* November 19, 1960.

professors at Louisiana State University; and "the filthy, lying one-way newspaper that's for integration, the *Times-Picayune*." The legislators said they were depriving teachers assigned to the two desegregated schools of their salaries because, by refusing to leave their posts, they were "fighting this Legislature and knowingly implementing the integration of schools." The Whitney National Bank ceased to be a state fiscal agent after it honored a check drawn by the Orleans Parish School Board. The Joint Legislative Committee on Un-American Activities investigated the professors at Louisiana State University, especially Professor Waldo F. McNeir, who had written a letter to his state senator charging that the segregation laws enacted by the legislature were a "disgrace and a national scandal." Said one legislator: "By what right does an LSU Professor dare to attack the character and intentions of the Legislature?" [29]

Legislators called for: an investigation of "un-American" parents who refused to boycott the schools, the impeachment of the Supreme Court, the imprisonment of Judge Wright, the dismissal of all teachers "not loyal to the American Way" of segregation. President-elect Kennedy was condemned for his refusal to repudiate Judge Wright or to disown the Supreme Court. The Louisiana House of Representatives charged that every officer of the federal executive and judicial branches, including President Eisenhower, had made "common camp with the atheistic communist menace," but the Senate, after a hard debate and by a close margin, amended these charges to cover only "some" federal judges and "some" federal executive officials.[30]

Privately, many of the legislators confessed a fear that the legislature was "going too far," and by its conduct, enacted under the scrutiny of television cameras, was bringing discredit to the state.[31] Many were less emotionally aroused than they publicly proclaimed, but many lawmakers, especially those from rural and northern Louisiana, were afraid their political

[29] *New Orleans Times-Picayune*, December 14, 1960.
[30] *New Orleans Times-Picayune*, November 24, 1960.
[31] *New Orleans Times-Picayune*, November 13, 1960.

careers might be jeopardized if they allowed any other legislator to appear to be more dedicated to the preservation of segregation than they. After one representative announced he was "one hundred per cent for segregation," another announced he was "a million per cent" loyal.[32] Even moderates from New Orleans who were working behind the headlines to persuade the governor to abandon his crusade voted for many of the segregation measures.

United States Senator Russell Long, in his address to the legislature, made common cause with his fellow Louisianians and was loud in his denunciations of Judge Wright and the Supreme Court. But he did point to some political facts. He explained to the segregationists that they had the votes to push anything they wished through the Louisiana legislature, but they were outnumbered in Congress. He explained that the civil rights forces were getting stronger, and that too extreme conduct by the state legislature might react adversely, perhaps even provoking Congress to enact punitive legislation. The only way Louisiana could maintain segregation, he stated, would be to abolish the public schools.

Nor could Senator Long give his friends any hope that they would be able to alter the character of the federal judiciary. True, he would have some influence, he said, in filling future federal judicial appointments in Louisiana [more so under a Democratic President than a Republican President], but he told the lawmakers "any judge absolutely committed to segregation would have difficulty being confirmed by the Senate."

Senator Long's comments were received in silent coolness by the legislature. "Maybe you men don't want to hear the truth," [33] he said.

During the first week of desegregation, a thousand high school students responded to the legislature's plea for public demonstrations by racing through New Orleans' streets. An application of water by the fire department and two hundred arrests by the police, combined with a firm hand by school authorities, quickly

[32] *Ibid.*
[33] *New Orleans Times-Picayune,* November 17, 1960.

restored order. Police Superintendent Joseph I. Giarrusso commented after the riots: "The people who inaugurated this are conspicuous with their absence at the scene today." [34]

New Orleans police and federal marshals protected the school children and put down riots; they were unable to prevent minor destruction of property like the throwing of rocks through windows, and they permitted agitators to assemble along the routes to the two schools. Every morning as the children went to class, angry white mothers—some police called them the "cheering section"—howled and jeered. Although Judge Wright had profited from the experiences of other cities by calling for desegregation to begin with the first grade, the school board had made the mistake of picking two schools in "blue-collar" neighborhoods. A highly placed official in the Department of Justice in the Kennedy Administration charged: "The worst possible schools were selected to start desegregation. They were in the poorest neighborhoods where bad race relations resulted partly from Negroes displacing white workers by working at lower pay. By having only two desegregated schools, extreme elements could easily focus their hate and pressure tactics; if desegregation had been ordered throughout the school system such tactics would have been much more difficult and much less effective." [35] In New Orleans residential segregation is not so complete as in northern cities, and if the board had chosen schools in middle-class neighborhoods, white mothers might not have resorted to street brawling. Mayor Morrison charged that a desire for publicity contributed to the continuance of these demonstrations. The demonstrators rushed home to see themselves on television, and in the legislature too the oration always grew more intense when the cameras were on. Once again the television cameras portrayed the moving contrast between the dignity of the Negro children and that of their tormentors.

The legislature did not openly call for violence. In fact, after some delay and much debate, it even adopted a resolution de-

[34] *New Orleans Times-Picayune,* November 17, 1960.
[35] *The Wall Street Journal,* March 6, 1961.

ploring violence. Moreover, overt violence and rioting were of little significance in New Orleans. Segregationists placed primary reliance on the boycott.

Led by the legislature, the segregationists "encouraged" parents to withdraw their children from the two desegregated schools. The legislature inserted in New Orleans newspapers an advertisement, at public expense, addressed "To the Parents of the Students Enrolled at McDonogh No. 19 and Frantz" commending them for "their courageous stand against the forces of integration" and for their "positive action of removing their children from said schools." The legislature resolved "To hereby urge these parents . . . to continue their courageous stand and refrain from attendance at said schools." [36]

When Dr. Emmett Erwin, chairman of the New Orleans Citizens Council, led a delegation of boycotting parents to the capital at Baton Rouge—they carried a coffin containing a blackened effigy of Judge Wright—the Louisiana House of Representatives responded with a standing ovation.[37]

Leander H. Perez, a power behind the scenes in the Louisiana legislature, gave up his position as District Attorney of St. Bernard and Plaquemines Parishes—his son took his job—to lead the boycott. "Don't wait for your daughter to be raped by these Congolese. Don't wait until the burr-heads are forced into your schools. Do something about it now," he urged.[38] A few days later Associate Justice Walter B. Hamlin of the Louisiana Supreme Court, the justice who had written the opinion for the Louisiana court sustaining the legislature's right to establish a substitute school board for Orleans Parish, told an enthusiastic audience: "Perez has contributed more to the government, economy, and educational facilities of his community than is in my power to describe." [39] State Senator Speedy O. Long urged the people to expand the boycott to white employers who hired

---

[36] *Southern School News*, December 1960, p. 10.
[37] *New Orleans Times-Picayune*, November 23, 1960.
[38] *New Orleans Times-Picayune*, November 16, 1960.
[39] *New Orleans Times-Picayune*, December 6, 1960.

Negroes and urged them to fire their maid, "no matter how good she is, or regardless of how well she has nursed and cared for the children." [40]

Perez arranged for St. Bernard Parish to open its schools to 450 of the thousand white students assigned to McDonogh and Frantz, and the legislators donated funds for school buses. A private co-operative took care of another 250. This still left 350 white students without an alternative except to quit school or return to their assigned places.

Spurred on by Perez and the state legislators, most of the white parents boycotted McDonogh and Frantz. At McDonogh the boycott was complete. Then on January 27, 1961, John H. Thompson, a drug clerk, who felt that his son Gregory was not getting a proper education in St. Bernard Parish, escorted his son to McDonogh. Within hours a group of women appeared at the school to boo and shout "traitor" at Gregory when he left school. The store at which Thompson worked was picketed. His landlady, Mrs. Margaret S. Lezina, served Thompson with an eviction notice. Five days after Gregory had entered McDonogh, the Thompson family left New Orleans for an undisclosed destination. [41] Except for this brief period the three little Negro girls had their new school all to themselves. McDonogh was as segregated as ever. But not so at Frantz, where a few resolute white parents continued to send their children. And as long as a single white child went to one of the unsegregated schools, segregationists were defeated. Nothing short of a complete and sustained boycott would serve their purpose.

A courageous Methodist minister, the Reverend Lloyd A. Foreman, and an indomitable couple, Mr. and Mrs. James Gabrielle, refused to participate in the boycott, and took their children to school. Other white parents returned their children to Frantz. The boycott was beginning to break. A moderate organization, Save Our Schools, furnished cars and drivers so that children would not be exposed to taunts on their way to school.

[40] *New Orleans Times-Picayune,* November 15, 1960.
[41] *Southern School News,* March 1961, p. 9.

The New Orleans police tightened their vigilance. By the end of the first week in December 1960, twenty-three white children were attending Frantz.

The boycotters now turned to the telephone. Emile Wagner, with the help of a state judge, got hold of the names of parents refusing to boycott. Mimeographed lists with names, addresses, and telephone numbers of the drivers furnished by Save Our Schools were handed out. Legislators threatened to investigate "non-co-operative parents." Representative Hiram Allen announced that he had heard that many parents were ready to return their children to public schools when it became safe, and declared, "The legislature ought to do something. This is an all-out last ditch fight." [42]

Many of the parents who defied the boycott lost their jobs. The father of the one Negro child attending Frantz, a veteran who held the Purple Heart, was fired from his position at a filling station. His employer conceded that Abon Bridges had been a good worker for four years, but he said whites had threatened to boycott his station unless he fired him. "I wouldn't have a nigger working for me with a child in a 'white' school, would you?" he asked.[43] Marion McKinley, a Baptist seminary student, withdrew his children from Frantz because of threats and a warning that he would lose his part-time job. So did another student. James Gabrielle quit his city job because of harassment by fellow workers and left town to return to his former home in Rhode Island.

The pressures began to work; the number of white children at Frantz dropped from twenty-three to twenty, then to fourteen. Each morning the number of white children was carefully counted: an increase was scored as a victory for the moderates, a decrease was another round won by their opponents. The number was reduced to eight, and there it stayed.

Gradually the moderates began to be heard from. At first it was a resolution of a PTA group; then the Junior Chamber of

[42] *New Orleans Times-Picayune,* December 19, 1960.
[43] *New York Times,* November 18, 1960; December 11, 1960.

Commerce spoke out. In mid-December 1960, one hundred of New Orleans' most prominent business and professional citizens took a full-page advertisement to call for an end to the boycott, the street demonstrations, and the threats, and for a restoration of civic dignity. A few days later 190 parents endorsed this declaration in another ad.[44] In February 1961, 1,650 of New Orleans' most distinguished citizens held a testimonial dinner for the four moderate school board members and for Superintendent Redmond.

The trend seemed clear. As the vigilance of the police became more strict, the publicity less favorable, and the weather colder, the "cheering section" grew smaller and smaller. A child could go to school as though it were an ordinary matter, and not an affair of state. Most white students would serve out the school year in their substitute schools, but the boycott would not prevent New Orleans from complying with Judge Wright's injunction. Gradually the students would return to McDonogh and Frantz.

The legislature had provided an expensive but ineffective forum, costing more than a half-million dollars, in behalf of segregation orations. As the expense of the fight became apparent, and Governor Davis called for an increase in the sales tax to support "private schools," once again voices of moderation were heard in Baton Rouge.

The legislature had already, as Governor Davis stated, taken the "last step before secession." But one hundred prominent New Orleans citizens spoke for many less articulate when they said in their advertisement: "We are proud that we are citizens of the United States, and we recognize allegiance to this Union." [45]

[44] *New Orleans Times-Picayune,* December 14, 1960, December 23, 1960.
[45] *Ibid.*

9 ✳ Not by Judges Alone

In December 1952 when the Brown case was first before the Supreme Court, Justice Felix Frankfurter declared: "Nothing could be worse from my point of view than for this Court to make an abstract declaration that segregation is bad and then to have it evaded by tricks." [1] Eight years and two hundred lawsuits later, had Justice Frankfurter's worst fears been realized? The Supreme Court had declared public school segregation unconstitutional, but many southern federal district judges had permitted the evasion of the consequences of these decisions. Segregation is still the most widely practiced pattern for the operation of southern schools.

In the days immediately following the Supreme Court's disposition of the original suits, judges were telling southern communities that there was no way out—each community could decide how it should be done, but it must integrate the public schools. In the face of segregationist onslaught, judges backed down. Since 1957 the judges have approved programs that will keep most Negroes in segregated institutions until long beyond the time when even those now starting first grade will have graduated.

[1] *United States Law Week*, vol. 21, December 1952, p. 3165.

The Supreme Court itself has retreated. By affirming pupil-placement laws, the Court sanctioned token integration. Taking their cue from the Supreme Court, the district judges, even the most aggressive among them, require only that a school board within the next several years admit a few Negroes to a "white" school. This is a far cry from the "full compliance" "at the earliest practicable date," and complete desegregation "with all deliberate speed" which was promised by the Supreme Court's 1955 decision.

Yet the ledger must be balanced. The Supreme Court has re-affirmed its stand that segregation is unconstitutional, and it has pushed the logic of its doctrine to cover buses, parks, golf courses, and other public facilities. The symbolic destruction of segregation is only the first step, but it is an important first step. In the border states, segregation is fast disappearing. In the South itself, federal judges are insisting that sooner or later cities must introduce at least a small measure of integration. The presence or threat of violence can no longer be used to justify interference with a federal injunction. "Private-public-school" programs have been set aside; so have school-closing programs.

What the district judges need—and what most of them want—is not the responsibility for making choices, but rigid mandates that compel them to act. The Supreme Court appears to have made a serious mistake when it delegated so much discretion to the district courts. It was, and is, politically unrealistic to think that a southern judge could, or would, cut through the Supreme Court's vague instructions to initiate action hostile to segregation.

The ambiguity of the Supreme Court's mandate enables the most segregation-minded judge to set the pace; it compounds the task of those judges who are willing to act more boldly. Since the judge has such a wide range of choices, he personally is held accountable when he chooses to insist upon prompt desegregation. It takes a man of unusually strong resolve to force integration when he can just as readily and respectably construe the law to avoid an immediate showdown.

Judges will do what they are told by the United States Supreme Court, even those who are personally devoted to segregation. But none of them, even those who favor desegregation, are particularly anxious to attack strongly entrenched local institutions. As a result the ambiguity of the Supreme Court's instructions has been resolved to conform to the dominant political forces in the South.

What is needed is a hierarchy of scapegoats. Just as the district judge is in a better position than the locally elected school board to insist on desegregation, so the court of appeals is in a better position than the district judge, and the Supreme Court is in the best position of all. If the Supreme Court had issued unequivocal mandates insisting that the district judge promptly order recalcitrant boards to act, the board could blame the district judge and he could blame the Supreme Court.

The Supreme Court is in a better position than the district judge "to take the heat." [2] It has a national constituency; it can withstand locally generated pressures. And after all, one of its primary functions is to establish national minimum standards.

The process of litigation is slowly making the district judges' duty more precise. The rulings of the Lemleys, Atwells, and Davidsons are being reversed; those of the Wrights, Hoffmans, and Taylors are being affirmed. Gradually the discretion of the trial court is being restricted. But the Supreme Court could expedite desegregation if it would reformulate its mandate in less cloudy terms and take from the district judges the responsibility for shaping the precise contours of the law.

The Supreme Court did handle the issue of segregated seating on the buses directly and precisely. The Court made a clean decision: insistence by any government upon segregation in buses or in other forms of public transportation is unconstitutional.

---

[2] However, even the Supreme Court is not invulnerable. It too has to mend its "political fences." As long as it is merely taking on the defenders of segregation, the Court has ample power to withstand the onslaught. But if it takes on too many enemies at the same time, the Court could find its own power curbed. One major battle at a time is good strategy in politics as well as in war.

Nothing was said about giving cities time to desegregate their transportation systems by stages. A few judges have permitted cities to maintain segregated buses; for the most part, however, judges have swiftly enjoined the enforcement of such laws. In city after city the buses have been desegregated.

The difference, however, between the pace of bus and school desegregation is not attributable solely to the difference in how the Supreme Court disposed of the two issues. There are other factors: Negroes have fought for bus integregation with more zest than for school integration. And in this fight, they have had more effective weapons. In addition to the lawsuit, they have economic power—they make up a large percentage of the bus companies' patronage. On the other side, their opponents have fought less intensely. Riding the buses involves contacts of a much less permanent and social nature; there has been less opposition to bus desegregation than to school integration. State legislatures cannot as readily interfere, for few cities receive state financial support for their transportation systems. Buses have been integrated because of the combined impact of the federal judiciary and the political and economic pressures of the Negroes. It is more trouble for cities to insist upon segregated buses than to desegregate them.

The debates on segregation may be couched in legal language, the conflict may take place inside a courtroom, and a judge may make the choice. But the judge must make more than a legal decision; he must make a political decision in the broadest and noblest sense. He must choose between competing concepts of the public interest.

All policy-makers in a free society are the focus of contending pressures. Judges are no exception. The judiciary is subject to competing claims in a somewhat different fashion from, say, the legislature; nevertheless the difference is one of degree and not of kind. And just as the laws enacted by the legislature reflect the dominance of certain values in the community, so do the decisions of judges. It is so today; it has always been so.

In 1896 the Supreme Court (*Plessy v. Ferguson*) supported segregation. A half century later (*Brown v. Board of Education*) the Supreme Court declared segregation unconstitutional. What happened in the fifty-eight years between 1896 and 1954 was not the discovery of some new legal theory, but major alterations in American society. The Supreme Court's 1896 decision reflected the subservient position of the Negro. The 1954 decision reflected the emergence of the Negro from servility to full citizenship. Both decisions were as much consequence as cause; both rested on the value systems of their times.

For the Supreme Court to have declared segregation unconstitutional in 1896 would have been unthinkable. Most Negroes did not aspire to enter the "white man's world." The Negro was considered by many whites, North and South, to be a depraved, comic, childlike, or debased person. Southern political leaders openly and unapologetically espoused white supremacy. In 1896 one Negro was lynched every fifty-six hours; few citizens, black or white, raised a voice in protest.

Even if the Supreme Court in 1896 had declared segregation unconstitutional, a decision so contrary to dominant national values would have had little significance. In 1896 Negroes had too little political power even to implement the "separate but equal" doctrine proclaimed by the Plessy decision. Indeed, within the context of its time, the Plessy decision was forward-looking. Yet with the separateness equality did not come. The difference between then and now is not that Plessy was obeyed and Brown is being disobeyed, but that in 1896 those working for racial equality were so weak that then the defiance of the Supreme Court and the circumventions of the Constitution went unchallenged.

With the new century came the industrialization and urbanization of the South, the northern migration of Negroes, World War I, the New Deal, World War II, and the growing decline and destruction of colonialism. Out of these changes came a growing and insistent demand for the abolition of color barriers. And above all, they created a Negro middle class to whom segregation as a symbol of servitude and a cause of inequality became a target.

By 1954 it was only a question of time before the basic charter of American government would be brought in line with the growing claims of racial equality. The Supreme Court's decision in 1954 did not cause the conflict over civil rights; it was a product of that conflict. For the Supreme Court in 1954 to have declared that our Constitution permits governments to force Negroes to stay in their place would have been just as out of step with national values as a decision in favor of integration would have been in 1896. By the middle decades of the twentieth century the pro-civil rights forces are so strong that even if the Supreme Court had sustained segregation, such a decision could not long have endured.

In the context of the nation at large the civil rights forces are politically powerful. Within the councils of southern governments, however, civil rights advocates still lack an effective voice: they remain a relatively unimportant part of the constituencies of most southern decision-makers. Civil rights advocates within the national community are strong enough to produce Presidents advocating equality before the law, Supreme Court decisions promoting desegregation, and congressional civil rights statutes, but within the South they are not powerful enough to secure effective enforcement of these national standards.

The course of judicial decision-making during the 1950's reflects this balance of political pressures. It has been difficult for southern federal district judges, who as national officers are subject to these integration pressures, to face exposure to segregation demands. Even the Supreme Court has been affected by the political facts of life. Its acceptance of token integration reflects this truth.

Token integration is winning in large southern cities, not just because federal judges insist on it, but because such a program marks the terms on which the dominant groups can agree. Urban white citizens are not unwilling to accept limited integration and, for the moment, this is all the Negro community is asking for.

Indeed it is the present situation in many communities in the North, where housing segregation has made many schools, in fact, segregated, even if they are not so in law.

In the rural South no school integration is in sight. Here the Negro is still economically depressed; he has no vote, and the white community is opposed even to symbolic integration. Federal judges handling suits concerning rural communities are likely to find reasons why no integration injunction should be issued. Even if they do order desegregation, orders are not likely to bring it about.

In the future as well as in the past, what the judges will do and the significance of their actions will be determined not so much 'by what goes on inside their courtrooms as by what happens outside. Even if the Supreme Court strengthens its instructions, even if all the district judges unitedly insist upon compliance, judges cannot desegregate the schools by themselves. The effectiveness of their decisions and their ability to bring about fundamental alterations in the operation of the schools rest basically on the power that can be mobilized behind the value of equal rights. Litigation is only one of the techniques available to a free people. Until those favoring school integration fight as hard for civil rights as segregationists are fighting against them, southern schools will remain segregated. That desegregation is proceeding so slowly is a fault not of the judges, but of society at large. In the long run, a nation gets the kind of judicial decisions it deserves.

One of the decisive factors in determining the outcome of the civil rights conflict will be the ability of Negroes to translate their potential voting power into actual ballots. When the voting power of Negroes in Mississippi is brought into play, United States senators and United States district judges from Mississippi will be less opposed to school desegregation. Segregationists are fully aware that they can control southern governments only if they can keep the Negroes disfranchised. But they are less likely to be as effective in the future as they have been in the past.

Here it is not a question of "separate but equal" ballots, but whether or not the Negro is to be given the vote at all. Here it is not a question of the Supreme Court's construction of the Constitution; the Constitution itself states in unequivocal terms that no state is to deprive any person of the right to vote because of race, color, or condition of previous servitude.

In the battle for the ballot Negroes do not have to do all the fighting by themselves. In 1957 Congress authorized the Department of Justice to enter the fray. On its own motion the department may seek injunctions in behalf of persons who are being unconstitutionally deprived of the right to vote. Furthermore, though this is not true in suits to desegregate schools, federal courts are open to aggrieved persons who claim that they have been refused the right to register or to vote, without their first having to exhaust administrative remedies.

The Department of Justice has so far had very little success with the 1957 Act. The department has moved slowly, bringing few suits. Southern federal judges have shown no greater desire to protect the Negroes' right to vote than they have to desegregate the schools. In Georgia, Judge T. Hoyt Davis even went so far as to declare the 1957 Act unconstitutional. Other judges discovered technical reasons for refusing to enjoin voting officials from discriminating against Negroes. Only Judge J. Skelly Wright has so far used the Act of 1957 to protect Negro voters. But in 1960 the Supreme Court reversed the judges who were dismissing complaints filed by the Department of Justice. Henceforth, though litigation is inherently slow, southern judges will have to find other reasons to refuse to act.

The United States Civil Rights Commission is skeptical about the vesting in judges of the responsibility for presiding over the registration of Negroes. Instead the commission has recommended that whenever the commission finds a pattern of discrimination exists, the President should be authorized to appoint temporary federal registrars. These registrars, officials responsible to the Chief Executive, would then enroll voters for any primary or election in which officers of the national government are to be elected.[3]

President Eisenhower, however, consistent with his general tendency to consider the struggle for civil rights to be a lawyer's problem, proposed that the job be turned over to the district judges, and in 1960 Congress adopted the Eisenhower version. Under the 1960 Civil Rights Act, after the Attorney General has won a civil suit under the 1957 law he may ask the judge to make a finding that a pattern of discrimination exists. If the judge makes such a finding, then any Negro in the region who has tried unsuccessfully to register and believes he has been unlawfully rejected may appeal to the judge. The judge appoints referees who within ten days conduct an investigation. State officials have ten days to object. After a hearing, the judge or referee may issue a certificate declaring the applicant a qualified voter. State officials are notified and required to let the applicant vote. If they refuse, they may be held in contempt, but not until after another judicial hearing. It is hard to imagine a more complicated procedure. The opportunities for delaying maneuvers inherent in this law are apparent.

The 1960 Civil Rights Act ignores the experiences of the last seven years in school desegregation lawsuits; it marks another futile attempt to sweep political issues under judicial rugs by an effort to avoid disagreeable tasks by assigning them to judges.

The 1960 Act saddles the already overburdened southern federal judge with another difficult and disagreeable responsibility. These judges have enough to do in the area of school integration without having to force southern registrars to enroll Negro voters. The prestige of the federal judges does not make most civil rights rulings more acceptable; indeed the unpopularity of civil rights actions may deprive the federal judges of the prestige itself.

Federal courts are not expendable. If they are given the task of forcing many unpopular reforms on their local communities, they may cease to be effective instruments for the administration

---

[3] United States Commission on Civil Rights, *Report,* 1959, pp. 134 ff.

of justice. Judges function best when they are handling issues of little political explosiveness. If large numbers of southerners, for reasons just or unjust, come to consider federal judges to be nothing but "Yankee agents," even civil rights advocates may lose more than they may gain from immediate legal victories. These men will be not only lonely, but ostracized.

The federal executive must enter the battle. If executive officials enroll Negro voters, no matter how difficult it may be for them personally, their lack of local prestige would have few consequences. Unlike federal judges, they would have one duty only—to enroll Negro voters. When this is finished, they could retire.

It is not likely, however, that federal judges will use the 1960 Civil Rights Act in such a fashion as to arouse the ire of southerners. As the story of school integration illustrates, they are apt to be something less than aggressive. Judicial decisions here, as elsewhere, are not likely to make any major departure from the norms of the community.

But there will be other Civil Rights Acts, and more Presidential action through the White House itself or the Department of Justice. President Kennedy can hardly refrain from taking a more positive part in the struggle over civil rights than did President Eisenhower. President Kennedy promised, "At such time as I think it most useful and most effective, I will attempt to use the moral authority or position of influence of the Presidency in New Orleans and in other places. . . . " [4] Moreover, the Department of Justice has started to take a more active role in desegregation suits. In the spring of 1961 United States Attorney Many made the government a party to desegregation suits in St. Helena and East Baton Rouge parishes.[5] And Attorney General Robert F. Kennedy asked the Court to let the department directly intervene in the Prince Edward case, not merely as a friend of the court, but as a *co-plaintiff*.[6] Each year more and more Negroes

[4] *New York Times*, February 9, 1961.
[5] *Southern School News*, April 1961, p. 8.
[6] *Chicago Tribune*, April 27, 1961.

will vote. As more of them become educated, they will comprehend more clearly the connection between voting and better schools, houses, and jobs. And with better jobs, better houses, and better education, more and more Negroes will come to insist upon the abolition of segregation. The impact of the political voice of the Negro will be felt long before every Alabama field hand and Atlanta maid becomes politically self-conscious. In India independence was won by a small but active leadership supported only at crucial times by great masses of the people. It is the same with most social change.

What is happening in the United States is one facet of the world-wide "revolution of rising expectations." Colonialism is dead. White supremacy is dying. Governmentally imposed segregation will be abolished in the United States eventually. There is no stopping place between the granting of a few rights and full citizenship. Once the first Negro was educated, once slavery was abolished, America made her choice. Negroes will demand and secure the same rights as other citizens. No other Americans have asked for more than this, or settled long for less.

* Epilogue: 1970

by Kenneth N. Vines

When this study was first issued a decade ago, Professor Peltason concluded with a somewhat pessimistic evaluation of district judges' achievements in implementing school desegregation in the South. Charged by the Supreme Court's 1955 decision with bringing the South into "full compliance" "at the earliest practicable date," southern courts had made little progress toward these goals. The best that could be said was that token integration was emerging in the larger southern cities and the border states. On the other hand, very little school desegregation had come to the school districts of the rural South, and in such deep South states as Mississippi, Alabama, and South Carolina the problem had barely been posed in the courts. Measured according to the most tolerant standard, ten years' litigation had brought little compliance with the Supreme Court's stated objectives. Indeed, the constitutional rights of most southern Negroes to a desegregated education were being systematically and almost routinely denied.[1]

But in this year, 1970, dramatic changes are developing in school desegregation in the South, drastically altering traditional educational patterns. At this writing the extent of the changes is not

[1] Gary Orfield, *The Reconstruction of Southern Education,* New York: John Wiley and Sons, 1969.

known but many school districts previously untouched by racial mixing are desegregating this year.[2] Such previously untouched deep South states as Mississippi and South Carolina are falling into line and so have most black-belt counties of all southern states. Moreover, the change to desegregated education has systematically involved every phase of the educational process and routinely included the desegregation of faculty, staff, and school facilities as well as pupil attendance in classrooms. Most interesting of all, the change has included important symbols of southern resistance. For example, when Strom Thurmond High in Edgefield, South Carolina, was desegregated this year, perhaps the ultimate symbol of southern opposition fell, for Thurmond was identified both nationally and in his Edgefield home district as the effective figure of resistance.[3] Some district judges have even ordered bussing of white and Negro students to achieve racially balanced school populations, and the Supreme Court has said that it will rule in the near future on the legitimacy of bussing. As a whole, the extent of desegregation in southern school districts this year is more than many would have considered possible a decade ago.

Of course, this picture of desegregated education in the South must be balanced by notice of counter trends resulting from continued resistance of white segregationists. In some deep South counties whole schools have been deserted by whites in favor of private school systems that have been hastily erected after evasion tactics were exhausted and segregation was imminent. In other areas the results of desegregation are threatened by the consequences of population movements from the city to the suburbs. In still other areas desegregation has been defined as racially balancing grammar schools while high schools are left with traditional segregation patterns. On balance, however, school desegregation in the South has made impressive strides.

Although the break-through in the desegregation impasse has been momentous, southern courts had little to do with its accom-

---

[2] *New York Times,* September 3, 1970.
[3] *New York Times,* September 3, 1970.

plishment. Immediately preceding the passage of the Civil Rights Acts of 1964 and 1965, southern judges were still approving pupil placement laws and allowing grade-a-year desegregation schemes and other devices by which school boards could delay the onset of desegregation and avoid the full consequences of a desegregated school system. Somewhat more progress had been made in the desegregation of government facilities, but even here the courts were susceptible to the states' sometimes ingenious attempts to avoid desegregation by preserving private facades on public institutions. In the field of voting rights attempts to increase Negro voting in hard-core areas of the deep South were particularly frustrating. Not only were district judges not dealing expeditiously with state disfranchisement devices but those instances in which judges did rule out evasion and denial tactics were often interminably slow and the voting rights grudgingly allowed. Evaluation of federal court actions in either education or voting rights could allow, then, little credit in contributing to the break-through.

The crucial actions that implemented the Supreme Court's mandate for desegregated schools were not denoted in the Court's opinions. Those actions emanated from the national Congress and the Executive. Acting in concert, congressional legislation and executive implementation of key provisions provided the force that led to the critical change in the equation of power.

Thus, the politics of southern desegregation was fundamentally altered by the involvement of other institutions. As handled by southern courts, decisions were the outcomes of adversary cases and were fragmented by decentralization of the judiciary as well as restricted in scope by the narrow formality of adversary litigation. Moreover, policies which evolved through individual litigation of each case in separate school districts allowed little opportunity for programmatic decisions that would provide system and planning for desegregation. Finally, court decision-making provided little opportunity for wielding the power of the purse, for there was no way that courts could channel economic power through appropriations of money or allocation of resources. The indirect economic consequences of litigation that followed from disallowance of grants-in-aid to private schools were negligible and did not provide direct economic power.

The shift in power was accomplished by the passage of the Civil Rights Act of 1964 and its enforcement by the Department of Health, Education and Welfare. Title IV prohibited the extension of federal financial assistance to any dual or segregated system of schools based on race, color, or national origin. In turn, the provisions of the Act were to be enforced by the Office of Education of the Department of Health, Education and Welfare which soon provided a compliance form based on regulations drawn up by the agency. As an alternative the school district might submit its own desegregation plan determined to be in substantial compliance with the law. In any case, it was clear that school districts expecting federal aid had to satisfy HEW requirements and that any bargaining had to take place with the proper official in Washington.

The segregationist reputation of southern judges also affected the provisions of the Act. One of its key provisions provided a check on judges' complicity in approving inadequate desegregation plans. This was accomplished by requiring that final court orders be accompanied by a compliance report.

It is quite clear that it was the weight of federal money which provided much of the impetus for compliance of southern school districts. But it was the importance of money in operating the modern school system which set the stage, the conditions under which national subsidies are crucial to efficient local school operations. The ideal of Jeffersonian localism may have been feasible for the schools of former years, but modern schools with their swollen enrollments, expensive plants and equipment, and high-cost teaching staff require substantial funding to exist under modern conditions.

The channel for federal influence through financial intervention was established by the passage of the Elementary and Secondary School Act of 1965. This Act provided a long-due recognition of the financial needs of public schools and it also provided large new federal grants favoring those school districts that were most in need of assistance. Under the formula for allocation of assistance, poor southern school districts particularly stood to gain. Ironically, many poor southern districts were those that had progressed the least in desegregation and in which resistance was strongest—for example, in the rural areas of the deep South.

Financial aid provided by the 1965 Act proved of great importance in operating schools in the deep South and many districts soon came to depend upon federal aid to meet educational needs. Segregated school districts faced few problems in the first several years of the Act's administration, for no punitive measures were enforced by the national administration. Southern school districts not only grew increasingly dependent on federal funds but they also managed to maintain segregated schools in the Act's first few years of operation.

In managing to gather federal school funds while maintaining segregation, southern districts were simply continuing an arrangement that had been perpetuated with the help of the national administration for a number of years. Before the passage of the Education Act of 1965 the federal government had been making substantial contributions to "impacted" school districts in the South. An impacted district was one whose enrollment had risen due to an influx of pupils from families connected with some government installation, often a military base. Acting on the theory that the federal government shared responsibility for school problems in the impacted district, Congress had provided for the appropriation of funds for these districts.

Many impacted districts receiving federal aid were segregated, and the states were thus engaging in discriminatory acts in education in administering federal funds—a situation that bothered many congressional civil rights advocates. Anti-discrimination amendments were introduced for the educational aid bills in 1963 but the amendments were defeated. In the same year the Civil Rights Commission reported that Mississippi was engaging in systematic discrimination utilizing federal educational funds and there were demands that the Administration cut off funds. President Kennedy, however, refused to cut off federal funds to the discriminating dis-

tricts. Finally, reacting to increasing pressures, HEW Secretary
Ribicoff announced that HEW funds would no longer be used to
pay local school districts that forced children on southern military
bases to attend segregated schools but left children living off bases
unaffected.

Because of the reliance of southern districts upon federal funds,
HEW certification procedures soon became a potent weapon in
bringing about desegregation in the South. Typical was the situation
in Edgefield, South Carolina, where the school board abandoned a
dual school system based on academic achievement, which had the
effect of segregating the races, because HEW refused to certify the
plan. The comment of a school board member on the HEW decision indicates southern awareness of HEW's role: "We couldn't do
that [equalize racial enrollments in the school]. We'd be putting
whites in a school they didn't belong. What HEW was telling us
was that if we set up classes according to ability we'd be violating
the law."

The Act of 1964 also brought the Attorney General into the desegregation process by authorizing him to initiate suits in behalf
of Negro children for the desegregation of school districts. Thus,
even when school districts chose to abandon federal funding, the
power of the federal government could be brought to bear through
the actions of the Justice Department.

Before the Attorney General was authorized to initiate desegregation suits, their instigation throughout the South had been one
of the chief obstacles in the presentation of desegregation to the
courts. Although district courts were charged with the implementation of desegregation, they could not act until suits were filed. As
a consequence, Negro children and their parents were burdened
with the responsibility for initiating and carrying on litigation in
situations where many Negroes were not suited for the role of liti-
gant by training, motivation, or experience. Moreover, outright
intimidation and lack of resources frequently made it difficult for
Negroes to conduct litigation in those deep South areas where the
needs for action in the courts were greatest. The NAACP had

shouldered some of the burden by providing legal services and encouraging litigation, but this organization did not possess sufficient resources for the widespread attacks in district courts that were needed to attack segregation. Southern states had instituted various kinds of attacks upon the NAACP designed to harass that organization and diminish its legal effectiveness. And while the Supreme Court had held the legal activities of the NAACP to be protected political expressions which could not be prohibited by the state, such attacks created an atmosphere of fear and intimidation.

The importance of the Justice Department's involvement in desegregation litigation by means of the 1964 Act is difficult to overstate. Not only were the legal resources of the Justice Department and the prestige of the national government committed to desegregation litigation but in the process the whole balance of resources was changed. Attorneys appearing for state and local southern governments were now matched with the Justice Department's attorneys appearing for the national government. Perhaps most important of all was the potential for planning and systematic action that the Justice Department could bring into the desegregation process. Through centralized direction of litigation the Attorney General could bring an orderly scheme to the determination of time, strategy, and location of desegregation suits. The presence of United States attorneys made it possible for the Attorney General to develop simultaneous suits in school districts throughout the South and so avoid the hit-or-miss efforts that had characterized former desegregation litigation.

In somewhat different ways, then, both the Department of Health, Education and Welfare and the Attorney General entered the politics of desegregation. Once the national administration decided upon really active involvement of these officials in enforcing the provisions of the Act of 1964, desegregation activity proliferated throughout the South and decisions were made with authority and dispatch. Because of the decision to enforce statutory provisions more rigorously in 1970, the impression created is that many school districts are simultaneously desegregated. And, indeed, this is essentially what happened because of the program planned and activated by national political officials.

A perceptive southern federal appeals judge, himself sympathetic to the cause of desegregation, has argued that responsibility for the slow pace of desegregation should not be attributed to federal judges. Both voting and school desegregation concern nationally created rights, he has argued, that are attributes of national citizenship. It follows that the responsibility for protecting these rights lies with the nation, with all three coordinate branches of government. Judge Wisdom saw the enactment of the Civil Rights Acts of 1964 and 1965 as a long overdue assumption of responsibility for the protection of national rights, a responsibility that the federal courts had not the power to fulfill. ". . . until Congress adopted the Civil Rights Act of 1964 and the Voting Rights Act of 1965, statutes with teeth, Congress and the Executive had not acted affirmatively to enforce those rights of national citizenship. This left it entirely to the judiciary, the branch of government least able to carry out enforcement in a reasonable time and on a national scale." [4]

Judge Wisdom's demurrer excuses federal judges from their responsibility far too easily. Considerable evidence from this work indicates that southern judges lacked not so much the formal power to implement desegregation but the will. Whether their powers were adequate for the difficult task is certainly an open question. But the evidence indicates that southern judges often willfully cooperated with local school boards in evading and delaying the desegregation process. Only a few judges seriously utilized judicial power in difficult situations. If district courts lack the potential power to implement difficult decisions, actions of southern courts were hardly a serious attempt to test the proposition and could scarcely be said to prove the point.

One of the severest indictments of district judges has come from within the legal establishment. In an article entitled "Judicial Per-

[4] John Minor Wisdom, "The Frictionmaking, Exacerbating Political Role of Federal Courts," *Southwestern Law Journal,* vol. 21, 1967, pp. 411–428.

formance in the Fifth Circuit," the *Yale Law Journal* took to task judges in deep South states for their extraordinary dilatory tactics and found that they had substantially obstructed the process of desegregation by their handling of cases.[5] Segregationist judges had utilized their control over the conduct of trials to postpone and evade desegregation and granting of voting rights. Moreover, the *Journal* assessed judges' tactics "as an underlying bias against the established rule for resolving the principal issues between litigants. . . ." Although the article was couched in legal language and spoke in terms of legal procedures, the overall effect was that of a legal "tongue lashing." Such a critique is rare in this prestigious journal where articles are usually concerned with legal developments and not often with policy questions or with evaluation of judges' performances.

The *Yale Law Journal*'s critique of southern judges is of unusual significance for two reasons. First, as one of the major law journals, it commands a large and legally illustrious readership, including high court judges and prominent lawyers. We can assume that this condemnation of southern judges not only reached a prominent part of the bench and bar but influenced their thinking about the problems of desegregation and Negro rights in the South. Since the editors of the *Journal* inform us that the article was based on interviews with federal judges, lawyers, professors, and officials of the federal government, we can assume that the attitudes of the authors were shared by at least a portion of the legal fraternity.

The point of the article, however, is not its criticism of southern judges but its proposal of a remedy. After documenting judges' dilatory tactics in some detail, the authors devote the remainder of the article, by far the largest portion, to an exposition of "The Need for Discipline" and to an extended discussion of means for controlling judicial performance.

Comments on cases and on judges' handling of them are perhaps not so unusual. On the other hand, proposals for "discipline" of judges because of their conduct of the judicial process or their case

[5] "Judicial Performance in the Fifth Circuit," *Yale Law Journal,* vol. 73, 1963, pp. 90–133.

decisions are decidedly unusual. We might expect Negro organizations or civil rights groups to call for such discipline but not a legal journal. On the eve of the passage of the Civil Rights Act of 1964 (the article was published in 1963) this attack on southern judges is a striking indication of disillusionment and anger at their behavior. Moreover, such an article is one sign of the pressures that were building for congressional and executive action.

By the year 1971 the politics of desegregation will have been to a large extent removed from the federal courts. Desegregation plans are still often legitimized in court but only after prior HEW approval or after the active intervention of Justice Department attorneys has largely settled the issue. The diminution of the courts' functions in the southern desegregation problem provides an occasion for speculation and evaluation of judges' roles in the desegregation crisis.

Judged by the Supreme Court's mandate to bring full compliance within the shortest feasible time, the district courts have failed to desegregate southern education. And at the time of the entrance of Congress and the Executive into the picture there is no evidence that the courts were approaching the goal in any orderly fashion. With hindsight it is tempting to conclude that courts are unsuited to the task of dealing with difficult social problems and should never have been allocated the task. Echoing Judge Wisdom, we could observe that national rights are at issue and should be secured by the active intervention of Congress and the Executive. The courts lack three crucial powers that have been effectively utilized by Congress and the Executive in bringing compliance:

1) Judges cannot initiate cases but must wait passively for litigation to develop and so have little control over timing.

2) Courts lack the power of the purse since they cannot appropriate moneys to persuade and coerce behavior.

3) Courts cannot make policies that are programmatic and have the critical elements of planning and systematic thinking. The adversary basis of decision-making does not provide centralized direction and integration of policies.

As a consequence some persons have observed that the courts

had insufficient powers for the momentous task of desegregating schools in the South. And yet the Supreme Court, presumably after a good deal of thought, believed that the federal courts were suited for the task. The justices of the Supreme Court must have been aware of the extreme difficulty of school desegregation and also of incidents in the history of federal courts' handling of difficult problems. There were undoubtedly, however, both positive and negative considerations underlying the Court's expectations for the role of the district courts. For one thing, it was quite clear that neither the Congress nor the Executive was prepared to take actions guaranteeing Negroes' rights in the middle 1950's. Any actions to enforce desegregation would have had to come from the courts. It was believable that popular support for the courts and the status of the federal judiciary would have contributed to the acceptance of desegregation in the South. Indeed, such action as there was immediately following the 1954 desegregation case emanated from the federal courts. However, the record of failures and segregationist decisions in the southern courts shows that the Supreme Court critically underestimated the strength and persistence of judges' allegiances to the southern region.

The Court overestimated, on the other hand, the functions of the judicial values of "independence" and rational legal thinking in overcoming the segregationist point of view and identification with the local community. Southern judges were usually born and reared in the South, often educated there, owed their appointments to southern political influence, and continued to live in local southern communities. Many opinions and attitudes of southern judges indicated that legal values, such as respect for higher court orders and precedents and independence of public opinion, were not strong enough to overcome local prejudices.

Although southern judges failed to desegregate the schools, they did set the stage for present desegregation. With hindsight and a broad sociological view of such problems, we can argue that the federal judges of the South performed a number of critical functions leading to eventual desegregation. For one thing, during the first years after the 1954 decision district judges were manning the breaches while Congress and the Executive were largely ignoring the question. The issue of school desegregation was kept constantly alive in the southern courts where it was locally and often nationally visible. Uneven and ineffective as much litigation was, it nonetheless presented occasions for the basic issues and problems of desegregation to be posed and argued. Moreover, continuous litigation in southern courts, by keeping the issue before southern public opinion, possibly provided time and the opportunity for the South to "work through" the difficult problems of social change.

Southern courts did settle a number of difficult questions that prepared the South for acceptance of the inevitable. For example, the device of state grants-in-aid to private schools was litigated and finally declared void; the Prince Edward County litigation settled the issue that a state could not vacate public schools to avoid desegregation; and litigation, particularly Judge Wright's experiences, determined that massive state legislative intervention should not stop the process of desegregation. Collectively, these attempts by southern states were an exhaustion of state remedies. For southern public opinion the demonstrations of failure of state evasions were, it can be argued, a necessary ritualistic preparation for acceptance of social change. This line of thought leads to the idea that school desegregation in the South could not have been accomplished instantaneously because social changes in traditional behavior patterns were involved.

Evaluation of southern judges in a long-term sociological perspective sometimes apologizes for their actions. However, thoughtful analysis of judges' roles in the South should alert us not to expect unrealistic performances from them. Compared to other local recruited and community-based officials in the South, such as state legislators and state executives, district judges were less prejudiced and more effective in approaching desegregation. Compared to U.S. attorneys, however, judges were probably less effective and more prejudiced. Although U.S. attorneys were, like judges, federal officials based in the local community, they were under the more direct command of national officials and were, moreover, especially recruited to represent national viewpoints.

Judges were not recruited specifically to represent national view-points, nor did they act under the direct command of national officials.

In the final analysis our observation of southern judges leads us to appreciate how powerful certain social and political factors are in the operation of the courts. Never was it in doubt that judges were responding to a variety of social factors in the complex desegregation litigation rather than to the intricate skeins of the law. Most critical of all were the backgrounds and socializing experiences of judges which linked them to southern segregationist values. The decentralization of the court system and the independence of each district court from central direction maximized judges' local orientations and rendered them especially vulnerable to local opinion. In this respect the organization and structure of district courts did little to encourage judicial independence from surrounding pressures. Those judges who did decide on desegregation for local school districts in defiance of local pressures displayed extraordinary courage and paid a high price in alienation from and rejection by their southern constituencies. Life tenure and freedom from election guaranteed independent judges their positions but could not help them live and work in the day-to-day task of adjudication in the South.

* Bibliographical Essay
by Numan V. Bartley

The Southern Education Reporting Service Library in Nashville, Tennessee, contains the most extensive collection of materials relating to the public school desegregation controversy. The library's holdings include newspaper clippings and magazine articles, pro- and anti-desegregation literature, and numerous miscellaneous items. Virtually all of this material has been reproduced on microfilm in Southern Education Reporting Service (ed.), *Facts on Film,* 185 rolls in 10 series (Nashville, 1958–67). *Southern School News,* the monthly publication of the Southern Education Reporting Service, is the most reliable chronological summary of the events that followed the *Brown v. Board of Education* decision. Published from September, 1954, until June, 1965, *Southern School News* contains a state-by-state summary of developments in the southern and border states. The Southern Education Reporting Service continued to collect these state-by-state reports after the demise of *Southern School News;* they appear under the heading "School Desegregation in the Southern and Border States" in *Facts on Film.* The agency also periodically issued a *Statistical Summary of School Segregation-Desegregation in the Southern and Border States* (Nashville, 1956–67).

The Southern Regional Council Library in Atlanta, Georgia, is another major repository for materials relating to race relations in the South. This collection includes newspaper clippings and other periodical literature, pamphlets, and a variety of unpublished materials. The Southern Regional Council publishes two periodicals, *New South* (monthly, 1946–66; quarterly, Winter, 1966—) and, more recently, *South Today* (monthly, July, 1969—). Additionally, the Voters Education Project of the Southern Regional Council publishes *V.E.P. News* (monthly, January, 1967—), which contains important voter registration data. The Southern Regional Council also issues frequent and often valuable "special reports" on various subjects pertaining to southern race relations. Some recent titles suggest the prevailing mood of pessimism current among many human rights advocates: *School Desegregation 1966: The Slow Undoing* (Atlanta, 1966); *Lawlessness and Disorder: Fourteen Years of Failure in Southern School Desegregation* (Atlanta, 1968); and *The Federal Retreat in School Desegregation* (Atlanta, 1969).

The most important source for documentary materials pertaining to school desegregation is the *Race Relations Law Reporter* (bimonthly, February, 1956–December, 1958; quarterly, Spring, 1959–Winter, 1967). Published by the Vanderbilt University School of Law, *Race Relations Law Reporter* contains state and federal judicial decisions, legislative enactments, rulings of administrative agencies, and reports of commissions. It also includes articles and annotated bibliographies on legal problems arising from or related to the field of civil rights.

The best general guides to secondary literature are Elizabeth W. Miller, *The Negro in America: A Bibliography* (Cambridge, Mass.: Harvard University Press, 1966), and Arthur S. Link and Rembert W. Patrick (eds.), *Writing Southern History: Essays in Historiography in Honor of Fletcher M. Green* (Baton Rouge: Louisiana State University Press, 1965).

Among numerous works providing background, the following studies are particularly significant: W. J. Cash, *The Mind of the South* (New York: Knopf, 1941); V. O. Key, Jr., *Southern Politics in State and Nation* (New York: Knopf, 1949); Gunnar

Myrdal, *An American Dilemma: The Negro Problem and Modern Democracy,* 2 vols. (New York: Harper, 1944); and George B. Tindall, *The Emergence of the New South, 1913–1945* (Baton Rouge: Louisiana State University Press, 1967).

Loren Miller, *The Petitioners: The Story of the Supreme Court of the United States and the Negro* (New York: Random House, 1966), is an excellent history of Negro rights as they have been defined by the federal judiciary. Other significant studies shedding light on the evolution of minority rights are Robert J. Harris, *The Quest for Equality: The Constitution, Congress, and the Supreme Court* (Baton Rouge: Louisiana State University Press, 1960); Joseph B. James, *The Framing of the Fourteenth Amendment* (Urbana: University of Illinois Press, 1956); Alfred H. Kelly, "The Fourteenth Amendment Reconsidered: The Segregation Question," *Michigan Law Review,* LIV (June, 1956), 1050–86; and Bernard H. Nelson, *The Fourteenth Amendment and the Negro Since 1920* (New York: Russell and Russell, 1946). Dan T. Carter, *Scottsboro: A Tragedy of the American South* (Baton Rouge: Louisiana State University Press, 1969), an account of the Scottsboro trials of the 1930's, offers insights into the functioning of the judicial system in one deep South state in matters relating to race and caste. C. Vann Woodward, *The Strange Career of Jim Crow,* 2nd rev. ed. (New York: Oxford University Press, 1966), is a concise and incisive study of the development of a social system based on racial segregation in the South.

The most thorough study of the southern reaction to the Brown decision is Numan V. Bartley, *The Rise of Massive Resistance: Race and Politics in the South during the 1950's* (Baton Rouge: Louisiana State University Press, 1969). This work also contains a substantial bibliographical essay. Benjamin Muse, *Ten Years of Prelude: The Story of Integration Since the Supreme Court's 1954 Decision* (New York: Viking, 1964), and Reed Sarratt, *The Ordeal of Desegregation: The First Decade* (New York: Harper, 1966), are important studies of the desegregation controversy by perceptive journalists. Less comprehensive but still valuable are William Peters, *The Southern Temper* (Garden City, N.Y.: Doubleday, 1959), and Anthony Lewis, *Portrait of a Decade: The Second American Revolution* (New York: Random House, 1964). Don Shoemaker (ed.), *With All Deliberate Speed: Segregation-Desegregation in Southern Schools* (New York: Harper, 1957), is a collection of essays written by Southern Education Reporting Service staff members and state correspondents for *Southern School News.*

Important works dealing with the legal aspects of the school desegregation controversy include Albert P. Blaustein and Clarence C. Ferguson, Jr., *Desegregation and the Law: The Meaning and Effect of the School Segregation Cases,* 2nd ed. rev. (New York: Vintage, 1962); Daniel M. Berman, *It Is So Ordered: The Supreme Court Rules on School Segregation* (New York: Norton, 1966); and Jack Greenberg, *Race Relations and American Law* (New York: Columbia University Press, 1959). Of equal importance are such articles as Robert A. Leflar and Wylie H. Davis, "Segregation in the Public Schools," *Harvard Law Review,* LXVII (January, 1954), 377–435; Francis B. Nicholson, "The Legal Standing of the South's School Resistance Proposals," *South Carolina Law Quarterly,* VII (Fall, 1954), 1–64; Walter F. Murphy, "Private Education with Public Funds," *Journal of Politics,* XX (November, 1958), 635–654, and "The South Counterattacks: The Anti-NAACP Laws," *Western Political Quarterly,* XII (June, 1959), 371–390; Robert B. McKay, " 'With All Deliberate Speed': A Study of School Desegregation," *New York University Law Review,* XXXI (June, 1956), 991–1090, " 'With All Deliberate Speed': Legislative Reaction and Judicial Development, 1956–1957," *Virginia Law Review,* XLIII (December, 1957), 1205–45, and "The Repression of Civil Rights as an Aftermath of the School Segregation Cases," *Howard Law Journal,* IV (January, 1958), 9–35; Joseph B. Robinson, "Protection of Associations from Compulsory Disclosure of Membership," *Columbia Law Review,* LVIII (May, 1958), 614–649; Daniel J. Meador, "The Constitution and the Assignment of Pupils to Public Schools," *Virginia Law Review,* XLV (May, 1959), 517–571; and Vanderbilt University School of Law, "School Closing Plans," *Race Relations Law Reporter,*

III (August, 1958), 807–840, "Inciting Litigation," *Race Relations Law Reporter,* III (December, 1958), 1257–77, and "Freedom of Association," *Race Relations Law Reporter,* IV (Spring, 1959), 207–236.

Kenneth N. Vines, "Federal District Judges and Race Relations Cases in the South," *Journal of Politics,* XXVI (May, 1964), 337–357, is an extremely valuable evaluation of the performance of federal judges during the desegregation controversy. Also helpful on the behavior of lower federal court judges in the South are George W. Spicer, "The Federal Judiciary and Political Change in the South," *Journal of Politics,* XXVI (February, 1964), 154–176, and Robert J. Steamer, "The Role of the Federal District Courts in the Segregation Controversy," *Journal of Politics,* XXII (August, 1960), 417–438.

Significant state studies that concentrate on white southern resistance to desegregation include Howard H. Quint, *Profile in Black and White: A Frank Portrait of South Carolina* (Washington, D.C.: Public Affairs, 1958); Robbins L. Gates, *The Making of Massive Resistance: Virginia's Politics of Public School Desegregation, 1954–56* (Chapel Hill: University of North Carolina Press, 1962); Benjamin Muse, *Virginia's Massive Resistance* (Bloomington: Indiana University Press, 1961); and Hodding Carter III, *The South Strikes Back* (Garden City, N.Y.: Doubleday, 1959). The latter work deals with the rise of the citizens' council movement and the politics of massive resistance to desegregation in the state of Mississippi and should be supplemented by James W. Silver, *Mississippi: The Closed Society* (New York: Harcourt, Brace and World, 1964), and Russell H. Barrett, *Integration at Ole Miss* (Chicago: Quadrangle, 1965). Hugh Davis Graham, *Crisis in Print: Desegregation and the Press in Tennessee* (Nashville: Vanderbilt University Press, 1967), offers insights into the desegregation controversy through an examination of the response of the Tennessee press.

The Little Rock desegregation crisis is dealt with in Corinne Silverman, *The Little Rock Story* (University: University of Alabama Press, 1958); Wilson and Jane Cassels Record (eds.), *Little Rock,*

U.S.A.: Materials for Analysis (San Francisco: Chandler, 1960), and Numan V. Bartley, "Looking Back at Little Rock," *Arkansas Historical Quarterly,* XXV (Summer, 1966), 101–116. Firsthand accounts of the Little Rock episode include Virgil T. Blossom, *It Has Happened Here* (New York: Harper, 1959), and Daisy Bates, *The Long Shadow of Little Rock: A Memoir* (New York: McKay, 1962).

Other case studies of desegregation crises are Louisiana State Advisory Committee to the United States Commission on Civil Rights, *The New Orleans School Crisis* (Washington, D.C.: Government Printing Office, 1961); Robert L. Crain and Morton Inger, *School Desegregation in New Orleans: A Comparative Study of the Failure of Social Control* (Chicago: University of Chicago Press, 1966); Bob Smith, *They Closed Their Schools: Prince Edward County, Virginia, 1951–1964* (Chapel Hill: University of North Carolina Press, 1965); and Ernest Q. Campbell, *When a City Closes Its Schools* (Chapel Hill: University of North Carolina Press, 1960). The latter is a study of the opinions held by white residents of Norfolk, Virginia, during the period when that city's schools were closed to avoid desegregation.

John Bartlow Martin, *The Deep South Says "Never"* (New York: Ballantine, 1957), and James Graham Cook, *The Segregationists* (New York: Appleton-Century-Crofts, 1962), both based on interviews with segregationist spokesmen, provide helpful information about the leadership of the organized opposition to desegregation. James W. Vander Zanden, the author of several important articles dealing with the Ku Klux Klan, the citizens' councils, and other aspects of white southern resistance to social change, summarizes his findings in *Race Relations in Transition: The Segregation Crisis in the South* (New York: Random House, 1965). David M. Chalmers, *Hooded Americanism: The First Century of the Ku Klux Klan, 1865–1965* (Garden City, N.Y.: Doubleday, 1965), and Arnold S. Rice, *The Ku Klux Klan in American Politics* (Washington, D.C.: Public Affairs, 1962), provide information about that secret order. The citizens' council movement will be dealt with in a forthcoming book by Neil McMillen to be published by the University of Illinois Press.

Noteworthy among numerous works written by the defenders of traditional southern racial practices are William D. Workman, Jr., *The Case for the South* (New York: Devin-Adair, 1960); Charles P. Bloch, *States' Rights: The Law of the Land* (Atlanta, Ga.: Harrison, 1958); Carleton Putnam, *Race and Reason: A Yankee View* (Washington, D.C.: Public Affairs, 1961); and James Jackson Kilpatrick, *The Southern Case for School Segregation* (New York: Crowell-Collier, 1962). Two extreme but nevertheless important statements of the segregationist position are Tom P. Brady, *Black Monday* (Winona, Miss.: Association of Citizens' Councils, 1955), and Herman E. Talmadge, *You and Segregation* (Birmingham, Ala.: Vulcan, 1955). *Charleston News and Courier,* "We Take Our Stand" (Charleston, S.C., 1956); *Richmond News Leader,* "Interposition: Editorials and Editorial Page Presentations" (Richmond, Va., 1956); and *Montgomery Advertiser,* "Publish It Not in the Streets of Askelon" (Montgomery, Ala., 1956), offer a good sampling of editorials relating to the desegregation controversy from three leading southern newspapers hostile toward the Brown decision.

Provocative works by white southern racial moderates and liberals include Harry S. Ashmore, *An Epitaph for Dixie* (New York: Norton, 1958); Sarah Patton Boyle, *The Desegregated Heart: A Virginian's Stand in Time of Transition* (New York: Morrow, 1962); James McBride Dabbs, *The Southern Heritage* (New York: Knopf, 1959), and *Who Speaks for the South?* (New York: Funk and Wagnalls, 1964); Wilma Dykeman and James Stokely, *Neither Black Nor White* (New York: Rinehart, 1957); Ralph McGill, *The South and the Southerner* (Boston: Little, Brown, 1963); and Henry Savage, Jr., *Seeds of Time: The Background of Southern Thinking* (New York: Holt, 1959). Brooks Hays, *A Southern Moderate Speaks* (Chapel Hill: University of North Carolina Press, 1959); Luther H. Hodges, *Businessman in the Statehouse: Six Years as Governor of North Carolina* (Chapel

Hill: University of North Carolina Press, 1962); and Frank E. Smith, *Congressman from Mississippi* (New York: Pantheon, 1964), are memoirs by southern politicians who were involved in the controversy over desegregation.

A number of works analyze the attitudes of southerners toward desegregation, among the best of which are Melvin M. Tumin et al., *Desegregation: Resistance and Readiness* (Princeton, N.J.: Princeton University Press, 1958), and Alfred O. Hero, Jr., *The Southerner and World Affairs* (Baton Rouge: Louisiana State University Press, 1965). William Brink and Louis Harris, *The Negro Revolution in America* (New York: Simon and Schuster, 1964), and *Black and White: A Study of U.S. Racial Attitudes Today* (New York: Simon and Schuster, 1967), are helpful national studies.

Another important investigation of southern attitudes is Donald R. Matthews and James W. Prothro, *Negroes and the New Southern Politics* (New York: Harcourt, Brace and World, 1966), which examines the re-entry of black southerners into the southern political process. Donald S. Strong, *Negroes, Ballots, and Judges: National Voting Rights Legislation in the Federal Courts* (University: University of Alabama Press, 1968); Pat Watters and Reese Cleghorn, *Climbing Jacob's Ladder: The Arrival of Negroes in Southern Politics* (New York: Harcourt, Brace and World, 1967); Everett C. Ladd, Jr., *Negro Political Leadership in the South* (Ithaca, N.Y.: Cornell University Press, 1966); William R. Keech, *The Impact of Negro Voting: The Role of the Vote in the Quest for Equality* (Chicago: Rand McNally, 1968); and Harry Holloway, *The Politics of the Southern Negro: From Exclusion to Big City Organization* (New York: Random House, 1969), deal with various aspects of growing Negro political participation in the South and contain helpful insights on race relations generally.

I. A. Newby, *Challenge to the Court: Social Scientists and the Defense of Segregation, 1954–1966* (Baton Rouge: Louisiana State University Press, 1967), discusses the efforts by "scientific racists" to win a reversal of the Brown decision in the federal courts. The impact of civil rights legislation on the national level on the progress of public school desegregation in the South is examined in Gary Orfield, *The Reconstruction of Southern Education: The Schools and the 1964 Civil Rights Act,* (New York: Wiley, 1969). Robert L. Crain, *The Politics of School Desegregation: Comparative Case Studies of Community Structure and Policy-Making* (Chicago: Aldine, 1968), focuses on desegregation experiences in nonsouthern cities and is helpful for comparative purposes.

The hearings and reports of the United States Commission on Civil Rights cover a variety of subjects affecting minority rights in the South and in the nation. The commission's *Report, 1959* and *Report, 1961* (Washington, D.C.: Government Printing Office, 1959, 1961) contain good discussions of the desegregation controversy in the South, and *Equal Protection of the Laws in Public Higher Education* (Washington, D.C.: Government Printing Office, 1960) is an excellent review of the progress of desegregation in higher education. *Survey of School Desegregation in the Southern and Border States, 1965–1966: A Report* (Washington, D.C.: Government Printing Office, 1966) demonstrates that the South has made progress toward public school desegregation; however, United States Commission on Civil Rights, *Racial Isolation in the Schools* (Washington, D.C.: Government Printing Office, 1967), documents regional and national failure to achieve genuine public school integration, while the *Report of the National Advisory Commission on Civil Disorders* (Washington, D.C.: Government Printing Office, 1968) shows how deeply racial segregation permeates American life generally.